EUROPE DANCING

Europe Dancing examines the theatre dance cultures and movements that have developed in Europe since the Second World War. It charts the post-war progression of the art form and discusses the outside influences that have shaped it. Nine countries have been selected as case studies in order to contrast divergent dance cultures and political and national situations.

The book looks at the interplay of international, national, regional and multi-cultural forces to examine:

- relationships between dance and culture;
- dance as a conservative or resistant form;
- the influence of dance on other art forms;
- the impact on dance of the post-war transformative impulses of youth, women and gay culture;
- artist–audience relationships.

Europe Dancing is essential reading for anyone interested in dance and its wider context, and reveals the potential for dance theory and practice to have a more powerful voice than ever before.

Andrée Grau is Senior Lecturer in Dance at University of Surrey Roehampton in London. She is a contributor to many dance journals, and author of *Eyewitness Dance* (1998) and *Following in Sir Fred's Steps* (1996) edited with Stephanie Jordan.

Stephanie Jordan is Head of the Dance Department at University of Surrey Roehampton in London. Her publications include *Striding Out: Aspects of Contemporary and New Dance in Britain* (1992) and *Moving Music* (2000).

EUROPE DANCING

Perspectives on Theatre Dance and Cultural Identity

Edited by
Andrée Grau and Stephanie Jordan

London and New York

First published 2000
by Routledge
11 New Fetter Lane, London EC4P 4EE

Simultaneously published in the USA and Canada
by Routledge
29 West 35th Street, New York, NY 10001

Routledge is an imprint of the Taylor & Francis Group

© 2000 Andrée Grau and Stephanie Jordan

Typeset in Galliard by Keystroke, Jacaranda Lodge, Wolverhampton
Printed and bound in Great Britain by TJ International Ltd, Padstow, Cornwall

British Library Cataloguing in Publication Data
A catalogue record for this book is available from the British Library

Library of Congress Cataloging in Publication Data
Europe dancing / [edited by] Stephanie Jordan & Andrée Grau.
p. cm.
Includes bibliographical references and index.
1. Dance—Europe—Cross-cultural studies. I. Jordan, Stephanie. II. Grau, Andrée.
GV1643 .E87 2000
793.3'094—dc21   99–089366

ISBN 0–415–17103–2 (pbk)
ISBN 0–415–17102–4 (hbk)

CONTENTS

CONTRIBUTORS

Anna Aalten is Assistant Professor in the Department of Sociology and Anthropology at the University of Amsterdam. She received her PhD in 1991 and now teaches gender studies, qualitative methodology and anthropological theory. She is currently doing a research project on the relationship between dance, culture and constructions of the body and has published her research in several Dutch scientific journals and in the *European Journal of Women's Studies*. She also works as a freelance journalist for the Dutch magazines *Dans*, *The Theatermaker*, *Carnet* and the *Vrienden* – journal of the Friends of the National Ballet – and bulletins of several ballet companies.

Marta Carrasco is a journalist and specialist in bolero and flamenco. She is a critic for *ABC* newspaper and is responsible for the press coverage of the Biennial of Flamenco in Seville. She is a member of the board of *Cairón* and co-editor of *Dansart*.

Estrella Casero-García is a dancer and the director of the Aula de Danza at the University of Alcalá de Henares in Madrid. She studied for an MPhil at the University of Surrey on Spanish Fascism in Franco's era. She is editor-in-chief of *Cairón*.

Delfín Colomé is a composer and critic as well as a diplomat and Spanish ambassador to the Phillipines. He has written numerous articles and is now enrolled for a PhD in Aesthetics at UAM, Madrid. He is the director of *Cairón*.

Lívia Fuchs is a Budapest-based dance historian, critic and teacher. She was formerly an associate editor of *Táncművészet*, for which she has written regularly. She is a lecturer at the Hungarian Dance Academy and a deputy editor-in-chief of *Ellenfény*, a journal on contemporary dance and theatre. She was also in charge of the Hungarian Dance Archives. She has published articles and studies in numerous periodicals and books including *Ballett International* and *World Ballet and Dance*.

Pascal Gielen received his MA in Sociology from the Faculty of Social Sciences at the Catholic University of Leuven, where he holds the position of researcher at the Centre for the Sociology of Culture. He is currently writing up his PhD thesis on the functioning of artistic organizations. He is also finishing a book in collaboration with Rudi Laermans on the recent developments within the field of contemporary dance in Flanders.

Georgiana Gore is Maître de Conférences at the Université Blaise Pascal, Clermont-Ferrand, France, where she is currently responsible for the Master's programme in the anthropology of human movement. She has also held positions in dance and anthropology in the UK and Nigeria. Her publications include contributions to *Dance History: an Introduction* (eds Adshead-Lansdale and Layson 1994); *Dance in the City* (ed. Thomas, 1997); *Dance in the Field* (ed. Buckland, 1999) and *Sociopoétique de la danse* (ed. Montandon, 1998). Her research focuses on the mutual construction of bodily and discursive practices in dance and ritual contexts.

Andrée Grau is Senior Lecturer in Dance at University of Surrey Roehampton in London, where she also directs a research project on South Asian dance in Britain. She has held positions in Cultural/Social Anthropology in Australia and the UK. She recently wrote *Eyewitness Dance* for Dorling Kindersley. Her publications include chapters in *La danse: art du vingtième siècle?* (ed. Pidoux, 1990); *Common Worlds and Single Lives* (ed. Keck, 1998); *Sociopoétique de la danse* (ed. Montandon, 1998) and *Dance in the Field* (ed. Buckland, 1999). She is currently working on a book on the embodiment of knowledge.

Lena Hammergren is Assistant Professor and Director of Dance Studies in the Department for Theatre Studies, Stockholm University. Her doctoral dissertation 'Form and meaning in dance' (1991) is an analysis of Mary Wigman's and Birgit Åkesson's dances. She has written articles on twentieth-century dance and historiography, for instance in *Choreographing History* (ed. Foster, 1995) and *Corporealities* (ed. Foster, 1996). She is currently working on a book on popular dancing and dance as high art around 1900.

Claudia Jeschke has a PhD focusing on systems of dance notation and is currently Professor at the Institut für Theaterwissenschaft, Leipzig University and Director of Tanzarchiv Leipzig. Her scholarly work and publications focus on European theatrical dance of the eighteenth to twentieth centuries (her latest publication is: *Tanz als Bewegungs Text*). She is editor of *Documenta Choreologica*, and is involved in a number of dance-reconstruction collaborations including Nijinsky's *L'Après-midi d'un faune* (with Ann Hutchinson Guest); Noverre's *Orpheus* and *Les Petits Riens* (with Sibylle Dahms) and German expressionist dances (with Betsy Fisher).

Stephanie Jordan is Professor of Dance Studies at University of Surrey Roehampton in London. Her books include *Striding Out: Aspects of Contemporary and New Dance in Britain* (1992); *Parallel Lines: Media Representations of Dance* (co-edited with Dave Allen, 1993) and, forthcoming in 2000, *Moving Music: Dialogues with Music in Twentieth-Century Ballet*. She has written for a number of scholarly journals and has presented at conferences worldwide. Current projects include an edition of translated writings by the choreographer Fedor Lopukhov for *Studies in Dance History* and a book on Stravinsky and dance.

Rudi Laermans is Professor of Sociology at the Faculty of Social Sciences of the Catholic University of Leuven, where he also directs the Centre for the Sociology of Culture. His research interests lie in the fields of social-systems theory, cultural theory and sociology of the arts (especially the performing arts). Recent publications include *Communicatie zonder mensen: een systeemtheoretische inleiding tot de sociologie* ('Communication without human being. An introduction to sociology from the point of view of systems theory) and *Secularization and Social Integration* written with B. Wilson and J. Billiet. He is currently finishing a book with Pascal Gielen on recent developments within the field of contemporary dance in Flanders.

Mirjam van der Linden studied Theatre Studies in Amsterdam and Glasgow and received her MA in Amsterdam in 1992. She undertook dramaturgical research for the Belgian choreographer Wim Vandekeybus. At present, she is an editor of dance programmes at the Dutch NPS Television and a freelance journalist. She published on dance in the magazines *Dans*, *The Theatermaker* and *Carnet*. She started her work as a dance critic in 1997 for *NRC Handelsblad*. Currently, she writes for *de Volkskrant*, another national newspaper.

Laurence Louppe is an art historian and critic with a training in dance and theatre. She lectures extensively on dance and on its relation to the other arts, and contributes regularly to the Belgian journal *Nouvelles de danse*. Her publications include numerous exhibition catalogues and articles as well as the two books *Danses tracées* (1992) and *Poétique de la danse contemporaine* (1997).

Nèlida Monés is a freelance dance historian and editor who has lectured at various Spanish universities. She studied journalism and art history in Barcelona, has an M.Phil. in History from UPF and is currently concluding her PhD. She researches mainly nineteenth- and twentieth-century dance and has written for different magazines and encyclopedias as well as presenting at international conferences. She is an editorial board member of *Cairón* and co-editor of *Dansart*.

Giannandrea Poesio was born in Italy where he worked both as a performer and a dance critic. In 1990, he moved to England, where he completed his PhD in dance history in 1993. He now lectures in Dance History at the University of Surrey. He is the dance critic for the *Spectator*, vice-chairman of the European Association of Dance Historians, one of the Directors of the Society for Dance History Scholars and has published extensively on nineteenth- and twentieth-century theatre dance.

Bonnie Rowell is a Senior Lecturer in the Dance Department at University of Surrey Roehampton in London, where she teaches dance analysis and choreography. She is currently engaged in doctoral research on postmodern dance and its critical analysis and her research interests also include dance and philosophy. She has recently completed a book on the Dance Umbrella Festivals.

Gabi Vettermann has an MA in Theatre Studies and German Literature. She was formerly a dramaturge, stage manager and assistant director for various theatre productions. She worked as a research assistant for numerous projects and publications on eighteenth-century dance and *Ausdruckstanz*. She is currently an independent scholar, reviewer, lecturer, and editor in Munich (with a forthcoming publication on inter-intracultural dance and ritual).

ACKNOWLEDGEMENTS

We would like to thank all our contributors for enabling us to assemble such an ambitious and exciting collection, so many of them, after all, for whom English is not their first language. We also thank our first Routledge editor Julia Hall for indicating her faith in the project, Talia Rodgers, who took over responsibility from her with such enthusiasm, and editorial staff Jason Arthur, Kate Trench and Rosie Waters. University of Surrey Roehampton provided financial support for which we are grateful. This enabled us to collaborate with the ideal research assistant, Sanjoy Roy, who, ever calm, efficient and rigorous, provided invaluable help in matters of historical tables, language and liaison with contributors.

1

INTRODUCTION

Stephanie Jordan and Andrée Grau

Newspaper headlines for the New York festival 'Dancing in the Isles: British Invasion 97' informed readers at various stages that 'The Troupes are on the Way', 'The Empire Strikes Back' and 'The British are Leaving'. There was reference to a 'Brit Pack' while Clive Barnes, noting that virtually all Siobhan Davies' teachers were American imports, suggested that 'coming here, she remains something of a colonial showing off her art in the home country' (Barnes 1997).

American quotations may seem incongruous to introduce a book on dance in Europe. Yet these bombastic headlines and titles highlight in their own way what this volume is about: they barely conceal a number of ironies clustering around issues of identity, difference, history, power, and centre–periphery debates. Just how British was any of the dance showcased during this festival, for example? Several of the performing companies are international in personnel: the Jonathan Burrows Group reputedly appears more frequently on the continent of Europe than within Britain and the Ricochet Dance company show was dominated by the work of Javier de Frutos, a Venezuelan choreographer now resident in London. Making a flying visit to speak on 'Anti-dance' was Lloyd Newson, Australian director of DV8 Physical Theatre, which was touring elsewhere in the US at the time and must surely be one of the most nomadic, root-eclectic of all companies based in Britain in the late 1990s.

Speaking the international lingua franca often renders people rather parochial, imagining that their world-view is the only existing one, or at least the only one of any real importance. This leads us to a second reason why the 'American' start is appropriate. Wanting to look at post-war dance in Europe has undoubtedly a political element in it. The US dominated the world economy for the past five decades and Europe has responded through the creation of the European Union and over the years through the incorporation of more and more countries within it. A book on dance in Europe could then be seen as paralleling this movement, showing that, although the American imports have been invaluable to the development of dance in Europe, there have also been many indigenous currents that are just as important.

Starting from an American standpoint also highlights the United Kingdom's ambiguous relationship with 'Europe'. Crossing the Channel, for example, the

British 'go to Europe' or 'to the Continent' as if the British Isles somehow did not quite belong to this larger land mass. In dance, the UK has generally been closer to the US than to its European neighbours whether it is in terms of artistic styles, criticism or scholarship. London critics are often at one with their American counterparts. This has been shown, for example, in their attitude towards Maurice Béjart's work, described by some as 'the tabloid of dance'! Whether one likes Béjart's choreographies or not is irrelevant (the plural is used deliberately because the works are so eclectic that one cannot really talk of one overall style). One cannot, however, ignore the fact that he has been immensely influential throughout Europe either through the ballet of the twentieth century or through the company dancers who then went on to develop independently, often introducing 'contemporary' dance where ballet was the norm. This is well illustrated in the different chapters of this book. Neither can one ignore that so many of the great dancers of our era, from Suzanne Farrell, Maya Plisetskaya, Sylvie Guillem to Rudolf Nureyev, have all wanted to work with Béjart. Yet British scholars and critics have generally chosen to follow their American colleagues and pretend that the 'phénomène Béjart' does not exist.

Considering the diversity of the dance scenes in Europe, however, questions are raised as to the possible nature of a book attempting to bring them under one umbrella and about the structure that such a book may take. Indeed, looking at the British situation mentioned above, the evidence is of a messy, pluralistic, ambiguous picture, a situation likely to be similar in other European countries. Can one then talk about British, French, Italian, let alone 'European' dance? Is it even remotely interesting to do so? Do we talk about 'national' or occasionally 'block' culture for reasons of nostalgia or for more invidious reasons? Is it relevant to talk in these terms, or is it not far more relevant to examine why these terms are used at all, to look at what is concealed behind 'natural' boundaries and what more productive imaginings of community they might hide?

Certainly, in recent times, competing conceptions of the place of individuals in the world have become exacerbated. In her paper 'Nomadic Subjects: The Ethnoscapes of Postmodernity', Rosi Braidotti pointed to a central paradox of our historical condition:

> On the one hand we see the globalization of the economic and cultural processes, which engenders increasing conformism in life-style, consumerism and telecommunication (a global commodification of culture), on the other hand, we also see the fragmentation of these same processes: the resurgence of regional, local, ethnic, cultural and other differences not only between the geopolitical blocks, but also within them: European integration and regional separatism simultaneously.
>
> (Braidotti 1996: 30)

Certainly, today's international economy has signalled the decline of nation states as economic–political units of organization. The European Union has for a long time signified the end of the old nationalisms that began to develop power at the end of the eighteenth century. After the Second World War, we embarked on a process of supranational integration, initially in an attempt to stop Fascism ever happening again in Europe, then to build a strength of opposition to the Soviet bloc. The issues of the arts and education reached the agenda much later and only recently European networks dealing with them have been developed. Many of these networks remain in embryonic state. Braidotti suggests that this situation tells 'something about how complex and potentially divisive culture is, in the broad context of a project that ultimately aims at undoing the European nation states and to re-group them in a federation' (ibid.: 33).

During these processes, we have learned to understand something of the fictions behind the old divisions of nations, these 'imagined communities' (Anderson 1991); the redistribution of lands and peoples with no necessarily logical match between language, culture and nation boundaries; the patriotisms cultivated by groups in power in order to maintain the status quo; the myth of cultural homogeneity which ignores the waves of migrations from the East and South and the persistence of Jewish and Muslim presences (Braidotti 1996: 34). Given these perspectives, we might too look differently at any new configurations and hegemonies that might emerge.

A key area for current European debate, for instance, is one about difference within 'the same' culture as opposed to between cultures, given the patterns of post-war migration challenging the alleged homogeneity of European nation states. This has been interpreted by some as a respect for the separate identity and kinship needs of communities in exile. Salman Rushdie has drawn attention to the explosive potential of such difference, arguing in a recent interview that

> it's as if there is this terrible rupture in the surface of the world and this other reality underneath which comes cracking through before the surface closes over it again. Both are real. They are different realities that lie on top of each other and are not compatible with each other. It is a strange thing about life that it's full of incompatibilities; that realities which describe one world could not possibly contain the other.
>
> (Mackenzie 1995: 15)

Some, including Rushdie himself, have seen the need to explore alternatives to dualistic oppositional conceptualizations that ultimately maintain power imbalance and control cultural diversity. They support more dynamic modes of thinking and a concept of 'hybridity' that, while prompted by the migrant condition, envelops all of us, as we all occupy multiple positions within culture. This was the concept of hybridity shared, for example, at the 1997 London conference 'Re-inventing Britain', celebrating 'impurity . . . [and] mongrelization' (Gilroy 1993: 223), and ethnicity as 'an infinite process of identity construction' (Rushdie 1991: 394), always changing, always renegotiating itself. Looking at dance with this in mind can open our perspective: the essence of ethnicity being room to manoeuvre, flexibility of strategies and tactics of choice, attitudes and engagements of choreographers and dancers can be interpreted in a new way.

And yet, in contrast to such toleration and embrace of diversity within our current global–local conceptions, very different patterns of behaviour manifest themselves at precisely the same time. As Benedict Anderson has pronounced: 'the end of the era of nationalism, so long prophesied, is not remotely in sight' (Anderson 1991: 3). Important upsurges of nationalism, many with long-rooted histories, have emerged in Europe mobilizing popular support in active opposition to the modern state and to supranational integration, as in Brittany, Catalonia, Corsica, Flanders, Scotland, Ulster or Wales. The process further accelerated after the fall of the Berlin Wall in 1989, especially among the people within the sphere of influence of Soviet Russia.

The arts, including dance, can reflect, reinforce, prompt, challenge as well as be appropriated in the quest for identity. They are never politically innocent: they operate in dialogue with both exclusive and inclusive ideologies. Ethnomusicologist Ankica Petrović, for example, has shown how the rural polyphonic musical form of *ganga*, found in Hercegovina, and in parts of Bosnia and Croatia, has at times been an expressive symbol of all rural people who once shared the same kind of pastoral life: people of Muslim, Roman Catholic and Orthodox Christian religions alike. At other times, during the Second World War or since the 1980s for example, it has also been used by Croatian ultra-nationalists as a symbol expressing 'exaggerated feelings about ethnic identity and hatred against another nearby ethnicity – the Serbs' (Petrović 1995: 68). In a similar vein, ethnochoreologist Colin Quigley (1994) discussed how, despite contemporary discourses in the United States about multiculturalism and diversity, a white nationalistic ideology exists. This is so to the extent that in the 1980s a bill was put forward no less than four times to Congress to designate the square dance as *the* American folk dance of the United States because it was seen as representing universal 'American' values cutting 'across all of the ethnic backgrounds that make up [US] society' (US Congress 1988: 30, cited in Quigley 1994: 93).

How the arts have been used as propaganda for German National Socialism and Soviet communism is common knowledge. Rather less well known to a broad public is the fact that America too used its arts as 'a weapon of the cold war'. President Eisenhower argued, for example, on 27 July 1954 to the House Committee on Appropriations:

> I consider it essential that we take immediate and vigorous action to demonstrate the superiority of the products and cultural values of our system of free enterprise.
>
> (Prevots 1992: 2)

Dance was one such product, and, as already noted, the impact of American dance across Europe has been immense and recognized by all. Sometimes, as a result of this, narrative, socio-political voices, of a kind raised earlier in Europe than

4

in America, became temporarily quietened by high modernist giants from across the Atlantic, like Merce Cunningham and Trisha Brown. Thus, Lena Hammergren spoke of the major influence of Cunningham on Sweden's 'Fridans', at a 1992 conference entitled 'American Dance Abroad: Influence of the United States Experience':

> This specific development has . . . prevented some of the tendencies from the late 60s and 70s to blossom, since it has helped creating a very singular minded cultural policy concerning the dance and its possibilities to grow as a multifaceted body of movement. So, the acceptance and appreciation of the new compositional form helped diminishing variety instead of enhancing it.
>
> (Hammergren 1992: 184)

'Trade agreements' are what export of the arts is really all about today, says Greg Nash of the British Council in London (1998), building the image profile of a country, ultimately for economic purposes, and usually with designated priorities. The extraordinary rise of French dance in the 1980s could be interpreted as a massive promotion and a ploy to reinforce the French position as a cultural centre within the European Union. Similarly, the Kylián project, part of the Dutch Programme Cooperation with Eastern Europe, as these countries broke from the USSR, could be perceived in a number of ways. This project, given Jiři Kylián's dual nationality, was established with the purpose to support the development of modern dance in the Czech Republic. Yet dance historian Onno Stokvis reports that 'cultural imperialism' has been spoken about and he acknowledges that 'a certain pay-off' for the project 'gives a more human face to the capitalistic revolution that now takes place in the Czech Republic and in which The Netherlands as producer of many services and products have a big share' (Stokvis 1995: 244–6).

Funding means power and presence, in two senses. Of course, it means that an artist is able to produce and perform work that is more or less expensive, an issue that is experienced most acutely of all in eastern Europe today, since the collapse of communism and, with it, massive state subsidy. But it also means power and presence 'abroad'. Belgian, French, German work travels, assisted by major subsidy from home. In this respect, Britain has been singularly unable to reciprocate, often having to rely on other countries' funds to enable its own artists to perform abroad and often missing out on hosting the big names from those other countries. Ironically, now, Nash suggests (1998), British artists may have become especially attractive and marketable in a recession-burdened Europe, accustomed as they have become to low subsidy and fees. Other countries, such as Hungary, for example, are even more disadvantaged as until recently they operated within a different circle.

Selling art products under a 'national' umbrella, then, contains its ambiguities and ironies. It uses as well as supports artists; it answers to government priorities for political and economic development while it may also be prompted by the urge to share exciting work across borders. It might be considered a dangerous game by some, outmoded, by others (though perhaps appealing to a 'feel-good' nostalgia, entertaining a hint of self-mockery), of primary political importance, by others still. The UK chapter, for example, shows how Scotland, the new 'nation' wants to build its own dance culture and how, for perfectly understandable reasons, when it looks internationally, it is not to its neighbour south of the border. In contrast, the new debates of its neighbour south of the border are about difference within its own heterogeneous culture, and England now prefers to sell itself abroad according to these terms.

As Mike Featherstone has said: 'strongly defined stereotyping "we-images" and "they-images"' give little space to 'more nuanced notions of otherness' (Featherstone 1995: 100). Emphasizing difference between one country and another often goes hand in hand with minimizing difference within the country. The dance historian Ira Tembeck (1995) describes how a cultural community such as Quebec invents remarkably misleading myths about itself. As part of Quebec's quest for a distinct identity, its choreographers and presenters have, until recently, stressed purity, a flow of virgin-birth works untainted by the outside world, a 'culture de résistance' – and all of these images have been powerful marketing tools. But Tembeck sees the reality of this 'tradition of no tradition' as one of a distinctive pluralism and eclecticism, drawing indeed on many other sources, and she proposes that Montreal choreographers must now answer to this in a modification or reinvention of their self-image.

It is also fascinating to note how, at the 1995 Toronto 'Border Crossings' conference, a new generation of Spanish dance scholars arrived in force to critique what they perceived as dangerous new nationalist impulses. Undoubtedly provoked by the image of their recent, repressed nationalist past (Franco died in 1975), they noted the return of the traditional devils of Spanish reactionary thought, in particular the neoplatonic Fascist definition of Spain as a 'unit of destiny of the universal' (Franco's words) (Carreira in Colomé *et al.* 1995: 277). There was condemnation for the 'isolationist' intellectual trends, with the big question reversed: is there such a thing as Spanish dance? There was condemnation too for the fact that

> Being 'national' is still a value that artists brandish when seeking the publicity or the protection of the administrators of public funds . . . It can be said that many artists are considered 'good' just because they are 'ours' . . . In Spain, not a few artists offer us Spanish, Catalan, Galician, Basque, etc. 'national' art.
>
> (Ablanado in Colomé *et al.* 1995: 276)

A significant undercurrent of the Spanish chapter in this volume, for example, is an anxiety about the country's position on the edge of, or even outside, the rest of Europe.

It might also be claimed, however, that calls today to turn our back on our American heritage are equally misguided, encouraging us to situate ourselves too solidly within a new sovereign centre of 'fortress Europe'. Although we may deplore the most crass aspects of Americanization of the world, we should not deny what has been meaningful as a contribution from America, not least in dance, and be open to what continues to be so. After all, in the end, the most interesting and challenging dance resists easy categorizations. So often, the label 'typical' simply cannot be applied.

Despite all the questions raised, the current book on dance in Europe is largely framed in chapters identified by nations within the larger configuration of Europe. As the book came into being, we pondered as to the continuing relevance of such a structure, but, for 1999, it seems still relevant to be so. Numerous dance networks now operate with this European conceptual and institutional framework in mind, including scholarly networks in dance. We have, however, opted to have a chapter on Flanders, rather than Belgium, because we felt that in dance today no one would deny the importance in recent years of the 'Flemish phenomenon' and that it was an apt illustration of the fact that, on occasions, the 'regional' is more significant culturally than the 'national' in terms of identity. The organization of the book also reflects the fact that the different countries of Europe have their own systems, institutional structures and heritages that play a major role in any consideration of dance culture. Indeed, an important factor of difference might be that the various countries feel the pressures of their own dance systems and heritages to varying degrees, France perhaps most of all, Belgium perhaps the least.

The book charts the post-war development of this concept of Europe for dance, whilst it also identifies the marks of distinctive heritages in interplay with the contradictory impulses of identity. Another major factor for any consideration of dance today too is the need for primary data collection, basic information gathering, sometimes for the first time, and certainly a first-time overview of a number of different country profiles for purposes of comparison. It seemed that the best way of doing this was to conduct the enquiry nation by nation.

Certainly, dance since the Second World War provides ample examples of the interplay of levels and kinds of cultural organization, and demonstrates that cultural boundaries are highly resistant to definition. From within a western tradition, on the one hand, we have the international dance styles, genres and body types that spring from Balanchine in ballet and Pina Bausch in contemporary dance, themselves reflecting and commenting on identity concepts of class, race and politics. We might note too the impact of American modern dance as a force for internationalization, Russian ballet serving a similar role in former Eastern bloc countries.

On the other hand, any of these dance manifestations might be conveniently modified and reframed as a national emblem, the global dissolved into the particular: the Royal Ballet as the major example and export of British dance culture, or, as we have already seen, the new contemporary dance movement in France, as glitzy, modernist signal of France's position on the world stage, or the Kylián project of energizing a choreographic culture in Prague, but which might be viewed as a gesture of Dutch cultural imperialism. Then, we have the theatre dance as part of a planned decentralization or regionalization of dance culture in Britain, France and Sweden, a feature that has long been a reality for Italy, by dint of its history of dispersed political structures. Or there is the work which draws upon local, indigenous dance culture (as in Hungary and Spain, and, following Russian models before the collapse of communism, East Germany), originally cultivating a small community identity, while it too is sometimes used as a national emblem.

Other kinds of work, which use non-western dance traditions, promote different cultural issues. Some of the dance of minority groups, such as, in Britain, African/Caribbean and South Asian dance, cultivates a sense of separateness from the majority, with closer links indeed to the 'home' nation or, at least, to a particular image of that nation. Other artists from such groups (even if their work is still marginalized) prefer to see their work as part of a more open tradition of art-making, mixing western and non-western traditions, international in quite a different sense of the word.

On the other hand, people who control resources also control taste, through establishing canons, promoting one form of dance over another – and this has in the past usually been ballet – or presenting non-establishment work in such a way as to reinforce the dominant power. The different countries of Europe experience these considerable complexities in different ways, for each, with its distinct heritage, has always had to look at its present in terms of negotiating a relationship with its own past and the outcomes of that past. It is interesting to look at both the contemporary reality and aftermath for dance of such different political situations as the Franco regime in Spain and the communist rule in Hungary and East Germany, different balances in the dance tradition, depending on the presence and strength of a national ballet company (contrast, for example, Britain and Sweden with their Royal traditions and Italy and Spain, with no national ballet company at all), the length of the dance tradition, the existence or not of long-standing training institutions and codes of dance vocabulary (contrast France and Belgium, for example). It is fascinating too, to look at the ideologies about the value of dance-for-everyone in rich liberal countries such as Sweden and The Netherlands; or how in both of these countries and the United Kingdom until the 1980s, the welfare state unofficially supported experimental dance, in the sense that dancers on unemployment benefit were able to support themselves and continue their creative work.

All the contributions to this book make reference to dance issues that many countries have shared in the latter half of the twentieth century, after the upheavals of the Second World War: the phenomenon of the East–West cultural division; the development of state subsidy, leading, in a number of countries to a boom for dance in the 1970s or 1980s, followed by a decline with recession in the 1990s, the latter forcing many to ask again the most fundamental questions about the role of the arts in society; the burgeoning of contemporary dance as an 'alternative' genre, featuring by now several generations of choreographers and dancers; the renewal, stabilization or hardening of the traditions of ballet; the pluralism of current approaches and eclecticism of styles. More broadly, there are the issues of relationship between dance as abstract force or representation of life issues, especially important being the dynamic relationship between critical forms of dance and post-war transformative impulses for youth, women and gay culture; dance as pure form or integrated with the other arts; dance as conservative or resistant form; aesthetics and politics; artist–audience relationships; not to mention the vulnerability of dance as apparently the 'young' and possibly least articulated art form of the twentieth century.

Any project as ambitious and international as this one must have clearly delineated boundaries. One editorial decision was to concentrate on dance as a theatre form, although this may well include influence from or even theatricalized examples of social or folk dance. Within these terms, a vivid picture emerges of the various styles and genres of theatre dance seen today. The book focuses first and foremost on the post-war situation, but authors explain this in terms of the earlier twentieth century, bringing in this historical perspective as it informs the more recent situation. With each contribution, there is a brief chronological table of important dance and political events, 1900 to present, as a clear exposition of both the historical precedents to as well as the key moments in the period covered, also a bibliography of key literature on the dance culture of the country. The charts make no attempt to represent an objective account of history – they are tied to the individual chapters and flow in relationship to the issues raised by their respective authors. They must be understood as working tools which help us to situate dance. Any such tool will be reductive and what is included or excluded is always up for debate. Together with the bibliographies, which contain examples of literature in the 'home' language, they also suggest further lines of enquiry, starting points for further research and study.

The nine countries represented have been chosen with the aim of documenting case studies. We were interested in such criteria as geographical spread, and bringing in the most divergent dance cultures and political/national situations. But we were also led by the network of scholarly dance writers across Europe whom we felt would challenge us in collaboration and who felt in a position to accept that challenge.

Certainly, there was no question but to commission from authors resident or recently resident within the countries they write about, so as not to impose an outsider's view, rather to pick up on the power of immediate identification with a specific place, time and the issues stemming directly from these. An approach such as this, of course, carries its inherent problems. As editors, we have respected that authors wanted to deal with their subject-matter in different ways according to their interests and expertise, including, for instance, more or less history, or choosing to angle their historical writing so that a chapter reads like the history of the present. It is not possible in any case, given the necessarily summary nature of each author's task, to cover everything everywhere; reading the chapters in juxtaposition exposes continuities and suggests rereadings of and future questions to be answered in relation to chapters first understood in isolation. Some contributors have chosen to write in teams, or with one leading writer working in liaison with others contributing and researching information. Others have researched and written on their own. This too reflects the state of dance scholarship within a country as much as personal preference. The chapter on Germany provides detailed discussion of early twentieth-century roots. This seemed justifiable given the particularly strong link between Germany's pre- and post-war dance and the influence of Laban and Bausch on developments in so many other European countries. The chapters on Spain and Hungary are noteworthy for offering detail that is not generally well known outside these countries, and some of this material is documented here for the first time.

The book is intended to be accessible to anyone interested in dance seen within a European context, as well as to those who seek information about the recent dance culture of a particular country. There are now a number of established dance departments in universities across Europe and, with the development of a European unit of cultural and organizational identity, we have witnessed the growth of European conferences on dance and the increasing flow of dance students across countries in Europe. The book also responds to the new emphasis on inter-disciplinary work in dance studies, and for the drive to widen the readership on dance to include people from the broader field of cultural studies. In recent years, with the moving of the body to the centre of cultural discourses, there is the potential for dance practice and theory to have a more powerful voice than ever before, and our discourses on identity and dance, the interplay of international, national, regional and multicultural forces, speak well beyond the confines of dance studies.

References

Anderson, B. (1991, 2nd edn) *Imagined Communities: Reflections on the Origin and Spread of Nationalism*, London and New York: Verso.

Barnes, C. (1997) 'Step Lively to Davies Debut', *New York Post*, 7 November.

Braidotti, R. (1996) 'Nomadic Subjects: the Ethnoscapes of Postmodernity', proceedings of the conference 'Reflections on the Human Face', 4th ELIA Conference, Lisbon: Calouste Gulbenkian Foundation, pp. 30–5.

Colomé, D., *et al.* (1995) 'Russian Soul and Spanish Blood: Nationalism as a Construct in the Historiography of Dance in Spain', proceedings of the conference 'Border Crossings: Dance and Boundaries in Society, Politics, Gender, Education and Technology', Society of Dance History Scholars, Toronto: Ryerson Polytechnic University, pp. 249–86.

Featherstone, M. (1995) *Undoing Culture: Globalization, Postmodernism and Identity*, London: Sage.

Gilroy, P. (1993) *The Black Atlantic*, London and New York: Verso.

Hammergren, L. (1992) 'The Import(ance) of Fragmentation: a Moment in Swedish Dance History Seen as Both a Tradgedy and a Romance', proceedings of the conference 'American Dance Abroad: Influence of the United States Experience', Society of Dance History Scholars, University of California: Riverside, pp. 175–85.

Mackenzie, S. (1995) 'The Man who Made the Booker', the *Weekend Guardian*, 4 November: 15.

Nash, G. (1998) Interview with Stephanie Jordan, London, 2 April.

Petrović, A. (1995) 'Perceptions of Ganga', in (ed.) Bailey, J. *Working with Blacking: the Belfast Years, Journal of the International Institute for Traditional Music* 37(2): 60–71.

Prevots, N. (1992) '$410 – Was That a Necessary Expense?', proceedings of the conference 'American Dance Abroad: Influence of the United States Experience', Society of Dance History Scholars, University of California, Riverside, pp. 1–10.

Quigley, C. (1994) 'A hearing to Designate the Square Dance the American Folk Dance of the United States': Cultural Politics and an American Vernacular Form', proceedings of the 17th Symposium of the Study Group on Ethnochoreology Nafplion: Peloponnesian Folklore Foundation/International Council for Traditional Music, pp. 87–98.

Rushdie, S. (1991) *Imaginary Homelands: Essays and Criticism 1981–1991*, London: Granta.

Stokvis, O. (1995) 'Establishing Contacts Between East and West Europe Through Modern Dance', proceedings of the conference 'Border Crossings: Dance and Boundaries in Society, Politics, Gender, Education and Technology', Society of Dance History Scholars, Toronto: Ryerson Polytechnic University, pp. 239–47.

Tembeck, I. (1995) 'Crossing the Rubicon Waters: Myth and Identity in Montreal's New Dance', proceedings of the conference 'Border Crossings: Dance and Boundaries in Society, Politics, Gender, Education and Technology', Society of Dance History Scholars, Toronto: Ryerson Polytechnic University, pp. 35–44.

2

FLANDERS

Constructing identities: the case of 'the Flemish dance wave'

Rudi Laermans and Pascal Gielen

During the 1980s, several Flemish theatre directors and choreographers achieved international success and artistic recognition. Almost unanimously, critics praised the productions of, for example, Anne Teresa De Keersmaeker (Rosas), Jan Fabre and Wim Vandekeybus (for brief sketches of the careers of these choreographers, see Van Kerkhoven and Laermans 1997; De Brabandere 1997; Jans 1997). More than one critic even became rapidly convinced that these choreographers were only singular representatives of a broader 'Flemish dance wave' (Laermans and Gielen 1997, 1999). Festival brochures and announcements also made use again and again of this expression, thus reinforcing the impression that something very important was going on in Flanders. Interestingly, Flanders, the Dutch-speaking province of Belgium, was more than once confused with Belgium as a whole. This is ironic considering that since 1980 Flanders and the French-speaking Walloon province have had autonomous governments within a federal Belgium state. These regional governments are, among other things, fully responsible for cultural matters and during the 1980s this resulted in distinct cultural policies. In the homeland of the new dance stars, the very same idiom acquired a broader meaning. During the previous decade, Flanders had been the breeding ground of a brand new generation of talented choreographers. Additionally, the international breakthrough of De Keersmaeker and Fabre went hand in hand with a sudden rise in the interest in contemporary dance. A new, relatively young public expressed its appetite for 'everything except ballet' and was rapidly served by contemporaries who set up dance festivals, such as the well-known Klapstuk (Leuven), and arts centres devoted to contemporary dance, avant-garde theatre and 'new music' (for a general overview, see Lambrechts, Van Kerkhoven and Verstockt 1996; see also Bauwens 1992, on the history of the new arts centres).

Hereafter, we present a selective picture of 'the Flemish dance wave' in Flanders, including its 1990s aftermath. Although we shall offer some background information, our interest is not primarily historical. Rather, we want to show

how the belief in a distinctive Flemish 'dance identity' could arise (see, especially, Laermans and Gielen 1998a). At the same time, our essay – an extended in-depth argumentation is of course not possible here[1] – focuses on the ways different choreographers actively constructed different individual artistic identities.

The Weight of the Ballet Tradition

Around 1980, not much modern or postmodern dance could be seen in Flanders (see Lambrechts, Van Kerkhoven and Verstockt 1996; this overview is our primary source of information for this paragraph). That year, the then 20-year-old Anne Teresa De Keersmaeker presented her first production, *Asch*, 'a theatre project for a dancer and an actor', in a small venue in Brussels. The performance was only shown a couple of times and did not get much attention in the press (Van Kerkhoven and Laermans 1997). For that matter, De Keersmaeker was not the only Flemish artist who tried to start up a career within the field of contemporary dance. Thus, the now forgotten, An Slootmaekers regularly performed at home and abroad. The fact that she and other white ravens were scarcely noticed, had much to do with the lack of a professional distribution system. Only such an apparatus, as the sociologist Pierre Bourdieu (1992) rightly stresses, can draw in a legitimate way a clear line between amateurs and professional artists within a highly insecure artistic field. In a word, contemporary dance was not yet institutionalized in Flanders by the time De Keersmaeker showed her first production. At the beginning of the 1980s, this aesthetic 'genre' was neither an autonomous field of cultural production (Bourdieu 1992), nor an independent subsystem (Luhmann 1995; cf. Laermans 1997).

In more than one way, this situation was strengthened by the fact that only a few foreign contemporary dance productions did reach Flanders (including its most important urban centre, bilingual Brussels, which is, paradoxically, situated in the heart of Flanders). It is therefore no exaggeration to say that around 1980, the ballet tradition still dominated the field of professional theatre dance in Flanders. Two companies set the tone, the Royal Ballet of Flanders (Antwerp) and the Ballet of the Twentieth Century (Brussels), at that time still directed by the legendary Maurice Béjart. The latter was also the founder and artistic director of the international Mudra dance school, which proved to be a real seedbed of artistic talent (among its students were De Keersmaeker, Michèle Anne De Mey, Fumyo Ikeda and José Besprosvany). As a matter of fact, Béjart was the leading figure within the field of Belgian and Flemish dance alike. Whereas the Royal Ballet of Flanders concentrated on virtuoso performances of classics, Béjart had developed his own modern version of ballet. By the beginning of the 1980s, Béjart was of course no longer the leading international choreographer he once was. But he still occupied the centre of the Flemish and Belgian dance field, not in the least because of his direct affiliation with the prestigious opera house De Munt/La Monnaie, where he was choreographer-in-residence.

13

As said, the quasi-monopoly of the ballet tradition was reinforced by the irregular presentation of the work of foreign choreographers working within the field of contemporary dance. The Royal Ballet of Flanders did, now and then, invite guest choreographers, provided they stayed in line with the tradition of classical ballet. Béjart, whose artistic narcissism is documented by many anecdotes, had a much more restrictive policy: only on rare occasions did he show the work of foreign choreographers in 'his' house. In a word, both the Royal Ballet of Flanders and Béjart always used their position of artistic gatekeeper between Flanders and 'the rest of the world' with a view to their own artistic status. This monopolistic strategy proved to be quite successful, at least seen from their point of view. Thus, the American traditions of modern and postmodern dance made no headway in Flanders. All in all, the region lived in a situation of splendid isolation. Moreover, the different government bodies that were responsible for financing cultural initiatives did not show any will to change the state of affairs created by the Royal Ballet of Flanders and Béjart's Ballet of the Twentieth Century. Indeed, at the beginning of the 1980s, classical and modern ballet were the only subsidized dance genres (for figures, see Laermans and Gielen 1998b). One may even say that within the field of dance, ballet was the official genre. Evidently, this policy again strengthened the more general institutional generic and taste monopoly of ballet.

Given this situation, it was no accident that the ballet tradition was a negative point of reference for the new generation of choreographers. The institutional weight of the ballet genre in Flanders (and in Belgium), however, also created a specific problem for every innovator. For how could she or he be recognized – in both the figurative and literal senses of the word – as a professional dance artist? Was the choreographer who transgressed the ballet canon not 'just doing something'? As a matter of fact, more than one dance critic, especially those who were very familiar with balletic decorum, did raise this very question when reviewing the first dance productions of, for instance, Jan Fabre. The impression of sheer amateurism seemed all the more plausible because of the ostensible lack of any education in dance of Jan Fabre, Marc Vanrunxt, Alain Platel or Wim Vandekeybus. In the light of this absence of educational capital, to suspect the innovators of 'not knowing their job' was far from unsound. This accusation of amateurism was all the more plausible because of the lack of a professional distribution network for contemporary dance. For, at least in their very early years, the newcomers within the field of Flemish dance were not backed by an organizational framework that could lend an aura of professionalism to their work.

Distinctive Appropriations: the Case of Anne Teresa De Keersmaeker

In the light of the institutional hegemony of the ballet tradition, choreographers such as Anne Teresa De Keersmaeker and Jan Fabre developed a very specific strategy in order to legitimize their first productions. More particularly, they referred, in a selective way, to artistic forms and norms that were already validated abroad. Through this selective appropriation of the international dance canon, their work identified itself as part of a broader, already established artistic framework. One may thus speak of an operation of auto-legitimization via 'intertextualization', which was at the same time a strategy of 'glocalization': international standards were used in order to counter a local hegemony. Of course, professional artists always work within a predefined context of acknowledged problems and shared solutions. As Becker writes:

> They define the problems of their art similarly and agree on the criteria for an acceptable solution. They know the history of previous attempts to solve those problems, or some of it, and the new problems those attempts generated. They know the history of work like theirs, so that they, their support personnel, and their audiences can understand what they have attempted and how and to what degree it works.
>
> (1982: 230)

Nevertheless, within the Flemish context, taking up the international tradition of contemporary dance as the principal frame of reference was not just an evident artistic stance. During the first half of the 1980s, it also proved to be a very efficient means to counter the then existing dominance of the ballet tradition and to define one's work as a professional contribution to an already recognized artistic genre or style.

The initial career of Anne Teresa De Keersmaeker is an exemplary illustration of this mechanism of auto-legitimization (see also Van Kerkhoven and Laermans 1997). After her first production, *Asch*, De Keersmaeker went to New York, where she studied at The Tisch School of the Arts. During this 'study leave', De Keersmaeker choreographed two of the four parts that make up *Fase: Four Movements to the Music of Steve Reich*, presented in 1982. This duet was an instant hit in Flanders and The Netherlands, and at international festivals such as the London Dance Umbrella. As its subtitle already indicates, the choreography is a highly original appropriation of American minimal dance as developed by, for instance, Lucinda Childs (the genre that Sally Banes refers to as 'analytic postmodern dance'; see Banes 1987: xiii–xxxix; Banes 1994: 301–10). This overt reference to a 'style' that the international dance community had already acknowledged, transformed *Fase* into a *fait accompli* within the Flemish context: only uninformed 'provincials' could deny its status as a professional work of art. Indeed, not unlike the performative power of quotations in scientific articles, the references to American minimal dance implicitly legitimized *Fase* in a very strong way. Those Flemish critics who contested the artistic value of this choreography also questioned an international standard, thus risking the accusation of not knowing what was going on within the field of contemporary dance. And, if they did, they had to defend their opinion not only against the young Flemish public that embraced *Fase*, but indirectly also against the international dance community.

In a word, by referring to an already recognized 'style', *Fase* created for itself a zone of protection, consisting of the artistic prestige or symbolic capital (Bourdieu 1992) that surrounded American minimal dance. Or, to use one of the leading ideas of Bruno Latour's sociology of science: *Fase* succeeded in making a strong link with 'uncontested (aesthetic) facts', thus strengthening its own claim to recognition (Latour 1987).

With its overt references to American minimal dance in *Fase* and its direct successor, *Rosas danst Rosas* (1983), De Keersmaeker did, of course, run the risk of being accused of imitation and copying. It was therefore crucial that both productions not only repeated an already existing dance idiom but also distinguished themselves from its foreign example. In this respect, the movement material proved to be pivotal. De Keersmaeker combined repetitive patterns with daily gestures and actions, like sitting on a chair, falling on the ground, or brushing one's hair out of one's face. Thus, *Fase* and *Rosas danst Rosas* provided minimal dance with a highly specific content. Both choreographies avoided the analytic emptiness of minimalism because they confronted its structural formalism with a semantically very rich movement material (Van Kerkhoven 1984; Van Kerkhoven and Laermans 1997: 9–12). In this way, De Keersmaeker also constructed for herself a distinctive choreographic identity that combined a stress on structures with emotionalism. Actually, this identity was the outcome of the by now well-known interplay between repetition (or similarity) and difference that is probably constitutive of every form of identification (see, *inter alia*, Deleuze 1969).

The construction of contemporary dance as an autonomous category during the 1980s: from Fabre to *Etcetera*

In his early work, Jan Fabre followed a comparable strategy of artistic legitimation and identity construction. 'Distinctive appropriation' also characterized successful productions like *The Power of Theatrical Madness* (1984). More particularly, Fabre excelled in confronting the tradition of performance art, as developed within the context of the fine arts, with the frame of conventional theatre and dance (see Laermans 1993; De Brabandere 1997). In his choreographies, such as *Das Glas im Kopf wird vom Glas: The Dance Sections* (1987), this overt intertextual layer was re-articulated: the works of Balanchine and especially William Forsythe became the main reference points. It was therefore appropriate, if rather ironic, that Forsythe invited Fabre to create a choreography for the Ballett Frankfurt, *The Sound of One Hand Clapping* (1990).

Fabre's choreographic work was – and still is – very critical of the ballet tradition. Thus, in *The Dance Sections*, the dancers only made elementary ballet movements, which were executed very slowly and with the hands bound together in a pair of ballet shoes. The overall allegorical message was quite obvious and has been spelled out in detail by Emil Hrvatin in his in-depth study of Fabre's work (Hrvatin 1994; cf. Laermans 1996). Indeed, Fabre considers ballet to be first and foremost a disciplinary machine that imprisons the body and restricts physical movement. Within the context of Flanders, where the ballet tradition was for a long time hegemonic, this message was understood. Fabre reiterated his harsh critique of ballet language in the already mentioned work for the Ballett Frankfurt, in the spectacular *Da un'altra faccia del tempo* (1993), and in his minimalistic choreography for Het Nationale Ballet of The Netherlands, *Quando la terra si rimette in movimento* (1995). He thus acquired – and probably deserves – the nickname of 'the *enfant terrible* of dance'. Actually, this laconic identification points to a very crucial operation in the way Fabre has 'fabricated' for himself a distinctive artistic identity. For, in his choreographies, positive allusions to Forsythe's work are combined with overt negative references to all those productions that uncritically reproduce the ballet canon. We may speak here of a prime example of identity construction through negative self-definition: one affirms one's personal artistic identity via an overt dis-identification with an already existing genre.

As said, to distinguish oneself in an aggressive way from the ballet tradition was far from evident within the Flemish context. At the same time, this instance of negative self-definition became rapidly dominant in the new discourse on dance that accompanied the breakthrough of De Keersmaeker, Fabre, Vanrunxt and other innovators in Flanders. Without doubt, the most important discursive agent was the bimonthly magazine *Etcetera*. This publication was set up in 1983 by Johan Wambacq and Hugo de Greef, then director of the Brussels Kaaitheaterfestival, which together with Klapstuk (Leuven) was for a long time the most important promoter of 'the Flemish dance wave'. It is thus no wonder that the editorial board of *Etcetera* affiliated itself, without much reservation, to the new generation of Flemish choreographers. As a matter of fact, this still existing magazine was throughout the 1980s the quasi-official mouthpiece of all the newcomers within the fields of both dance and theatre.

In no time at all, *Etcetera* developed a highly influential discourse that framed the work of a De Keersmaeker or a Fabre and the – at that time – massive introduction of the work of foreign choreographers in Flanders (such as Merce Cunningham, Lucinda Childs or representatives of German *Tanztheater* and Japanese *butoh*). Whereas, for instance, the American discussion focused on the differences between modern and postmodern dance (see, for example, Banes 1987), most contributions in *Etcetera* again and again invoked the expression contemporary dance. This 'master signifier' was neither clearly defined, nor given a specific aesthetic context. As a matter of fact, the notion of contemporary dance just referred to 'everything that was not ballet'. Cunningham, De Keersmaeker, Bausch, Fabre, . . . it was all subsumed under the heading of contemporary dance.

Etcetera did not devote much space to the productions of the Royal Ballet of Flanders or Maurice Béjart. But where this was done, negatively coloured expressions set the tone: ballet was 'superficial', 'commercial', 'empty', 'old-fashioned', and so on. These characterizations stood in marked contrast to the description of contemporary dance as being 'honest', 'personal', 'natural', 'sound', and so on. Already these very words pointed to a more general line of argument concerning the category of contemporary dance. Indeed, the lack of an aesthetic definition of this notion was compensated by a morally loaded discourse that played off the shallowness of the ballet tradition against the authenticity of contemporary dance. We may safely assume that this primarily moral typification of the difference between ballet and contemporary dance resulted from the absence of an established tradition of reflection on twentieth-century dance. At the same time, this framework was – and to a great extent still is – very influential. As such, it not only legitimized the work of De Keersmaeker or Fabre against the ballet genre. Perhaps more important was the discursive identification of these and other choreographers as authentic artists in search of an authentic expression of . . . authenticity.

All in all, the contributions to *Etcetera* from around the mid-1980s illustrate a well-known mechanism in the production of so-called self-descriptions or discursive self-observations (see Fuchs 1992). We already implicitly mentioned this basic operation when we spoke of negative self-definition: an in-group (here, the mouthpieces of contemporary dance) always has the tendency to construct its own identity via negative references to an out-group (the ballet tradition). At the same time, many essays in *Etcetera* on the work of De Keersmaeker or Fabre had a pedagogical edge. The positive allusions in their productions to American minimalism or Forsythe's deconstruction of the ballet language were thoroughly explained and interpreted. In this way, the uninformed fans of 'the Flemish dance wave' not only learned that they actually dabbled in contemporary dance; the readers were also informed about the implicit intertextuality of the productions they cherished and thus armed with arguments against all those who still spoke of 'sheer amateurism' or 'worthless dance'.

Being Cosmopolitan in Order to be 'Flemish'

According to Niklas Luhmann (1995), the arts system can be described as an autopoietic or self-(re)producing system because artistic communications then elicit aesthetic communications. The latter may negate, comment upon, or criticize the former. Seen from the point of view of systems theory, the particular form of the connection of a new artistic communication – and every work of art can be considered to be one 'compact communication' – with a previous one is not that important. Much more decisive is the fact that the arts system may be analysed as a social system that reproduces and closes itself via the mechanism of internal self-reference. Literary theory describes the same state of affairs when speaking of intertextuality or – following Bakhtin (1981) – 'the dialogic character of the work of art' (for a highly influential combination of both notions, see Kristeva 1966). Our interpretation of the initial phase of 'the Flemish dance wave' gives a specific twist to these theoretical insights. For notwithstanding the principal international nature of the arts system, regional or national differences are still of great importance. More particularly, intertextual references to a transnational 'art world' (Becker 1982), such as the contemporary dance community, can be used strategically within a specific regional or national context in order to guarantee a minimal amount of symbolic capital (Bourdieu 1992) or artistic and professional esteem. This specific form of a 'global–local nexus', thus we argued, proved to be very efficient in the initial take-off of the so-called Flemish dance wave. But was it enough to legitimate the aesthetic qualities of the work of the newcomers?

In our view, the crucial link in the success story of Anne Teresa De Keersmaeker, Jan Fabre, Wim Vandekeybus or – more recently – Alain Platel was the powerful combination of selective references to internationally acknowledged 'models' or 'styles' with an international recognition as original choreographers by leading festivals and foreign critics. The latter was a pivotal argument in the struggle against the long-standing dominance of the ballet tradition in Flanders, especially around the mid-1980s (see also Laermans and Gielen 1997). For only the symbolic capital imported from abroad could compensate the then existing relative absence of a strictly Flemish validation (as we said, only the bimonthly magazine *Etcetera* fully backed the newcomers within the field of Flemish dance). Besides, not only the needs of a difficult-to-discuss artistic esteem pushed De Keersmaeker or Fabre in the direction of an international career. Their lack of sufficient financial means was another motive. As we already said, the dance policy of the Flemish government had 'officialized' the artificially reproduced monopoly of the Royal Ballet of Flanders and Béjart's Ballet of the Twentieth Century. This situation would only gradually change during the 1980s (see Laermans and Gielen 1998b). Thus, for example, Rosas, the company of Anne Teresa De Keersmaeker, only received the paltry sum of 1.5 million Belgian francs (BF) in 1984. In 1985 and 1986, the same company obtained 2 million BF, and this notwithstanding the international success of *Rosas danst Rosas*. In 1987, this sum was doubled. Two years later, De Keersmaeker sounded the alarm: if the foreseen subsidy of 5.1 million BF did not increase, Rosas would consider leaving Flanders. This threat proved to be successful: during the following years, De Keersmaeker's company received 13 million BF from the Flemish government (Van Kerkhoven and Laermans 1997: 33–5). But she and other choreographers still had to wait until 1993 for a new decree on the performing arts that recognized contemporary dance as an autonomous genre. Therefore, during the 1980s, Flemish choreographers who were not working within the ballet tradition had continually to look for foreign co-producers in order to finance their productions. Thus, the work of Jan Fabre was only made possible thanks to the solid cooperation between the Brussels Kaaitheaterfestival and Theater am Turm in Frankfurt.

In the making of symbolic capital (Bourdieu 1992), some new Flemish organizations who associated themselves with the ongoing 'dance wave' developed a strategy that resembled the accumulation of artistic esteem via international affiliations. International festivals such as the Brussels Kaaitheaterfestival (established in 1977) and the Leuven-based Klapstuk (started up as a dance festival in 1983) showed foreign 'dance stars' (such as Merce Cunningham, Lucinda Childs, Trisha Brown) together with upcoming Flemish talents. In this way, they implicitly fulfilled the role of cultural bankers (an expression we borrow from Bourdieu, 1992, who only uses it in passing). The cultural banker collects already existing symbolic capital and then redistributes it. Given the difference between international and regional artistic reputations, this can be done without any loss for the artist who 'lends' his or her symbolic capital. Thus, Kaaitheaterfestival and Klapstuk 'borrowed' international symbolic capital from Cunningham and Childs in order to redistribute it within the Flemish dance community. In showing the work of internationally consecrated choreographers next to productions of Vanrunxt, Raeves or Platel, the latter got their share in the symbolic aura that surrounded – and still surrounds – the former.

Organizations such as Kaaitheater and Klapstuk were also highly effective in the mediation between the world of Flemish dance and 'the rest of the world'. By building up worldwide networks and making deals with important foreign theatres and festivals, they more then once paved the way for Flemish dance productions. A more particular and very important strategy was (and is) the practice of co-production. As a matter of fact, this is, more often than not, synonymous with a cartel agreement (or a so-called buyout): in exchange for a certain amount of money, the Flemish choreographer will show her or his work only in the theatre of the co-producer, and not in other festivals or theatres of the surrounding region. As we said, during the 1980s, this kind of deal was crucial for Flemish dance companies. Without the sometimes important financial contributions of foreign co-producers, they just were not able to survive. At the same time, the practice of co-production and – more generally – the anchorage in international networks via organizations such as Kaaitheater or Klapstuk, clearly indicates that an international reputation is not just the outcome of the passive process of 'being discovered'. Rather, this sort of symbolic capital was (and is) at least partially the result of an active networking and many 'backstage negotiations'. As such, it may be called a partly organizational, partly person-mediated construction in which passive and active components are inextricably intermingled.

How Flemish Was and Is 'the Flemish Dance Wave'?

As a matter of fact, not that many Flemish choreographers became connected with the international arts system. Outside Flanders, only Anne Teresa De Keersmaeker, Jan Fabre, Wim Vandekeybus and, more recently, Alain Platel enjoy a broad recognition as important choreographers – four names, though with some leeway, we could add Meg Stuart to this shortlist, a choreographer from New York who now works in Brussels (and regularly receives project subsidies from the Flemish goverment). These five, however, are usually about as far as Flemish and foreign dance critics or festival brochures ever get when discussing 'the Flemish dance wave'. Considerably less ink is spent over the work of lesser gods like Marc Vanrunxt, Karin Vyncke, Bert Van Gorp and Alexander Baervoets (see also the pertinent remarks on Vanrunxt's career by Van Imschoot 1997). In Flanders, this so-called mid-field of Flemish dance is measured against the work of De Keersmaeker and of Fabre, with all the consequences this entails. But this is not our point here. What interests us is that, upon closer examination, the mid-field of

Flemish dance is obviously quite small: all in all, we are only talking about three to five names. All of them are choreographers with several years' experience, more than a decade in Vanrunxt's case. Flemish and, to some extent, Dutch dance critics mostly assign this group without much argument to the periphery of Flemish contemporary dance. Outside Dutch-speaking areas, they are even hardly mentioned as part of the Flemish dance wave.

We thus arrive at a central paradox: expressions such as 'the Flemish dance wave' do suggest the existence of a vital and highly diversified dance field (for what follows, see also Laermans and Gielen 1997, 1998a, 1999). In fact, about fifteen people in Flanders, at most, have the ambition to be professional choreographers within the 'genre' of contemporary dance. Of course, these artists work with one or more dancers, which increases the number of people involved. Nevertheless, this clearly does not back up the notion of 'Flemish dance wave', and the situation was not very different in the 1980s when the 'wave' rhetoric was invented. As a matter of fact, at that time, the self-aggrandizing posture that the use of the discursive construct 'Flemish dance wave' implies, could claim a specific strategic value. Indeed, by suggesting the existence of a flourishing 'dance landscape' – another popular expression in the articles published in *Etcetera* – the mouthpieces of contemporary dance *simulated* a backing in their struggle for more money and official recognition by the Flemish government. With this kind of virtual politics, not only could the interest of politicians be engaged, but the 'wave' rhetoric also proved to be very efficient in dealings with foreign festival directors or critics (who then, naïvely or not, reproduced it in their brochures and articles).

Another paradox concerns the implicit assumption that 'the Flemish dance wave' has something to do with Flanders and that the associated artists share a common identity. Actually, most Flemish – in the sense of Dutch-speaking – choreographers work with foreign dancers. And yet, creations by De Keersmaeker, Fabre or Platel are assigned a regional identity with remarkable regularity. Does this mean their productions contain a specific artistic identity that is perfectly in step with *the* Flemish culture? To disregard for now the question of whether a homogeneous Flemish cultural identity even exists, it is striking to note the ambivalence with which dance critics or festival announcements treat the matter in the way they frequently use the designations 'Flemish' and 'Belgian' interchangeably (although this was more the case during the 1980s than in recent years). In this respect, it is also interesting to note the hybrid position taken up by Anne Teresa De Keersmaeker and her company Rosas. While enjoying structural subsidies from the Flemish government, Rosas is also the resident company of the national opera house De Koninklijke Muntschouwburg/Théâtre Royal de la Monnaie, one of the few remaining federal Belgian cultural institutions. On top of that, the choreographer herself was recently raised to the rank of nobility by the Belgian crown.

Journalistic observations, in particular, about the so-called Flemish dance wave and its representatives often exhibit a lack of deliberation. Individual performances and entire *œuvres* are often described in the same terms. Critics ignore possible differences, overemphasize similarities, and in doing so, whether explicitly or implicitly, discursively construct a distinctive Flemish artistic identity within the realm of contemporary performing arts. A few of the more ubiquitous catchwords – not to say, empty signifiers – concern the alleged visual qualities of the work of Fabre, Vandekeybus or Platel. Thus, the work of Flemish dance-makers is said to distinguish itself through its 'great visual power' or 'strongly visual character'. Another catchword is the body. Again and again, newspaper reviews and essays in *Etcetera* – not to mention several of the contributions in the synthetic publication *Dance in Flanders* (Lambrechts, Van Kerkhoven and Verstockt 1996) – suggest that most Flemish choreographers are primarily interested in the staging of situations in which 'the authentic body' deconstructs 'the disciplined (social) body' and, at the same time, the illusionistic frame that is constitutive for all forms of performing art. Actually, this highly popular interpretation is, in more than one respect, a by-product of the already mentioned discourse on contemporary dance that *Etcetera* created during the 1980s. In direct line with this moral rather than aesthetic discourse, the notion of authenticity is once again given a prominent place.

Of course, one cannot deny the fact that some Flemish dance productions resemble each other in *some* respects. But these similarities do not automatically point towards a common cultural or aesthetic identity. To assume the existence of such an 'essence' is to forget the necessarily selective construction made by the reader. Indeed, to stress the similarities over the differences between artistic 'texts' is a matter of choice, a contingent reading. It is precisely this selective character of every comparison that is suppressed in an interpretation that presents the outcome of the initial selections as pointing to an always–already existing identity.

Probably the most problematic aspect of every essentialist use of notions like 'aesthetic' or 'cultural' identity in order to explain certain characteristics of a group of artworks is the negation of the evidently constructed nature of every aesthetic act (Luhmann 1995). As we tried to demonstrate above in our interpretation of the early work of De Keersmaeker and Fabre, this 'construction work' includes the production of 'auto-identifiers' through, for example, overt intertextual references to other works of art, to already established styles or (sub)genres, and so on. This results in a *preferred identity or self-description* that critics or public may, or may not, pick up. If not, the work of art becomes the stake of an open conflict between interpretations in which it is just one voice. Needless to say, this article is also part of the polyphonic commentary that still surrounds so-called contemporary dance in Flanders.

Note

1   The data and insights presented in this article are the result of the research project 'Genesis and Structure of the Field of Contemporary Dance in Flanders, 1980–1995', for which we received a two-year grant from the Fund for Scientific Research/ Flanders. In the course of 2000, a book (in Dutch) will be published in which the most important findings are summarized and interpreted from a sociological point of view.

References

Bakhtin, M. (1981) *The Dialogical Imagination*, Minneapolis: University of Minnesota Press.

Banes, S. (1987) *Terpsichore in Sneakers: Post-Modern Dance*, 2nd edn, with a new introduction, Hanover: Wesleyan University Press.

Banes, S. (1994) *Writing Dancing in the Age of Postmodernism*, Hanover and London: Wesleyan University Press.

Bauwens, D. (1992) *Huizen van kommer en kwel. De groei en werking van de kunstencentra*, Brussels: Vlaams Theater Instituut.

Becker, H. (1982) *Art Worlds*, Berkeley: University of California Press.

Bourdieu, P. (1992) *Les Règles de l'art. Genèse et structure du champ littéraire*, Paris: Seuil.

De Brabandere, A. (1997) *Jan Fabre*, Brussels: Vlaams Theater Instituut.

Deleuze, G. (1969) *Différence et répétition*, Paris: Presses Universitaires de France.

Fuchs, P. (1992) *Die Erreichbarkeit der Gesellschaft. Zur Konstruktion und Imagination gesellschaftlicher Einheit*, Frankfurt: Suhrkamp.

Hrvatin, E. (1994) *Herhaling, waanzin, discipline. Het theaterwerk van Jan Fabre*, Amsterdam: International Theatre and Film Books.

Jans, E. (1997) *Wim Vandekeybus*, Brussels: Vlaams Theater Instituut.

Kristeva, J. (1966) *Sémiotiké*, Paris: Seuil.

Laermans, R. (1993) 'Death Foretold and its Brief Hereafter. On the Limits of Representation in the Scenographic work of Jan Fabre', in S. Bousset (ed.), *Jan Fabre. Texts on his Theatre Work*, Brussels/Frankfurt: Kaaitheater/Theater am Turm: 109–21.

Laermans, R. (1996) 'Repetition Reveals the Master: the *Danse Macabre* of Jan Fabre', in Lambrechts, Van Kerkhoven and Verstockt, *Dance in Flanders*, Bruges: Stichting Kunstboek: 168–89.

Laermans, R. (1997) 'Communication on Art, or the Work of Art as Communication? Bourdieu's Field Analysis Compared with Luhmann's Systems Theory', *Canadian Review of Comparative Literature/Revue Canadienne de Littérature Comparée*, 25(1): 103–13.

Laermans, R. and Gielen, P. (1997) 'Paradoxes of the Flemish Dance Boom', *Ballet International/Tanz Aktuell*, 11: 10–14.

Laermans, R. and Gielen, P. (1998a) 'Researching "the Flemish Dance Wave", or Opening the Black Box of Discourse', in O. Stokvis and M. van Geijnen (eds) *Dance in The Netherlands 1600–2000: Research Papers*, Amsterdam: Theater Instituut Nederland, pp. 165–76.

Laermans, R. and Gielen, P. (1998b) 'Hedendaagse dans in Vlaanderen: een cijfergeschiedenis', separate addendum in *Gids Kunst Vlaanderen*, Brussels: Kluwer.

Laermans, R. and Gielen, P. (1999) 'The Flemish Wave: Myth and Reality', *Carnet: Performing Arts in The Netherlands and Flanders*, 1: 25–30.

Lambrechts, A. M., Van Kerkhoven, M. and Verstockt, K. (1996) *Dance in Flanders*, Bruges: Stichting Kunstboek.

Latour, B. (1987) *Science in Action: How to Follow Scientists and Engineers through Society*, Milton Keynes: Open University Press.

Luhmann, N. (1995) *Die Kunst der Gesellschaft*, Frankfurt: Suhrkamp.

Van Imschoot, M. (1997) *Marc Vanrunxt*, Brussels: Vlaams Theater Instituut.

Van Kerkhoven, M. (1984) 'The Dance of Anne Teresa De Keersmaeker', *Drama Review*, 3: 98–103.

Van Kerkhoven, M. and Laermans, R. (1997) *Anne Teresa De Keersmaeker*, Brussels: Vlaams Theater Instituut.

Key texts

De Brabandere, A. (1997) *Jan Fabre*, Brussels: Vlaams Theater Instituut.

Bousset, S. (ed.), *Jan Fabre. Texts on his Theatre Work*, Brussels/Frankfurt: Kaaitheater/ Theater am Turm.

Hrvatin, E. (1994) *Herhaling, waanzin, discipline. Het theaterwerk van Jan Fabre*, Amsterdam: International Theatre and Film Books.

Jans, E. (1997) *Wim Vandekeybus*, Brussels: Vlaams Theater Instituut.

Laermans, R. and Gielen, P. (1997) 'Paradoxes of the Flemish Dance Boom', *Ballet International/Tanz Aktuell*, 11: 10–14.

Lambrechts, A. M., Van Kerkhoven, M. and Verstockt, K. (1996) *Dance in Flanders*, Bruges: Stichting Kunstboek.

Van Kerkhoven, M. and Laermans, R. (1997) *Anne Teresa De Keersmaeker*, Brussels: Vlaams Theater Instituut.

Table 2 Important dance and political events in Flanders (1900 to present)

Year	Dance: artists, works, events	Dance: institutions	Arts scene	Sociocultural and political events
1907	Isadora Duncan in Brussels*			
1910	Diaghilev's Ballets Russes in Brussels*			
1914				First World War
1918				End of First World War
1921	Isadora Duncan in Brussels			
1922	Les Ballets Russes in Brussels and Antwerp			
1923		Ballet of the Royal Flemish Opera (Antwerp)		
1925	Les Ballets Russes in Antwerp			
1928	Les Ballets Russes in Brussels			
	Lea Daan goes to Folkwangschule, Germany			
1929		Herman Teirlinck leads theatre laboratory in La Cambre, Brussels		
1930	Daan dances La Chatelet in Antwerp	Elsa Darciel school, Brussels		
1931		Lea Daan school, Antwerp		
1932	Kurt Jooss's The Green Table in Antwerp			
1933	Isa Voss, Daan and Darciel at Jooss summer school	Lea Daan dance group		
1934		Isa Voss school, Antwerp		
1936	Voss dances Dans van leed with her group			
1937	Darciel plays several pieces in Flanders	Akarova studio built in Brussels		
1938		Rudolf Laban teaches at Lea Daan school		
1939		Concours International de Danse in Brussels		Second World War
1945				End of Second World War
1947		Council of Friends of the Dance, Antwerp		
		Annual national dance festival in Antwerp		

Table 2 *continued*

Year	Dance: artists, works, events	Dance: institutions	Arts scene	Sociocultural and political events
1951		Ballet School of the Royal Flemish Opera (Jeanne Brabants)		
1958		Maurice Huismans director of Muntschouwburg, Brussels	World Exhibition in Brussels	
1959		Ballet du XXe Siècle (Maurice Béjart), Brussels		
1966		Ballet de Wallonie, Charleroi Studio-Ballet (Jeanne Brabants), Antwerp		
1969		Ballet van Vlaanderen, Antwerp (Jeanne Brabants)		
1970	*Prometheus*, first performance by Ballet van Vlaanderen			Cultural policy for Flanders and Wallonia separated
1975			Beursschouwburg, Brussels, starts contemporary theatre programme	Theatre Decree
1977			First Kaaitheaterfestival, Brussels (Hugo De Greef) Stuc Arts Centre, Leuven	
1978			Schaamte (De Greef)	
1980	*Asch*, performed by Anne Teresa De Keersmaeker *Theater geschreven met een K is een Kater* (Jan Fabre)		Limelight Arts Centre, Kortrijk	Separate governments for Flanders and Wallonia
1981	De Keersmaeker at Tisch School of the Arts (New York) Marc Vanrunxt, first performance (Antwerp)			
1982	*Fase* (De Keersmaeker)		De Vooruit Arts Centre, Gent	

Table 2 *continued*

1983	Rosas danst Rosas (De Keersmaeker)	International Dance Festival Klapstuk (Leuven) Rosas Company (De Keersmaeker)	De Singel Arts Centre (Antwerp) begins contemporary dance programme De Monty Arts Centre, Antwerp
1984	Stabat Mater (Alain Platel, Les Ballets Contemporaines de la Belgique) Sous les vêtements blancs (Karin Vyncke)	De Beweeging dance festival, Antwerp	Nieuwpoorttheatre Arts Centre, Ghent
1985		Valery Panov director of Koninklijk Ballet van Vlaanderen (Royal Ballet of Flanders) First Kaaitheater Festival	
1986	The Dance Sections (Jan Fabre) Need to Know (Jan Lauwers)		De Werf Arts Centre (Bruges)
1987	What the Body Does Not Remember (Wim Vandekeybus)	Robert Denvers, director of Royal Ballet of Flanders Maurice Béjart leaves Belgium	
1988		Aimé de Lignière establishes Institute for Dance (Lier) Nouvelle de danse	
1990			
1991			
1993	Disfigure Study (Meg Stuart)		Antwerp Cultural Capital of Europe	Performing Arts Decree (Flanders) Cultural Ambassadorship of Flanders
1994	Blauw (Alexander Baervoets)		Kunsten Festival des Arts (Brussels)
1995		Performing Arts Research and Training Studios (PARTS) founded by De Keersmaeker, Brussels	
1996		Dance in Kortrijk	
1997		De Greef leaves Kaaitheater, replaced by Agna Smisdom and Johan Reyniers (formerly Klapstuk)	

* First visit

3

FRANCE

Effervescence and tradition in French dance

Georgiana Gore and Laurence Louppe with Wilfride Piollet

In terms of the sheer volume and eclecticism of its theatre dance activity, France is undeniably one of the richest European nations. A demographic dance boom in the 1990s, during which the growth in contemporary, jazz and traditional dance choreography has been complemented by more recent staging and commercialization of popular forms such as hip-hop and the tango, has boosted the number of professional touring dance companies in 1998 to 450 (Dondi 1998: 42). These exclude the nineteen Centres Chorégraphiques Nationaux (CCN) (national choreographic centres), fourteen of which are run by contemporary choreographers including, of course, the Centre National de Danse Contemporaine (CNDC) (national contemporary dance centre), which houses the only state-funded contemporary dance school in France, the École Supérieure de Danse Contemporaine d'Angers. The other five CCNs play host to classical or neoclassical choreographers and include the internationally renowned Ballet National de Marseille, directed since its inception in 1972 by Roland Petit until his abrupt resignation in December 1997 and the appointment, in March 1998, of Paris Opéra *étoile*, Marie-Claude Pietragalla. Moreover, twelve state-subsidized ballet companies are integrated within opera houses including the Ballet de l'Opéra National de Paris (the other eleven belonging to the Réunion des Théâtres Lyriques de France [RTLF]), and numerous associations with the equivalent of charitable status stage regular dance performances. However, the public, when compared to those of the other performing arts, appears to have little access to this wealth of choreographic production, which, although clearly supported during the last fifteen years by a national cultural politics, has been left to the vagaries of the market in terms of its distribution through programming.

Two figures stand out as crucial in determining French cultural policy and in shaping the contemporary dance landscape. The writer André Malraux, the first Minister for Cultural Affairs from 1959 to 1969, accelerated post-war decentralization in the performing arts. The first five regional theatre arts centres (Centres Dramatiques Nationaux), funded half by central and half by local government, had been established between 1946 and 1952 (Degaine 1992:

369–72). These prefigured not only André Malraux's Maisons de la Culture (regional arts centres), which proliferated in the 1960s, but also the CCNs in that the state, for the first time, funded theatrical activity outside the élitist flagship institutions, the national theatres, with the aim of promulgating art to a broader public. It was within the Maisons de la Culture and on the theatrical circuit that independent modern dance companies, such as Dominique and Françoise Dupuy's Ballets Modernes de Paris, were able to present their work in the 1960s. André Malraux also supported dance at the Avignon Festival (initially a theatre festival founded in 1947 by the director Jean Vilar), which has nurtured in France, through commissioned productions, the works of the international, especially American, theatrical and (post)modern dance avant-garde. In the 1980s, Jack Lang, Minister of Arts and Culture in François Mittérand's socialist government, instituted a national dance policy, the major tenets of which were enshrined in two legal texts: the general *arrêté* (ministerial order) of 1987, which advocated increased amateur dance activity, the preservation of dance's cultural heritage and the fostering of appropriate dance training; and the law of 1989 outlining general principles for dance teaching. In 1982, within the Ministry of Culture's Direction de la Musique et de la Danse, Lang established the first autonomous body to determine state dance policy and funding, the Division de la Danse, which, in 1987, became the Délégation à la Danse. He quadrupled national funding for dance between 1982 and 1986, accelerated the establishment of the CCNs throughout the regions and generally fostered contemporary dance as one of the glitzy modernist emblems of his media-oriented term of office. The overall effect was to give contemporary dance a high public profile, and to create what might be called a 'mediatized' theatre dance culture, to which the works of such choreographers as Jean-Claude Gallotta, Maguy Marin, and Angelin Preljocaj belong.

The Centres Chorégraphiques Nationaux are the most visible, and most highly funded,[1] legacy of this era of rapid expansion in dance. They are regional dance centres, funded by local and central government, established in order to constitute a network of choreographic activity throughout France as part of the *aménagement chorégraphique du territoire* (national and regional choreographic development) (Martin 1996: 41). The term Centre Chorégraphique National was first used in 1968, but it was not until 1978, with the creation of the CNDC as a training institution under Alwin Nikolais's directorship, that a national network began to be constituted, and only from the early 1980s that the CCNs were effectively established in their current form. Initially, each CCN was created for and entrusted to a renowned choreographer, in order to enable choreographic creation and research in a local context and with a strong degree of artistic autonomy. A recent example was the creation of the nineteenth with the transfer of Maguy Marin's company, in February 1998, from Créteil to Rillieux-la-Pape, a culturally 'deprived' town on the edges of the Lyon conurbation, bastion of the French bourgeoisie and unrivalled haven to dance in the provinces since the 1980s. The appointment of a CCN director is now usually made by advertisement and interview. None the less, the CCNs operate as a form of state patronage and their attribution is therefore an accolade testifying to national recognition of choreographic prowess. Their institutionalization of artistic creation and their celebration of a noble élite harks back to Louis XIV's promotion and institutionalization of ballet some three centuries earlier. Moreover, in the way that artistic brilliance and institutional excellence reflected the Sun-King's image of himself, so the self-aggrandizement of decision-makers within the state apparatus for dance has generated an overblown representation of the importance of institutional powers, which, in turn, has overshadowed dance activity and thinking.

Ballet has not been exempt from the 'mediatization' of dance. The star status of its top dancers and the press stories bear witness to this. But, after nine years of socialist government during François Mittérand's two presidential terms from 1981–95, when contemporary styles were (as they still are) ideologically spearheaded by those occupying positions of power within local and national arts and culture institutions,[2] many of its advocates and some practitioners feel that the classical tradition is under siege. The hegemony of contemporary dance means that only one in six to ten performances includes pieces from the classical repertoire. None the less, with a tradition of institutionalization dating back to the seventeenth century, ballet is clearly well entrenched. The Ballet de l'Opéra National de Paris receives nearly 50 per cent of the state's dance funding; it occupies two sites in the French capital sharing with the lyric arts the grand Bastille Opéra complex. This 'battle' has not only been framed in relation to issues of cultural politics and to a loss of institutional power bases, but also in relation to the issue of heritage in terms of transmission through training and the continuity of the repertoire. The introduction in 1989 of a national dance-teaching diploma (Diplôme d'État de Professeur de Danse) has further compounded this institutional rivalry. Largely designed to ensure a homogeneity of training in contemporary and jazz dance, while simultaneously preserving stylistic and choreographic diversity in both forms, the Diplôme has further alienated a large section of the ballet community, although (or perhaps because) *la danse classique* is also included, thus seemingly wresting ballet from its élite training grounds, the regional conservatoires. Qualified ballet teachers in the private sector can now dispense a state-sanctioned training, thus promoting norms of correct training outside the bastions of tradition. Interestingly, the style most frequently chosen by students for the Diplôme is jazz dance, paradoxically one of the least represented in terms of diffusion.

Lang's mediatization of the arts has, we propose, created further tensions, increasingly manifest in the 1990s. Within contemporary dance, two distinct approaches to artistic creation may be discerned. There are, on the one hand, those above-mentioned choreographers (Jean-Claude Gallotta, and so on) whose work is inscribed within the conventions of commercial spectacular theatre dance and whose compositional methods operate according to a prescribed formula with little or no critical reflection as to relations between choreographic process, dance structure and constructions of the body. On the other hand, there is a developing trend towards 'interdance' or 'subdance', which includes an exploratory approach to choreography (as found in the works of Dominique Bagouet, Odile Duboc,

Christine Gérard, and, lately, those of Régine Chopinot and Daniel Larrieu) as well as the hands-on work of those connected to the community through teaching, research, or projects emerging from grass-roots dance associations, the last resulting from individual creative initiative rather than state funding.

Since the 1990s, however, in response to the economic recession and the *fracture sociale* (social fragmentation), socially profitable community dance projects have gained increasing favour with the establishment. This apparently left-wing discourse on the powers of dance as a tool for artistic democratization or social reform played into the hands of the right-wing government elected in 1993, whose cultural policy seemed to be no investment without returns, the equivalent of the Thatcherite discourse on the arts and education in Britain. During the return to left-wing government in 1997 with Lionel Jospin as Prime Minister but with Jacques Chirac as President since 1995, community dance projects, *missions de sensibilisations des publics* (*Mesures* 1998: 4) have begun to be funded by central as well as local government, with the apparent aim of cultivating an educated dance public, but in effect also a commercial strategy designed to increase audiences. The generation of capital – either economic, as with the commercial companies, or cultural, as with the community-based companies – and the need for communication appear to have become the motivations for dance funding and programming in the 1990s.[3]

This chapter aims to explore these and other issues in the context of the highly centralized politics of French dance using concepts and methodologics drawn from philosophical, historical, sociological and anthropological approaches to dance. Our account, because historically situated, espouses a distinct perspective which may not be shared by all actors within the context of French dance. In the process, we will use a particular example to elucidate some of the specificities of French contemporary dance, we will give a broad picture of French dance in relation to its recent history, and will explain why so much of it is narrative in style.

French Contemporary Dance

The 1970s and 1980s witnessed an unprecedented increase in contemporary dance activity in France, with several generations of choreographers rapidly succeeding one another (Verrièle 1997). Certain choreographers achieved extensive notoriety through the media and some, such as Jean-Claude Gallotta and Philippe Decouflé, became recognized personalities beyond the confines of contemporary dance. However, what is most striking is the proliferation of dance projects, which Louppe (1996) has often called 'the hundred flowers' of French contemporary dance, an allusion to Mao Tse-Tung's socialist dictum during the Chinese Cultural Revolution (1967: 302–3). Thus, at one fell swoop, an artistic practice which had been struggling to impose itself since before the Second World War seemed to have found a direct correspondence with the aspirations of a culture, of a generation.

From 1981 onwards, Jack Lang's Ministry of Culture favoured the promotion of an artistic current which had long since been present. (See Robinson [1990] on modern French dance from the 1920s to 1970s.) The sudden visibility of these artistic feats has favoured the use, still recurrent today, of the term 'explosion'. And so, during a tumultuous decade, a profusion of extremely brilliant performances revealed the vitality of a community of particularly inventive contemporary dancers, who had found a collective voice during the forum created by the 1981 *assises de la danse* (dance conference),[4] a semi-spontaneous gathering organized in order to assess the state of the art.

The dominance or impregnation of models

The effects of little training, of pressures to produce prolifically, and of overexposure by the media, made the French dancer–choreographer of the 1980s overly sensitive to the powerful influence of transatlantic models. By the end of the 1970s, American choreographers had gained a high media profile and quickly became an unavoidable professional yardstick. Since the 1960s, the American Centre in Paris had provided a forum for the latest in contemporary art, well received by a generation thirsty for avant-gardism, and a haven for the USA's younger choreographic artists, notably Susan Buirge, Carolyn Carlson and Andy Degroat, who were to remain in France. In a way that would seem incomprehensible today, the meteoric rise of American creators had completely undermined the forms of training and the choreographic trends already well established in France, which had emerged from the German expressionist schools, influential since the 1930s.

Perhaps the most important figure from this era was the German dancer–choreographer, Jean Weidt, a pupil of Sigurd Leeder's, who spent eight years on and off between 1934 and 1949 in Paris, where he established one of the few pre-war professional modern dance companies, the Ballets 38, and later in 1946 the Ballet des Arts. His work has been continued by his two main dancers, Dominique and Françoise Dupuy (formerly Michaud), who created and toured the Ballets Modernes de Paris between 1955 and 1979. Other prominent post-war choreographers include the Lyon-based Hélène Carlut, foreign-born Wigman trained dancers Karin Waehner, Jacqueline Robinson and Jérôme Andrews, the last having also trained or worked with all the major American pioneers.[5]

French culture and society were not, however, able to come to terms with modern dance until after 1968. In order for unconventional bodies to be accepted, for individual artists, freed from a legitimating presence beyond themselves, to be condoned, it had taken this immense revolution of structures of the imagination, of the hierarchy of values which had overthrown traditional society, a process described so well by Roland Barthes in *Mythologies* ([1957] 1972). Former dancer Jaques Chaurand's struggle to create the Bagnolet choreographic competition in 1969 symbolically marked this turning point.

Perhaps it was the combined effects of 1968 and the German legacy of an intensely subjective energy that gave birth to a 'French body' rapidly identified with those expelled from the old order. This is a body deliberately constituted outside any norms, one that is rebellious or even scabby, mean and nasty, one that seeks excessive or sharp gestures (as with François Verret, or the duo of Catherine Diverrès and Bernardo Montet), or those that are pathetic and inconsequential (as with Jean-Claude Gallotta or Philippe Decouflé), and with a recurring sexual irritability (often qualified, like French culture itself, as outrageously heterosexual, at least in its figures, by American observers). The 1970s saw the arrival of 'American bodies', serene and neutral, or shining with the coherence of a technique mastered. These exotic bodies either seduced the French dance community by their smooth and detached appearance or provoked an even greater commitment to a 'wild' body, closer to Antonin Artaud's cruel body or George Bataille's 'acephalous' than to the purity of Cunningham's. Did this result from any real choice, or from a headlong rush into mixed forms of training, which engendered these somewhat 'rough', disparate corporealities which still mark French dance (Louppe 1996)? This, at least, might explain the impregnation of non-European bodily figures, which arise from the modernist quest for deformity (as with Japanese *butoh*) or from the attraction of 'other', more enigmatic, bodies.

It is therefore a paradox that artists such as Françoise and Dominique Dupuy, who, moreover, established the first dance festival in France in 1962 at Les Baux-de-Provence, and who had long since been friends of José Limón and Merce Cunningham, with whom they already shared many ideas and values, became marginalized with the advent of a certain American cultural imperialism in dance. The choreographers in question were those whom the artistic agents chose to tour in Europe, and who had the stamp of common approval, such as Alvin Ailey, Martha Graham, Paul Taylor, and especially Merce Cunningham and Alwin Nikolais. This resulted, for example, in complete ignorance of the Humphrey-Limón choreographic tradition in most French contemporary dance circles. Such exposure to the better-known transatlantic works and choreographic processes did not mean that they were understood, even if they were emulated. By imitating only their surface aesthetics, French choreographers remained very attached to their own artistic propensities, in particular the inevitable recourse to an outside referent, whether literary, pictorial, cinematographic or whatever, and the privileging of ever more brilliant and decorative spectacles. The infatuation for Cunningham, for example, did little to encourage the use of chance procedures in composition, or even any form of experimentation, nor did it challenge current aesthetic conventions. We believe that during the 1980s in France, and perhaps elsewhere, available models were exploited only in terms of their external features, without any real questioning of the processes which gave rise to them. This seems to us to be the real limitation of French choreographers, who are otherwise extraordinarily inventive and active. There is no doubt that the incarnation of a 'model' has somehow placed an interdiction on memory and on the choreographic and other resources from which French dance of the 1980s would elaborate, in a most surprising way, a large part of its poetics.

33

An example: Assai (1986) by Dominique Bagouet

Rather than further generalization, we will continue with a specific example, which is one of the most revelatory as well as one of the most convincing: *Assai*, the late Dominique Bagouet's 1986 creation. One of the most important works of a much-lamented choreographer, it was reconstructed for performance in 1995. (French companies do not necessarily retain a repertory of works, therefore it is more accurate to talk of 'reconstruction' than 'revival'.) This was therefore a work already historically inscribed by a ritual of recollection. Because of the distance that the gaze may confer on a work, and because distance assists in refashioning the work's perception over time, by the same token, it can assist us in elaborating an archaeology of the present.

First let us situate the choreographer. He belongs to a generation which emerged in the 1970s and was converted to contemporary dance by the American choreographer Carolyn Carlson, a dancer from Alwin Nikolais's company, who, in 1974, was named *étoile-chorégraphe* (prima ballerina–choreographer) at the Paris Opéra by Rolf Liebermann, the then general administrator. A year later, she was given the GRTOP (Groupe de Recherches Théâtrales de l'Opéra de Paris) to run, the first modern dance company to be established within the Opéra. After she left in 1980, Jacques Garnier, whose short career spanned both classical and contemporary dance, established and ran its successor, the GRCOP (Groupe de Recherche Chorégraphique de l'Opéra de Paris), the Opéra's choreographic research group, a small contemporary dance company of twelve selected Opéra dancers, whose brief was to create at the heart of the Ballet de l'Opéra a contemporary dance group open to research of the day. Just before his untimely death in 1989, he became director of choreographic studies of France's foremost dance academy, the Conservatoire National Supérieur de Musique et de Danse de Paris (CNSMDP), the bastion of classical dance training outside the Paris Opéra, where he established a parallel training in contemporary dance. Others from that era include Quentin Rouillier, who replaced Jacques Garnier as dance director of the CNSMDP, Anne-Marie Reynaud, Dominique Petit, and so on. This was the first wave of contemporary choreographers whose work was extensively popularized by the media. They were, however, for the most part (including Dominique Bagouet), hardly trained in either contemporary dance technique or theory, but were driven by a desire and a sort of drunkenness to create in a field which to them appeared as new.

Commissioned for the 1986 Biennale de Danse de Lyon devoted to modern German dance, *Assai* conforms to the imposed theme of expressionism. Its main features can thus be noted in relation to this. Two elements dominate the work's aesthetic engagement: first, its visual impact and second, its references to expressionist cinema. The performance is divided into 'tableaux' in the nearly literal sense of paintings, which, because of the sheer volume of indecipherable costumes and the clever play of light and shade (elements favoured in expressionist art), are of a sumptuous plasticity. Thus the articulation of the choreography is overshadowed by the strongly 'sculpted' look of close-to-the-body movements, of the costumes and stage lighting. In the same way, the succession of 'tableaux' evokes an architectural or sequential construction, rather than a veritable 'composition', the latter only emerging at certain key points in the work. The mechanics proper to dance often give way to filmic structures, or to a succession of photographs centred on the image of 'characters' who in turn emerge and disappear. The piece lasts just over an hour, as is customary in France, and constitutes the whole evening's entertainment. (Every company is expected to produce a work of this length annually as testimony to its artistic progress.) We should not omit to mention that the musical score as well as the title of the work were borrowed from a renowned French composer, Pascal Dusapin. This public acknowledgement of musical sources is a rare occurrence in French dance, as is Dominique Bagouet's knowledge of music and particular interest in its contemporary forms.

Also to be noted are the importance of his sources, of his referential system, and his particular treatment of these. Dominique Bagouet's choreography is not 'narrative' in the strict sense, but plays upon a broad spectrum of references, which, when placed end to end, finish by constituting a 'text'. Allusive, veiled, oblique, these references remain underlying. (This is not a trait peculiar to French choreography: Marcia Siegel (1996) has analysed this same process in Paul Taylor's work.) In the same way, the homage paid to the expressionist aesthetic is not merely a pastiche. If the field of references is rich and takes us to Fritz Lang and Georg Pabst, as well as to E. T. A. Hoffmann and Henry Fuseli (with 'doctor' characters, other worldly creatures, and so on), all this happens implicitly. There is no facile 'imitation' of traits generally associated with expressionist imagery, such as violence or excess, and the tone remains elegant despite the strangeness of images. It is clear that the expressionist reference plays on other registers, and not just on a straightforward encoding. Any reference, with Dominique Bagouet as with others of his generation (such as Daniel Larrieu or Catherine Diverrès), presupposes an educated spectator, preferably a cinephile, capable of detecting artistic or literary references, even when these are oblique, dispersed or cryptic; and, as is the case here, treated against the grain.

Dominique Bagouet, in order to celebrate expressionism, chooses not the choreographic field (however rich), but expressionist cinema as if expressionist dance were not worth a mention. These characteristics owe their existence perhaps to the same origin: a certain detachment in relation to the inheritance of modernism in dance. To celebrate German expressionist dance by turning away from choreography towards film-making, Dominique Bagouet effectively states that the sources of inspiration, like the poetic elements, do not, or do no longer, derive from the materials and techniques instituted by contemporary dance. Whether this is ignorance or refusal on his part, none can say; what remains for all to witness is the veiled negation in a very singular aesthetic. Like his counterparts of the period, Dominique Bagouet thinks of himself as having no roots. In the same way that the choreographic writing here seems to invent itself like an orphaned, decontextualized system, so the cinematographic reference affirms the impossibility of self-recognition in preceding trends, as if these were somehow unspeakably vile. French choreographers of the 1980s, convinced, not without reason, of their mastery of the spectacular, nevertheless have problems of self-identification, and so endlessly project themselves into either mythical or other figures beyond their own practice. These 'constructs', hardly analysed today, correspond to key elements in their development and their problematics.

The quest for an external system of reference, a French cultural trait

The very founders of the French school may have initiated this trend. Conscious of the fundamental values of contemporary dance as they were trained within its sources, they were none the less the first to exploit their personal culture, granting poetry and painting pride of place in their preoccupations. Françoise and Dominique Dupuy are emblematic in this respect and the precursors of an extremely rich artistic current; and, it is perhaps to them that we owe the contemporary use, in French dance, of external references. With them, it was not (or at least not yet) a matter of providing resistance to the radicalness of an art that was being engendered from its own materials, as would be the case, later, with most non-figurative approaches. Nor was this a means of avoiding engaging with modernity and the autonomy of an art by yielding to a well-loved and rich contextual world, which must at all costs resonate with identity, as was already the case in the 1950s and 1960s. It is striking that, from the 1970s onwards, similar elements could be found in the visual arts and the cinema: subjectivity, autobiography, the fascination with a culture which projects itself as its own mirror. In France, there exists this persistent vacillation 'between modernity and nostalgia', so well described by Rony Golan (1996). None the less, French contemporary dance must be given credit for the extremely convincing renewal of its figures, even if, over several generations, this has been at the expense of its specific objectives.

But there are other more negative reasons at work. In the first place, modern dance in France was belatedly and not very well integrated into a culture renowned for its sophistication and brilliance. Although much respected during the 1960s by the theatrical and visual arts avant-gardes, modern dance has never belonged to what Roman Jakobson (1977: 79) calls the 'dominant'. This may refer to a specific discipline, an artistic or intellectual movement or a given practice, and, in French culture, is constituted by literature, philosophy and their various sub-disciplines. In this respect, the situation with regard to dance is contradictory. Recognized by the educated public as an important manifestation of contemporary creation, it none the less has difficulty in establishing itself as a theoretical force, as witnessed by the fact that there is no professorship and only three full-time lectureships in dance studies within French universities. The staging of performances has been overprivileged in relation to the nurturing of critical thinking, which, alone, in France can confer on an art the criteria for its recognition.

Choreographers have thus been unable to recognize themselves in their own practice, and have been forced to search elsewhere for legitimizing references. This may explain the impact of theatrical figures such as the American director Robert Wilson, or the Polish author–director Tadeusz Kantor, from whom Joseph Nadj drew much of his early inspiration, and of the German choreographer Pina Bausch. Moreover, this situation has produced two earlier-mentioned characteristics of French dance: first of all, a lack of basic or coherent training; and, above all, the dominance of predominantly literary sources of reference. The latter continues to haunt this art, where the figures of narrative developments abound (even when reduced to a simple appearance without a 'story', as with Dominique Bagouet's expressionist 'characters'). During the 1980s, this tendency compensated for the absence of any choreographic substance, and enabled many who were self-taught and without formal training in contemporary dance (including those who had come from classical dance or other non-choreographic backgrounds) to recreate a universe for themselves.

Although the primary field of reference for choreographers may be essentially literary and cinematographic, we should not, for all that, think of French dance only as 'high art'. On the contrary, the 1980s were a decade in which art generally was 'minorized'. For example, Jack Lang consistently encouraged interaction between the visual arts and mass culture, whether in painting, graphic art, graffiti, design or sculpture. Contemporary dance was not left unscathed by this trend; under the influence of the clothes and designer industries, as well as those of rock music and sports, the boundaries between the fashion parade, the video clip and choreographic composition were dissolved. This strongly decorative trend has, in turn, emphasized the primacy of the intrinsically spectacular elements, that is the costumes and set design, at the expense of choreographic writing and resources of the body. However, personalities as strong as Philippe Decouflé have made pertinent use of this situation. With him, contemporary dance has managed, without losing any of its value of invention, to touch a broader mass audience (with, for example, the 1992 Albertville Winter Olympic Games and the 1989 celebrations of the French Revolution), and has avoided the possible artistic risks of 'minorization'.

An exit from history

French dance of the 1980s has maintained this ahistorical illusion of a spontaneous birth, whence, perhaps, the popularity of the image of an 'explosion' evoked above, but which was first visible in the works themselves and their choreographic language. Jean Pomarès (1994) quite rightly sees François Verret's *Tabula Rasa* (1980) as emblematic, not only because of its title but also its content: two male dancers, through the unharnessed brutality of a hesitant confrontation without rules, are adjusting to the sudden appearance of a virgin dance without antecedent. With them began both the world and contemporary dance, daughter of nothingness (and bearer, in this duo, of that very nothingness). Curiously enough, the theme of historical amnesia may be found in numerous choreographic works, including those of Jean-Claude Gallotta (for example, in *Mammame*, 1986). François Verret further tackles it through a series of 'slayings of the father', the titles alone constituting a litany of annihilation: *Fin de parcours* (*Journey's End*, 1983); *Une Éclipse totale de soleil* (*A Total Eclipse of the Sun*, 1984); *La Chute de la maison Carton* (*The Fall of Carton House*, 1986). François Verret, and possibly Jacques Patarozzi before him, are largely responsible for the search for an exaggerated tonality which maintains, more or less implicitly, a notion of the 'crisis' as a sacrificial rite of passage (the liturgy of an original murder?). Even in the superficially calm, even works of Dominique Bagouet, mentioned earlier, this notion of an unresolved drama may be found, which, like an unnamed secret, somehow taints the gestural shading.

A thorough reading of these works (yet to be undertaken) might elucidate, besides the denial of origins, the importance of the role of the woman as 'object' or, at the least, consenting partner or accomplice to the disaster, often in a strongly sexually charged atmosphere, which Anglo-Saxon countries criticize in French and Belgian dance. However, the separation between men and women choreographers requires some qualification, since in the horde of brothers are included the 'sister' creators who often deploy the same artistic registers (for example, Karine Saporta and Catherine Diverrès). And there are those couples such as Joëlle Bouvier and Régis Obadia who have found a specific organic language to treat the implosion of this 'crisis' with their Compagnie L'Esquisse. It is interesting to note, moreover, that these latter four, unlike most of their counterparts, are much more concerned with remembering their dance heritage. For example, Karine Saporta and Catherine Diverrès both insist upon their filiation with European dance through Mary Wigman.

But this process of negation, through which a generation wanted to be born from its own works (in all senses of the word), has most efficiently served the visual aesthetic evoked earlier, where the notion of 'spectacle' prevails over that of a language or a material to be elaborated. Daniel Larrieu, for example, has conceived of a universe made of spare parts, where each work reinstates a world, a commitment, a point of view, even if, from one work to the other, it is possible to detect beneath the surface a consistently perceptible thread. In this approach to the choreographic project, it is clear that the artists have deftly taken charge of their own historical conditions of work. Linked to the mediatization of art under Jack Lang's regime, the prominence of contemporary dance activity henceforth led to the unbridled management of culture based on the value of the spectacular. To succeed, it was necessary to play the game, and a work such as *Assai* provides the supreme example of an artistic fight dazzlingly won over the ascendancy of production structures. When Dominique Bagouet, the following year, yielded to the vulnerability of artistic gesture with *Le Saut de l'ange* (*Leap of the Angel*), and poignantly questioned the very roots of a language, he was instantly rejected.

The notion of 'author'

The foregoing are not without relation to the notion of a *danse d'auteur* (authorial dance), developed, unsystematically and in the absence of any real debate, by Leonnetta Bentivoglio (1987: 131) following André Bazin's (1957) theorizing of the *cinéma d'auteur* some decades earlier. The author in film, as in dance, is first of all the author of a speech act which gives a point of view on the world, and, in this respect, is not interested in the very instrumentation which might constitute the actual material of a language. French dance has adopted this position somewhat belatedly, considering the ideas current in the 1980s when Gilles Deleuze published his books on the cinema (1983, 1985), in which, on the contrary, he reinstates 'movement' and 'time' as the 'primary materials' of film language. However, the idea of the author represents for French dancers, who jealously guard their own artistic autonomy, the idea of their own 'lines of flight' and the originality of imaginary universes, which are otherwise perfectly real. Often confronted with the violence and devaluation of purely journalistic criticism, choreographers have found, in the notion of the 'author', a system to demonstrate and to defend their own dreams.

Contemporary dance and other cultures

The French dancers' refusal to build upon the heritage of modernity in dance, and more often their ignorance or unconscious denial of what constitutes it, have forced them to seek sources in other cultural forms, which seem to them to be endowed with more credible or more useful corporeal and spiritual values. Numerous dancers have therefore gone to India or Japan to get 'what they could not find' in Europe (for example, Catherine Diverrès and Bernado Montet), whence the often successful integration of codes or a vocabulary borrowed from traditional forms to enrich a destitute field. Sometimes, the journey occurs in time and not in space, the most recently discovered continent being baroque dance (as with François Raffinot); and, as is often the case with Asian dances (especially Bharata Natyam, Kathakali, *butoh*), these have become the purveyor of new 'forms' for contemporary dancers, helpless in the face of the unknown, the too-infinite promise proposed by art. In these East–West relations, like those between North and South, periphery and centre (with the recent appropriation and mediatization of hip-hop), it is often a matter of skilful exploitation of a vocabulary, rather than an inquiry into the meaning of bodily states and of 'interior' philosophies. Those who have asked the real questions, without any veiled exoticism or orientalism, are the African-born choreographer Elsa Wolliaston, and the Japanese dancer, Hideyuki Yano, who, each within their own culture, have sought to communicate what is essential and universal in the presence of bodies beyond any visible form. Indeed, their shared concerns have brought them to work together despite their apparently dissimilar dance and cultural contexts.

Networks and transformations in the 1990s

Mediatization, and the merciless and often arbitrary processes of selection which this has created, have split the French contemporary dance community into two. The 'self-taught', those who had wholeheartedly entered into the game of the 'explosion', are undoubtedly those who were thrust into the limelight for ideological reasons, while a large number of contemporary dance artists were, and still are, marginalized. Interestingly, it is in this latter group that are vested greater knowledge and mastery of the tools and resources of dance, and that may be found the best teachers. There exists, therefore, in France a kind of 'inter-dance' or 'sub-dance', which has little or no access to the grand spectacular projects, and which, it would seem, is in charge of both the basic tools of the choreographic craft as well as of critical thought. This form of dance exists through the numerous associative networks (the equivalent of British community dance projects, for example) and in events such as *Danse à l'École* (dance in schools), established by Marcelle Bonjour, who organizes an annual festival at Chartres and, since 1983, a week's intensive course jointly funded by the ministries of culture and education. As the aims of these latter organizations are essentially educational and reflexive, they are left relatively unscathed by production constraints.

Since the end of the 1980s, it is in these networks that, through a slow process of maturation and awareness of its own internal dynamics, contemporary dance has evolved. It has begun to produce considerable transformations, by capillary means, even in the most highly mediatized choreographic milieus. Certain choreographers such as Odile Duboc have always navigated between both spheres, shifting between an overexposed world (in all senses) and those spaces where teaching and debate weave the backcloth of contemporary dance. Gradually, others – among whom some of the best-known are Daniel Larrieu and Régine Chopinot – have been influenced by this shadow world, and have become aware of the resources that it can offer as well as of the validity of the values that it defends.

To these transformations must be added the creation of the earlier mentioned Diplôme d'État de Professeur de Danse, which alone confers legitimacy in the private sector. Created in 1989, after a gestation period of twenty-four years and under the aegis of Françoise Dupuy, it has brought together and challenged dancers in contexts other than those related uniquely to choreographic production, and has thus regenerated historical and theoretical consciousness of dance. State-funded centres for the training of professional dance teachers, such as the former IFEDEM in Paris, now incorporated into the APCND (Association pour la préfiguration du Centre National de la Danse), have become important vectors in the transformation and even training of professional dancers, until then poorly equipped for their particular practice. Under the 'patronage' of philosopher Michel Bernard and the influence of such charismatic figures as Hubert Godard (Head of the Department of Dance at the University of Paris VIII, one of two degree-awarding departments in France; the other is within the University of Nice), a revival in the study and analysis of movement has also otherwise reoriented the perception of contemporary dance and the evolution of its criteria.

Since the 1990s, the idea of returning to more experimental situations, to choreography that owes its justification to exploratory work on the body and the materials of dance, begins to see the light of day. As a result, we are now witnessing a renewal of avant-garde attitudes, which challenge the habits of seduction or the spectacular conformity which had accrued during the 1980s. Young choreographers are attempting to refashion both the tools and perspectives of contemporary dance with a fresh interest in improvisation, unframed and off-stage performance, and so on. All of them, including, for example, Boris Charmatz and Emmanuelle Huynh, have belonged to the most aware, forward-thinking and formative companies (for example, those of Dominique Bagouet, Régine Chopinot and Odile Duboc). All have been radically committed to various forms of political militancy (especially Alain Buffard, Nathalie Collantès, Matthieu Doze, Christophe Haleb and Frédéric Werlé), as well as engaged in establishing contacts with the international dance scene in Berlin, Brussels, Lisbon, New York and elsewhere. This has provoked a number of their 'elders', comfortably ensconced in the CCNs, to follow suit with the creation of research and training programmes, thus far neglected, and of a CCN national association in 1995 to identify strategies for dance in the recession-ridden 1990s.

The Classical Heritage

In the wake of the Second World War, the Paris Opéra and its ballet, as well as the Comédie Française, were perceived, by French bourgeois culture, as emblems of national identity or even as sites of artistic 'resistance' to enemy incursion. If the identificatory value and historical deep-rootedness of its institutions, both founded by Louis XIV, are certain, the issue of cultural 'resistance' is somewhat more questionable. Although there is no definitive evidence to confirm the accusations of collaboration levied during the fraught post-war period of score-settling against Serge Lifar – *maître de ballet*, choreographer and *premier danseur étoile* at the Opéra from 1930 to 1958 except for two years after the liberation – it is clear that French cultural institutions accommodated the occupying forces: a number of dance companies, including the Ballet de l'Opéra, continued to function and create almost uninterruptedly between 1940 and 1944.

Indeed, ballet, for reasons other than its historic traditions, was then truly, though not exclusively, French. In line with his efficacious reforms, the Russian-born Serge Lifar, a former Diaghilev dancer, trained and imposed French artists to succeed the stars with Russian surnames such as Olga Spessivtseva and Nina Vyroubova. The new *étoiles* were named Lycette Darsonval, Solange Schwarz, Yvette Chauviré and so on. The 'neoclassical' aesthetic that he instituted was redolent with a certain French 'good taste' in dance, an interpretative art replete with a finesse and lyricism never to be equalled. To add the finishing touch to this new 'line', he engaged collaborators with a certain tasteful modernist restraint (Jean Cocteau, Igor Markevitch, and others). Indeed, it was apparently in relation to an aesthetic decision contrary to his convictions, and faced with his political

41

adversaries of 1947 (Charles de Gaulle and André Malraux), that Serge Lifar, hurt by the choice of a Marc Chagall painting for the ceiling of the Palais Garnier, finally left the Opéra in 1958.

Despite its renewed reputation, the Ballet de l'Opéra's prestige was to be challenged, even within the classical heritage. First, there was competition from touring companies such as the Grand Ballet du Marquis de Cuevas, whose Parisian seasons were very successful during the 1950s. Then there were departures from ambitious young bloods such as Roland Petit. Insubordination, personal ambition or the allure of novelty had not ceased to provoke such dissidence since the eighteenth century. After his resignation in 1944, Roland Petit founded, with Opéra star Janine Charrat (banished, like Serge Lifar, during the post-war period), the Ballets des Champs Élysées, a successful but short-lived company, best known for its 1946 triumph *Le Jeune Homme et la Mort*, starring the renowned dancer Jean Babilée. Abandoning the company after three years, he formed the Ballets de Paris, which was to immortalize the legendary couple of Renée (Zizi) Jeanmaire and Roland Petit, first made famous with their performance of the erotic *Carmen* (1949). Continued international success as a neoclassical choreographer led to national recognition and Petit's institutional reinstatement with the directorship, in 1972, of the CCN at Marseilles, the most important classical company after the Ballet de l'Opéra.

But the principal opponent (while maintaining the canons of classical ballet as an aesthetic yardstick for training and composition) was and still is Maurice Béjart, whose exile was not only from the conformism of ballet but from France itself, beginning in 1959 with a sojourn in Belgium of thirty-three years. His dissent and nonconformism were of a completely different order, and have provoked a double revolution, first in terms of social mores, and second as regards his choice of choreographic themes. Abandoning the audience of bourgeois balletomanes, he opened his company's performances to all social classes including a younger and more culturally diverse public, by using either independent fringe venues, such as the Théâtre Hébertot, or more popular venues such as sports stadiums or town halls. His use of themes and references corresponded to a modern vision of theatre, cinema and literature, with which a progressive audience could identify. He was rapidly incorporated into the left-wing movement of popular-culture exponents, spearheaded by those such as Jean Vilar who from the 1960s invited him to the Avignon Festival. Then, in 1967, Ariane Mnouchkine, founder and director of the Théâtre du Soleil, solicited the collaboration of his dancers for her production of *A Midsummer's Night's Dream*, since Maurice Béjart had unconventionally engaged, for his Ballet du XXᵉ Siècle (1960–92), dancers with strong personalities and of cosmopolitan origins who did not correspond to the physical canons of ballet. Finally, the infamous *Messe pour le temps présent* (1967), with electronic music by Pierre Henry, was a foretaste, if not of May 1968 itself, then at least of some of its images, and consecrated Béjart with rock-star status. Let us note that in 1968 he stood beside Jean Vilar, confronted with protests against the Avignon Festival during which actors from the Living Theatre were engaging in a theatrical revolution of a totally different kind. Since then, as a cultural exile, Maurice Béjart has managed to continue creating abroad, after Belgium in Switzerland, where he remains, and has founded some of the most influential dance schools, Mudra in Brussels and in Dakar, Senegal. Despite his continued provocation and exile, he was the first ever choreographer to be elected to the Académie Française.

But it is perhaps within the Ballet de l'Opéra itself that young dancers emerging in the 1970s and 1980s have wrought more profound, and for us more significant, transformations by introducing a less spectacular but more radical artistic current. The influence of Carolyn Carlson, the advent of guest choreographers such as Merce Cunningham in 1973, and, later, Douglas Dunn, Lucinda Childs, Karole Armitage, Andy Degroat, and, from closer to home, Dominique Bagouet, Maguy Marin and Odile Duboc among others, precipitated a form of self-questioning amongst this post-1968 generation, an interrogation concerning their work and the meaning of their lives in dance. Before establishing the GRCOP, Jacques Garnier had already left to found with Brigitte Lefèvre (since 1995 the Opéra's Directrice de la Danse), the Théâtre du Silence, the only contemporary dance company founded by ex-Opéra dancers to break successfully with the classical code. Others, like the enchanting couple, Wilfride Piollet and Jean Guizerix (*maître de ballet* at the Opéra from autumn 1998, succeeding Nureyev's appointee, Eugène Poliakoff), remained within the classical tradition in order to effect a revolution from inside, not only by working with contemporary choreographers such as Merce Cunningham and Andy Degroat, but by developing their own approach to the classical language. Through historical research and the analysis of movement, with Odile Rouquet as partner (1985 and 1991), they have questioned the foundations of their 'bodily trajectories'. One of their projects is the reappraisal and restitution of the values of the French school, with its tradition of sensitivity and delicacy, inherited from *étoile* Carlotta Zambelli's era as ballet-mistress from the 1930s to the mid-1950s, and particularly represented during the 1960s by the teaching of Maître Yves Brieux,[6] considered today as having been a veritable guru. This reassertion of the French heritage challenges, even today, the ostentatious and arrogant aesthetic developed by certain leanings among those at the helm of the Ballet de l'Opéra since the 1980s.

This reflexive approach to the classical tradition, to which others such as Jean-Christophe Paré have committed themselves, was nurtured on two fronts. First came the important rediscovery in France of baroque dance under the aegis of the academic Francine Lancelot, founder of the company Ris et Danceries. While the reconstruction and study of former choreographic traditions are not unique to France and have long since been undertaken within Anglo-American academia, the impulse to create, to perform, to train and to renew contact with this lost aesthetic was considerable and also touched (perhaps even more so) contemporary as well as classical dancers. The latter, however, were stimulated to delve into their own memories, and to undertake a return to sources which previously would have been impossible. Regional companies such as the Ballet de l'Opéra de Nantes and later the Ballet du Rhin, both under Jean-Paul Gravier developed a passion for such research, which resulted in productions as successful as *La Fille mal gardée* (1990).

The second influence emanated from the creation of the Diplôme d'État, which invited every great discipline to reflect upon its specificity and its foundations, and to undertake a re-examination of the aesthetic and bodily prerequisites of its work. Even more than the integration of a modern and contemporary repertoire into the Ballet de l'Opéra (a policy initiated in the 1960s during *maître de ballet* Michel Descombey's reign, continued by Rudolf Nureyev during his term as the Opéra's Directeur de la Danse during the 1980s, and now prolonged under Brigitte Lefèvre's leadership), we believe that what brings the different disciplines closer together is not the participation in a similar orientation, but this shared concern with genuine reflection and inquiry in relation to an artistic practice. Even when this attitude is applied to a traditional code, it remains implicitly contemporary. If the French school of ballet no longer produces, as in other European countries, brilliant choreographers, with the proviso that, rightly or wrongly, this would distance them from the classical tradition, this fine line of flight throws into the limelight far greater stakes.[7]

Conclusion

This analysis of the classical heritage clearly attests to our methodological biases. We have privileged aspects of reality, not always derived from the most spectacular or media-oriented events, but indicative of formative trends, which, even if they are not always salient, are those that make history. The extraordinary proliferation of works in contemporary dance, with diverse aesthetics, some of which show an undeniable quality of artistry, forbids us, even if only because of its quantitative aspect, from drawing a dividing line between 'important' and 'less highly mediatized' choreographers. The century of a 'hundred flowers' has not produced striking pieces, but an immense bouquet of diverse projects, all of which have not been equally exposed, to reuse Walter Benjamin's (1991: 147) notion of 'exposability', not that this permits their categorization according to an evaluative hierarchy (Dupuy 1998). Here one finds the eternal crossover between the visible and the invisible, between the forgotten and the remembered which underlies the history of dance in France. This history has perhaps required its own form of repression for its elaboration, in order to produce, at least in contemporary dance, this florescence of small masters, who, in the absence of any single totemic figure, are abandoned to a happy and fecund anarchy. And it is a paradox, perhaps, that this creative freedom and profusion contrasts with the arbitrariness of state evaluation and its immense financial powers of discrimination, and with the cultural 'violence' (in Pierre Bourdieu's sense) of the media. This notwithstanding, dance is developing in remarkable ways, both within and outside institutional structures. It is a pity, however, that the latter do not encourage, in accordance with their artistic and political missions, sites for creation protected from the fickleness of the programming market. The dance world in France is a fertile terrain for both

44

reflection and artistic practice, but a terrain constantly threatened, from the inside and the outside, by the contradictions of an unresolved history.

Notes

1 In 1996 and 1997, the CCNs received nearly 75 per cent of the Délégation à la Danse's total budget for grants to 'choreographic companies', that is companies producing new works, excluding the Ballet de l'Opéra de Paris.

2 In France, dance remains highly centralized both in terms of policy and funding, despite continuing efforts made since the 1970s towards institutional decentralization through, for example the creation of the Directions Régionales des Affaires Culturelles (DRAC), regional arts and culture councils that report to and depend upon central government. There are parallel, regionally funded music and dance councils, the Associations Départementales de la Musique et de la Danse (ADDM), which have greater local autonomy but little power and fewer resources. For further details on French dance policy and state institutionalization, see Rudnicki (1989) and Fleming (1995) whose accounts are a little out of date but provide a thorough overview.

3 Unless otherwise indicated, sources used for this introduction include Aubry (1989); Fleming (1995); *Journal Officiel de la République Française* (1989: 8674–6 and 1992: 3104–5); Martin (1996); C. and Marmin (1998); *Mesures* (1998); Rudnicki (1989); as well as interviews with Jean-François Driant, administrative director, Ballet Atlantique, and Philippe Verrièle, editor of *Les Saisons de la Danse*.

4 The *assises* of 1981 were the first meeting of its kind in dance. A second such event was held in February 1998 prior to the amalgamation later that year of the theatre arts, dance and music into a single ministerial unit to be called the Direction du Théâtre et du Spectacle Vivant (Division of Theatre and of Live Performance) and in the context of the opening of a national centre for dance, the CND (Centre National de Danse), which will administer the Diplôme d'État as well as act as a research centre with dance library, and so on. One of the two days was devoted to working parties on three topics: concepts and conditions of dance as public service; evaluation of the artistic project (criteria, expertise and competencies of evaluating bodies especially the DRACs, which from 1998 are directly subsidizing choreographic and community dance projects in the regions); and structuring of state organizations and funding (C. 1998: 33).

5 See Robinson (1990) for further details on the 'rise of modern dance' in France.

6 Maître Yves Brieux was a teacher at the Paris Conservatoire (CNSMDP) from the 1960s to the early 1990s and also taught privately. His Opéra pupils included the innovators Jacques Garnier, Brigitte Lefèvre and *étoiles* Jean Guizerix and Wilfride Piollet, as well as other Opéra stars such as Jean-Yves Lormeau, Monique Loudières and the late Claire Motte.

7 Sources include Guest (1976), and Michel and Ginot (1995), a good, but sometimes inaccurate, general reader.

References

Aubry, C. (1989) 'The CNDC. A Centre of Training, Creativity and Co-production', *Dance Theatre Journal* 7(1): 37–8.

Barthes, R. ([1957] 1972) *Mythologies*, London: Jonathan Cape.

Bazin, A. (1957) *Qu'Est-ce que le Cinéma?* Paris: Le Cerf.

Benjamin, W. (1991) 'L'Œuvre d'Art à l'Epoque de sa Reproduction Mécanisée' [1930] in *Écrits Français*, Paris: Gallimard. ('The Work of Art in the Age of Mechanical Reproduction' in H. Arendt (ed.) *Illuminations*, London, Fontana 1973).

Bentivoglio, L. (1987) 'Europe et États-Unis: un Courant' in M. Febvre (ed.) *La Danse au Défi*, Montreal: Éditions Parachute.

Degaine, A. (1992) *Histoire du Théâtre Dessinée*, Paris: A. G. Nizet.

Deleuze, G. (1983) *Cinéma I. L'Image–Mouvement*, Paris: Éditions de Minuit.

Deleuze, G. (1985) *Cinéma II. L'Image–Temps*, Paris: Éditions de Minuit.

Dondi, S. (1998) 'L'ONDA, un Observatoire Privilégié', *Les Saisons de la Danse* 303, April: 41.

Dupuy, D. (1998) 'La Danse Contemporaine, l'Insaisie', *Néant* 97 4, February.

Fleming, M. H. K. (1995) 'Dance Policy in France', unpublished MA dissertation, Department of Arts Policy and Management, City University, London.

Golan, R. (1996) *French Art Between the Two Wars*, Massachusetts: MIT Press.

Guest, I. (1976) *Le Ballet de l'Opéra de Paris*, Paris: Théâtre National de l'Opéra and Flammarion.

Jakobson, R. (1971) 'La Dominante', in *Readings in Poetics*, Cambridge, MA: MIT Press; Paris: du Seuil, 1977.

Journal Officiel de la République Française (1989) 'Loi no 89–468 du 10 Juillet 1989 Relative à l'Enseignement de la Danse', 11 July.

Journal Officiel de la République Française (1992) 'Décret no 92–193 du 27 Février 1992 Portant Application de la Loi no 89–468 du 10 Juillet 1989 Relative à l'Enseignement de la Danse', 29 February.

Louppe, L. (1996) 'Hybrid Bodies', *Writings on Dance: The French Issue* 15, winter: 62–7.

Mao Tse-Tung (1967) 'On the Correct Handling of Contradictions among the People' (1957) in *Quotations from Chairman Mao Tse-Tung* (2nd edn), Peking: Foreign Languages Press.

Martin, C. (1996) 'Y'a-t-il une Vie après un Centre Chorégraphique National?', *Les Saisons de la Danse* 286, November: 40–4.

Martin, C. (1998) 'Cristallisation. Rencontres Professionnelles de la Danse', *Les Saisons de la Danse* 303, April: 33.

Martin, C. and Marmin, O. (1998) *Guide des Métiers de la Danse*, Paris: Cité de la Musique, en collaboration avec *Les Saisons de la Danse*.

Mesures (1998) 'L'Aide aux Compagnies Chorégraphiques: Bilan 1997', publication of the Direction de la Musique et de la Danse, Ministry of Culture and Communication, 47, March.

Michel, M. and Ginot, I. (1995) *La Danse au XXᵉ Siècle*, Paris: Bordas.

Pomarès, J. (1994) 'Parcours du Danseur: de la Formation à la Création', *Positions. Cahiers de la Drac PACA*, Aix-en-Provence: 50–9.

Robinson, J. (1990) *L'Aventure de la Danse Moderne en France (1920–1970)*, Paris: Éditions Bougé. [English translation in preparation.]

Rouquet, O. (1985) *Les Techniques d'Analyse du Mouvement et le Danseur*, Paris: Fédération française de la danse.

Rouquet, O. (1991) *La Tête aux Pieds*, Paris: Recherche en Mouvement.

Rudnicki, E. (1989) 'Government Financing of Dance in France', *Dance Theatre Journal* 7(1): 30–3.

Siegel, M. (1996) 'Visible Secrets', in G. Morris (ed.) *Moving Words*, London: Routledge.

Verrièle, P. *et al.* (1997) '99 Biographies pour Comprendre la Jeune Danse Française', *Les Saisons de la Danse numéro hors série*, summer 1997.

Key Texts

Adolphe, J.-M. (1991) 'The Source and the Destination: Concepts of Memory, Movement and Perception in French Dance', *Ballet International*, special edition, January: 23–9.

Cottias, J. (1992) 'The Sociological Evolution of the New Dance Public', *Choreography and Dance* 2(1): 39–53.

Dance Theatre Journal (1989) 7, 1.

Dupuy, D. (1998) 'La Danse Contemporaine, l'Insaisie', *Néant* 97, 4, February.

Louppe, L. (1996) 'Hybrid Bodies', *Writings on Dance: the French Issue* 15, winter: 62–7.

Martin, C. and Marmin, O. (1998) *Guide des Métiers de la Danse*, Paris: Cité de la Musique, en collaboration avec *Les Saisons de la Danse*.

Michel, M. and Ginot, I. (1995) *La Danse au XXᵉ Siècle*, Paris: Bordas.

Niclas, L. (dir.) (1989) *La Danse, Naissance d'un Mouvement de Pensée*, Paris: Armand Colin.

Robinson, J. (1990) *L'Aventure de la Danse Moderne en France (1920–1970)*, Paris: Éditions Bougé.

Verrièle, P. *et al.* (1997) '99 Biographies pour Comprendre la Jeune Danse Française', *Les Saisons de la Danse numéro hors série*, summer.

Table 3 Important dance and political events in France (1900 to present)

Year	Dance: artists, works, events	Dance: institutions	Arts scene	Sociocultural and political events
1900	*Isadora Duncan Loïe Fuller at Universal Exhibition			Universal Exhibition
1905			Fauvism	Church and State separated Unified Socialist Party
1907			Cubism	
1909	Ballets Russes debut, Théâtre du Châtelet	Ballets Russes founded in Paris		
1910	Schéhérazade, L'Oiseau de feu (Fokine)			
1911	Le Spectre de la rose, Petrushka (Fokine)			
1912	L'Après-midi d'un faune (Vaslav Nijinsky)		Futurism reaches Paris from Italy/Russia	
1913	Le Sacre du printemps (Nijinsky)		À La Recherche du temps perdu (Proust)	
1914				First World War
1917	Parade (Léonide Massine)	Diaghilev's modernist phase		
1918				End of World War I
1920			Height of Dadaism Théâtre National Populaire (TNP)	French Communist Party
1923	Les Noces villageoises (Bronislava Nijinska)	Rolf de Maré's Ballets Suédois		
1924	Relâche (Jean Börlin) *Sakharoffs	Opéra dir. Jacques Rouch engages first Russian dancer, Olga Spessivtseva	Manifeste du Surréalisme (Breton)	
1925	*Josephine Baker with Revue Nègre	Dance for girls enters Paris Conservatoire		
1927	La Chatte (George Balanchine)	Isadora Duncan dies in Nice	Metropolis (Fritz Lang)	
1928	Apollon musagète (Balanchine)	Loïe Fuller dies in France		
1929	Prodigal Son (Balanchine) Prométhée (Lifar) at Paris Opéra	Death of Diaghilev and disbandment of Ballets Russes		

Table 3 *continued*

1930	Lifar joins Paris Opéra		
1931	*Mary Wigman		
1932	The Green Table (Kurt Jooss) wins AID choreographic competition		Colonial Exhibition
	Archives Internationales de la Danse Ballets Russes now in Monte-Carlo		
1934	*Jean Weidt		
1935	Icare (Lifar)		
	Manifeste du Chorégraphe (Lifar)		
1936		Cinémathèque Française	
1938	La Mort du cygne, film with Janine Charrat	Le Théâtre et son double (Artaud)	Married women gain autonomous legal status
	Jean Weidt's Ballets 38		
1939			Second World War
1940			German occupation of Paris; Vichy government
1942	Yvette Chauviré named étoile	L'Étranger (Camus)	
1944	Lifar excluded for life from all state theatres by Opéra's purge committee	Huis Clos, 1st play by Sartre	Allied landing, Paris liberated
			Général de Gaulle heads provisional government
1945	Nouveau Ballet de Monte Carlo under Lifar	Gérard Philippe in Caligula (Camus)	Women gain vote
	Ballets des Champs Elysées		
	Jean Weidt's Ballet des Arts		
1946	Le Jeune Homme et la Mort (Petit)	Centres Dramatiques Nationaux (Jeanne Laurent)	De Gaulle resigns
			War in Indochina
1947	Dance for boys at Paris Conservatoire	Festival d'Avignon	Fourth Republic
	Marquis de Cuevas' Ballets de Monte-Carlo	Marcel Marceau	
	Les Mirages (Lifar reinstated at Opéra)	La Peste (Camus)	
1948	Adame Miroir (Janine Charrat)	Les Mains sales (Sartre)	Marshall Plan
1949	Carmen (Petit)	Le Deuxième Sexe (de Beauvoir)	Atlantic Pact
	Petit's Ballets de Paris		
	AID folds, and becomes CIDD		
	*Merce Cunningham		

Table 3 continued

Year	Dance: artists, works, events	Dance: institutions	Arts scene	Sociocultural and political events
1950	*Martha Graham *José Limon with Ruth Page		Absurdist theatre	
1952	*New York City Ballet *Ballets Africains	Ballets de Paris defunct Harald Lander Dance Director at Opéra	Jean Vilar takes over TNP at Chaillot	
1953	*Les Algues* (Charrat)		*Waiting for Godot* (Beckett)	Defeat in Indochina Algerian insurrection
1954	Martha Graham and Company	Dupuys' Ballets Modernes de Paris		Beginning of Algerian War
1955	*Symphonie pour un homme seul* (Maurice Béjart) *Moiseyev's Soviet Ballets	Jacqueline Robinson's Atelier de la Danse		
1957	José Limon	Labanotation at ESEC	*Mythologies* (Barthes) Nouveau Roman	Rome Treaty and Common Market (EEC)
1958	*Frères Inmains* (Michel Descombey)	Karine Waehner's Les Ballets Contemporains	Étienne Decroux to USA Actor's Studio	Vth Republic: De Gaulle elected President
1959	*Jerome Robbins	Modern dance in physical education training	Nouvelle Vague Biennale de Paris	André Malraux First Minister of Cultural Affairs
1960	*Pas de Dieux* (Gene Kelly) at Opéra	Béjart leaves France Waehner at Schola Cantorum	*À Bout de Souffle* (Godard)	France gets atom bomb
1961	*Lac des cygnes* (Bourmeister) *West Side Story* (Robbins)	Rosella Hightower's Centre International de la Danse	*Histoire de la folie à l'âge classique* (Foucault) Maisons de la Culture	
1962	*Paul Taylor	Festival des Baux-de-Provence University dance classes Jazz training at Opéra		Algerian independence

Table 3 *continued*

1963	La Reine verte (Béjart)	Jérôme Andrews' Compagnons de la Danse	Tel Quel journal	
	Cendrillon, last performance of de Cuevas Grand Ballet	Festival International de Danse de Paris (winner de Cuevas Grand Ballet)	Jerzy Grotowski	
	*Erick Hawkins, Kurt Jooss			
1964	La Damnation de Faust (Béjart) at Opéra	Centre International de la Danse (CID)	Festival de Nancy (Jack Lang)	
	*Alvin Ailey		Ariane Mnouchkine's Théâtre du Soleil	
	Cunningham tour			
1965	Notre-Dame de Paris (Petit) for Opéra	Law on dance teaching	Lire 'le Capital' (Althusser)	De Gaulle re-elected President
1966	Le Sacre du printemps (Béjart) at Opéra	Michel Descombey's Ballet Studio at Opéra	Écrits (Lacan)	France leaves NATO
	Cunningham at Festival International de Paris		Les Mots et les choses (Foucault)	
			Living Theatre	
1967	Messe pour le temps présent (Béjart)			
1968	Modern dancers at National Museum of Modern Art	Concours de Bagnolet	Ariane Mnouchkine at La Cartoucherie	Students riot and workers strike in Paris
	*Batsheva Dance Company	Ballet Théâtre Contemporain (first CCN)	Théâtre des Nations becomes Théâtre de la Ville	
	*Alwin Nikolais			
1969	Fiat lux (Jacques Garnier) part of Opéra Young Choreographers evening	Théâtre Français de la Danse	Revolutionary university at Vincennes	De Gaulle resigns: George Pompidou President
	Objectif 28 (Michel Caserta)	Garnier and Brigitte Lefèvre's Théâtre du Silence		
1970	*Viola Farber	Last Festival International de Danse de Paris	L'Écriture et la différence (Derrida)	
	*Susan Buirge			
1971	Density 21–12 (Carolyn Carlson)	Béjart's Mudra in Brussels	Robert Wilson at Nancy Festival	
1972		Petit at Ballet National de Marseille	Libération, Sartre's newspaper	

Table 3 continued

Year	Dance: artists, works, events	Dance: institutions	Arts scene	Sociocultural and political events
1973	Limón and Taylor in Rudolf [Nuyerev] and Friends Un Jour ou deux (Cunningham) for Opéra *Trisha Brown	Rolf Liebermann Opéra Director First university dance courses at Paris VII	Choreographers included in authors' union (SNAC)	
1974	Carolyn Carlson étoile-chorégraphe at Opéra			
1975	Sumdaga (Elsa Wolliaston and Hideyuki Yano) *Susanne Linke	Carlson's GRTOP Festival Danse at Aix	The Dead Class (Kantor) Surveiller et punir (Foucault)	
1976	Chansons de nuit (Dominique Bagouet)	Bagouet, Quentin Rouillier etc. at Le Palace		
1977		Centre National de Danse	Centre National d'Art et de Culture Georges-Pompidou (CNAC)	
1978	Nieblas de Nino (Maguy Marin) *Pina Bausch at Nancy Festival	Contemporaine (CNDC) under Nikolais Ballets Modernes de Paris disband		
1979	Manfred (Nuyerev) for Opéra Dance (Lucinda Childs) for Bordeaux Sygma Festival	Le Groupe Émile Dubois (J.-C. Gallotta) Biennale Nationale de Danse du Val-de-Marne	'Paris Berlin' German Expressionist exhibition Empreintes. Écrits sur la danse (ed. Daniel Dobbels)	
1980	Tabula Rasa (François Verret) Pulcinella (Douglas Dunn) for Opéra	Garnier's GRCOP Montpellier CCN and Festival under Bagouet Francine Lancelot's Ris et Danceries	Mille plateaux (Deleuze/Guattari) Tel Quel Cunningham interviews	
1981	May B (Marin) Mad Rush (Childs) for GRCOP	Lyon Maison de la Danse Assises de la Danse Le Jardin de la Danse	Foucault dies	François Mittérand President Jack Lang Minister of Culture

Table 3 continued

1982	*Chiquenaudes* (Daniel Larrieu) *Eclats d'infante* (Karine Saporta)	Dance Division in Ministry of Culture Andy Degroat's Red Note	Choreographers included in authors' society (SACD)
1983	*France/Dance* (William Forsythe) and *Nouvelle lune* (Degroat) for Opéra	Nureyev Opéra Dance Director	*L'Image–mouvement* (Deleuze) *Le Moi Peau* (Didier Anzieu)
1984	*Le Sacre de printemps* (Taylor) for Opéra Karole Armitage at GRCOP	Lyon Biennale de Danse Grenoble CCN under Gallotta Basse-Normandie CCN under Rouillier	
1985	*Marché noir* (Angelin Preljocaj) *Quelques pas graves de Batiste* (Lancelot) for Opéra	Nevers CCN under Anne-Marie Reynaud François Raffinot co-directs Ris et Danceries Dance enters Lyon Conservatoire (CNSM)	*L'Image–temps* (Deleuze) Gérard Violette at Théâtre de la Ville Polemic over Buren's Palais-Royal sculpture
1986	*Assaï* (Bagouet) *La Chute de la maison Carton* (Verret)	Dance at Sorbonne Poitou-Charente CCN under Régine Chopinot Lyon Biennale on German dance	Festival Vidéo–Danse at Pompidou Centre Wigman's texts translated — Jacques Chirac Prime Minister: 'cohabitation' of left and right
1987	*Saut de l'ange* (Bagouet with Christian Boltanski) *Canard pékinois* (Josef Nadj)	General decree on dance	Collaborations renewed between visual artists and choreographers cf. Bagouet/Boltanski
1988	*La Conjuration* (Piollet and Guizerix)	International Year of Dance	Mittérand re-elected President
1989	*La Danse des sabots* (Philippe Decouflé) *Tantz Schule* (Jiri Kylian) for Opéra	Diplôme d'État de Professeur de Danse Contemporary dance at Paris Conservatoire	Decouflé included in bicentenary celebrations parade with *La Danse des sabots* Bicentenary of French Revolution

Table 3 continued

Year	Dance: artists, works, events	Dance: institutions	Arts scene	Sociocultural and political events
1990	*Roméo et Juliette* (Preljocaj)	Franche-Comté Belfort-Sochaux CCN under Odile Duboc		
1991	*Saint Georges* (Chopinot)	Dance at Paris VIII University		Maastricht Treaty and European Union (EU)
1992	'La jeune danse française' at Opéra; Albertville Winter Olympics (Decouflé)	Ballet de Marseille school; Béjart to Switzerland; Labanotation at Paris Conservatoire		
1993	*Projet de la matière* (Duboc); À bras le corps (Boris Charmatz/Dimitri Chamblas); *La Bayadère* (Nuyerev)	Angers CNDC under Joëlle Bouvier/Régis Obadia; Tours CCN under Larrieu; Larrieu founds Le Chorégraphique festival; Quattuor Albrecht Knust		Edouard Balladur as Prime Minister: second 'cohabitation'
1994	Guizerix in *Les sept dernières paroles du Christ* by seven contemporary choreographers	Rennes/Brittany CCN under Catherine Diverrès/Bernado Montet		
1995	*Végétal* (Chopinot and Andy Goldsworthy)	Brigitte Lefèvre Opéra Dance Director		Chirac President, Alain Juppé Prime Minister: return of right
1996	*Jérôme Bel* (Jérôme Bel); *Le Sacre du printemps* (Bausch) at Opéra	Aix-en-Provence CCN under Preljocaj	Fondation Cartier pour l'Art Contemporain hosts dance	
1997		Petit leaves Ballet National de Marseille		Lionel Jospin Socialist Prime Minister: new 'cohabitation'
1998		Opening of Centre National de la Danse		

* First visit

4

GERMANY

Between institutions and aesthetics: choreographing Germanness?

Claudia Jeschke and Gabi Vettermann

Structurally, the political situation of dance in Germany[1] in the twentieth century has been characterized by two phenomena: the lay or mass movement, and the emancipation of dance or its attainment of equality within the arts. Both phenomena have operated as premises for aesthetic conceptualization, and as factors reflecting the sociocultural situation. At the same time, they functioned as continuities that connect the periods before and after the Second World War. The participation of laypeople in the world of dance, originally conceived as innovative – sometimes anti-bourgeois, sometimes democratic – was prevalent during the first half of the century, before it found its socialist transformation in the eastern part of the separated Germanies. Inclining to the principle of capitalist efficiency, the western part did not integrate the lay movement. The second developmental line, the effort of dance to find its own autonomy, is still ongoing.

Before the twentieth century, theatre and dance were not incorporated into a national consciousness: between the emergence of German bourgeois society at the end of the eighteenth century and the consolidation of a state ruled by the bourgeois at the end of the nineteenth century, it was not possible to make theatre appeal to all social strata in Germany. In contrast to the situations in France, Italy and England, for example, theatre-going remained the privilege of the nobility and a few intellectuals of the bourgeois class.

In the political climate poised between aesthetic and sociocultural premises, two particular national dance identities evolved in Germany during the twentieth century: the *Ausdruckstanz* of the 1930s and the West German *Tanztheater* of the 1970s and 1980s. At the end of the century, both have receded into history as styles, although both have proved to be highly influential far beyond the nation's borders, and still contribute to the organization and understanding of dance in Germany. While *Ausdruckstanz* was primarily concerned with dance as a philosophical, metaphysical or even spiritual statement, *Tanztheater* featured body and movement in the discourse of the psyche and society, everyday behaviour and its norms.

Aesthetically, both *Tanztheater* and *Ausdruckstanz* were formulated beyond the organization and *Gestalt* of classical dance, which was and still is characteristic of (or at least influential for) stage dancing in the non-centralized German theatre system. There were and continue to be many different *loci* for dance in Germany, producing and presenting a multistylistic picture that is profoundly internationalized by the establishments of festivals and special performance spaces. For both *Ausdruckstanz* and *Tanztheater*, political development proved crucial: *Ausdruckstanz* usually refused to accept, or simply avoided the political implications of dance and art in general, while *Tanztheater* lost most of its political impact when the situation in Germany changed dramatically with the Wende, the process of unification that started in the late 1980s. At the end of the 1990s, there is a general intellectual fatigue that does not spare dance.

Life Forms and Reforms: Before the Second World War

The term *Ausdruckstanz* embraces different, even contradictory currents, concepts and ideas of dance, from expressionism to social agitprop. Its peak was during the Weimar Republic, between the 1920s and 1930s.[2] *Ausdruckstanz* emerged in close association with the then significant movement of *Körperreform*. With a 'back to nature' ideal, young men and women of the bourgeoisie were searching, emotionally, if not ecstatically, for their roots, rejecting, in their eyes, the dehumanizing effects of industrialization and its resulting urbanization and alienation. The body, movement and dance – terms that were often used interchangeably – functioned as metaphors and concrete ideas for this search for origins, as aids in helping people to reconnect with all that was alive, natural and organic; on a rather poetic and self-referential, though not reflexive, level, body, movement and dance became motifs and contexts for modern, young life at large. *Ausdruckstanz* was not a clearly defined ideological, pedagogical or technical system. The metaphor of the dancer, the mover, in *Ausdruckstanz* was authenticated through the creation of general insights into life in a celebration of the universalities and common values considered or felt to be the essence of individual experience.

The history of *Ausdruckstanz* is a history of individual artists who confronted their sense of alienation from body movement and nature in many different ways: by following the idea of synaesthesia (Loie Fuller), by treating movement in a quasi-pictorial manner (Rita Sacchetto, Sent M'Ahesa, Clotilde von Derp and Alexander Sakharoff), by trying to revitalize dance through notions of antiquity and neoclassicism (Isadora Duncan, the Wiesenthal sisters), or by renewing it by means of metaphysics, religion, or mathematics (Duncan as well as Oskar Schlemmer); and a few (they were the exceptions) felt that dance should respond or correspond to moral, social and even political factors (Jean Weidt, Valeska Gert). In their particular searches for 'true' expression, the protagonists of *Ausdruckstanz* fervently believed that the essence of an individual being led to the notion of a collective consciousness, allowing the performer to propagate a life through dance – a life in which everyone is deemed to be a dancer. It was this ideology of exuberant subjectivity that enabled the National Socialists easily to incorporate the existing ideals of *Ausdruckstanz* into their particular view of social uniformity within a popular Aryan community of peoples.

Aesthetic concepts

In relation to individual approaches to the body, movement and dance, *Ausdruckstanz* did not develop any approaches of theoretical significance until the 1930s, when Rudolf von Laban and Mary Wigman in particular framed its diverse methodological and artistic image. Before then, the Swiss musician and composer Émile Jaques-Dalcroze (1865–1950) had exercised a seminal influence on the fundamentals of *Ausdruckstanz* as early as the beginning of the century. By rediscovering and mysticizing the ancient significance of musical and body rhythms in his so-called Eurhythmics, he wanted to reconstruct and restore the wholeness, the unity of body, mind and soul. The Rhythmische Bildungsanstalt Jaques-Dalcroze was founded in 1910 in Dresden and was moved to Hellerau in 1911. The evolution of Jaques-Dalcroze's method and work was disrupted in 1913/14 by the beginning of the First World War, by the death of Wolf Dohrn, the founder of the Gartenstadt Hellerau, and by a probably careless authorization of protest against Germany's participation in the First World War, of which the Swiss, as a foreigner, might not have fully considered the consequences. The method itself proved to be one of the most influential teaching systems for European and international contemporary dance, more so than the Duncan school, which had lasted for a longer period, and had become successful in Germany after the First World War under the direction of Isadora's sister Elizabeth and her partner Max Merz, and continued until the mid-1960s.

In contrast to Dalcroze's synergistic view of movement, Laban and Wigman were concerned with the exploration and experience of corporeal consciousness as well as with the establishment of body control, based no longer on the traditional aesthetic of dance but on the movement potential of each single person, first applicable to the individual alone, and later to be exploited by society at large.

Rudolf von Laban (1879–1958) turned out to be one of the most influential figures of dance in this century, within Germany between the two world wars, and internationally during and after the Second World War. Early on in his life, he saw a connection between life and leisure, work and play; in this sense, he closely related dance to community and created a new kind of social dance that harmonized conceptually with the mass culture that was popular and politically accepted in Germany in the 1930s. As early as the years after 1910 he organized dance events in Munich, and concurrently he began to develop his ideas on what a dancer's education and training should look like. The result he came up with was an exploration of the autonomy, and, at the same time, the transdisciplinarity, of body and movement which he called Free Dance. Free Dance was based on the relationship between body, movement and space – the last influenced on the one hand by his interest in architecture and art, and on the other by mysticism[3] or his particular understanding of nature.

For Laban, the experience of nature meant dance. Thus, everyone who was able to experience nature could dance. Nature exposed spatial and dynamic prototypes, which he also found in the body and the movement. He held that the structures of the body, movement and nature are harmoniously connected: harmony was the result of the active interrelations between body action (movements) and its organic models found in nature (spatial and dynamic prototypes, such as crystalline forms). By applying this complex concept not only philosophically and theoretically but also practically, he became engrossed in the development of notation, in order to turn dance and its documentation as well as its creation into a pedagogic and/or scholarly topic. He was always interested too in psychophysical performance issues and, subsequently, the expressiveness of dance.[4]

After her studies with Jaques-Dalcroze in Dresden and Hellerau (1910–13), and with Rudolf von Laban at Monte Verità and in Munich (1913–14), Mary Wigman (1886–1973) began to search for Absolute Dance, the term emphasizing the primacy of creative movement. In her understanding, creative movement was no longer dominated by rhythm (as it had been for Jaques-Dalcroze), nor by expressive space (as it had been for Laban), but emanated from individual creative genius; in other words, from innermost feelings and from the mind. While Laban was interested in the equality of dance in relation to other art forms, Wigman valued its independence above all. Despite Wigman's evident artistic distance from Laban,[5] her point of view remained similar to his. In her work, she experienced the driving forces of her inner self, searched for knowledge of eternal laws. Like Laban, she too thematized the relationship between individuality and the mass, and used a mystical understanding of nature to support her topics philosophically. Her work, however, unlike Laban's, never explicitly challenged social or political subjects:

> Wigman's dances are not only other-worldly or superhuman, they are absolute. In terms of time, she reaches for eternity, in terms of space, for the cosmos . . . The pathos of Wigman's artistic creed is her conscious avoidance of any points of contact between dance and reality whatsoever. The essence of the personal individuality alone, the very nucleus of the personality, determines the dance form and its contents . . . in a word, there are to be no connections whatsoever between dance and civilization, and culture and the world around it.
>
> (Lewitan 1927: 28)

It was because of this idealistic approach that the National Socialists were able to appropriate her work. Wigman herself was ambivalent: on the one hand, she did not realize her ideological proximity to the Nazis, on the other, she felt the need to withdraw from official social and political life, but without leaving the country.[6]

Dance culture

From a nineteenth-century environment that was largely defined by aristocratic–bourgeois elements, the twentieth century brought a whole series of areas of challenge, including the relationship between dance and politics. Those challenges were mainly caused by financial distress, mixed in with, equivalent to, or complementing, the desire for recognition and political acceptance. Dance, among the other art forms, assumes a special status because its formal training has not been integrated into the curricula of school, colleges and universities to this day. Thus, it could, at worst, be dilated into a philosophical, ideologically led band of individuals, or, at best, expand into a federally subsidized institution. The only exception was ballet, which offered a clearly defined hierarchical structure in its training and scope, and in slightly varied form it still does so today. Ballet was integrated into theatrical institutions and took on a lesser role there, serving as a component of operas and operettas as well as musicals, rather than in performances devoted to dance alone. As it was, classical ballets could only be mounted on large stages because of their vast personnel requirements.

Despite, or indeed because of, the institutional problem, Laban, Wigman and other performers of *Ausdruckstanz* attempted to improve the acceptance of dance and its followers not only artistically, but also socially. In order to draw attention to the hitherto poor quality and low status of dance in Germany as well as to bring (their) dance into public consciousness, and to institutionalize it, they had to form schools, create dance groups, give lecture demonstrations, publish articles. Their work also entailed initiating dance organizations and becoming politically active in them. Wigman's school, founded in Dresden in 1920, started to perform in 1922. By 1926, it had 360 students, plus 1,200 more in departments in Hamburg, Erfurt, Frankfurt, Berlin and other towns. Laban set up his first school in Hamburg in 1923. In 1925, the association of Laban Schools listed 21 branches, plus movement choirs.[7]

One reason why Laban was so thoroughly absorbed by dance notation was that it advanced the dissemination of his ideas in the numerous sections of his school, and facilitated the conception and execution of his mass choreographies, which utilized as well as influenced the public. In tandem with the internal organization of the schools and their classes, so-called 'central' institutes were established, and diplomas were introduced as training qualifications. Master classes were created and summer terms started. Analogous to the consolidation of National Socialist supremacy, the external organization of the schools followed suit in the 1930s with conceptual and structural control coming from the state.[8] The state, a totalitarian amalgam of power, henceforth constituted the only framework for the recognition of dance and its standing among the other arts.[9] The individualism of the 1920s now began to be defamed in favour of the group-enhancing potential of choric dancing.

A national dance – that is, German dance originating from specifically German cultural history – had been championed by Laban and Wigman, as well as by the state. They did not, however, subscribe to the radical nationalization of the Aryan community of peoples and its implied nurturing of the ideal of the 'German dancing man' (*deutscher Tänzermensch*), in which 'Dance was assigned the task of heralding National Socialist man and an ideal social order – without the majority of the dancers becoming fully aware of it' (Müller and Stöckemann 1993: 127).

By the mid-1930s, *Ausdruckstanz* had conformed to the dictates of the regime and succeeded in permeating the stage anyhow,[10] and Laban could toy with the idea of placing all private schools under governmental control. In the German Master School for Dance (Deutsche Meister-Stätten für Tanz), organized by the National Socialists in 1936 – initially under Laban's directorship, and from 1937 under that of Rolf Cunz, the Advisor for Dance in the Ministry of Propaganda – many different styles began to be taught while thoroughly compromising their original intent.[11] Although, at least from 1938 onwards, attendance at this institution was obligatory for dancers who tried to pursue a professional career, in the final analysis, this dictatorial centralistic interlude of German cultural politics with *Ausdruckstanz* had no lasting effect on a traditionally uninterrupted trend in Germany of a largely conservative, bourgeois aesthetic (and its traditionally normative institutionalization), at that time pushed to Fascist extremes.

The Reichsballett Kraft durch Freude (KdF), oriented towards classical dance, was an exception. It had been founded in 1941 by Dr Robert Ley, the national leader of the governmental department Deutsche Arbeitsfront, N. S. Gemeinschaft Kraft durch Freude, as an institution that was independent from the opera and did not report to the propaganda ministry of Joseph Goebbels. The Reichsballett, directed by Friderica Derra de Moroda, existed until Goebbels's famous proclamation of 'total war' in 1944. Neither the shorter- or longer-term employment of so-called 'free'(lance) dancers at established theatre companies, nor the rush of students to independent schools, nor the specialists, professionally trained master students, who filled in the dance groups, gave rise to a counterculture (of whatever political persuasion) that would have challenged the organizational and aesthetic institutionalization of the theatre. That was true for the period before the Second World War, in which, say, Laban, or Wigman's student Max Terpis, or Laban's student Kurt Jooss, held positions of ballet-master or director in municipal and state theatres.[12] It held true as well for the period after the Second World War, when dancers and choreographers such as Dore Hoyer tried to set themselves up within theatre companies.

Only the protagonists of the West German *Tanztheater* succeeded in breaking with this practice – which doubtless would have been impossible without the preparatory, institutional, but especially the substantive work of Kurt Jooss before the Second World War. As early as the 1930s, Jooss developed the basic idea of the *Tanztheater*, conjoining ballet and modern dance trends, that, through its potential for theatrical abstraction, opened up for dance an everyday consciousness, an assimilated, critical understanding of politics, of social outlook, of the body and of movement. In 1924, Jooss accepted the post of movement director of the Municipal Theatre of Münster, and in 1927 became the head of the dance

60

department at the newly created Folkwang School in Essen. Unlike the private schools of his colleagues – mostly founded single-handedly and for which the introduction of classes became a necessity not just for ideological but also for financial reasons – the dance department at the Folkwang School was incorporated into the general art, theatre and music school under municipal leadership. Thus it was able to survive Fascism even after Jooss's emigration, and Jooss could pick up in 1949 where he had left off before the war. With the foundation of the Folkwang Tanztheater-Studio as an experimental group (1928) and the directorship of the ballet at the Essen Opera (1930), Jooss fully exploited the available structures that enabled him to realize his ideas. Jooss's arrangement with the establishment was never wholly untroubled, neither before nor after 1945.[13] Even so, the Folkwang School, along with its associated Folkwang Dance Studio, is one of the few institutions to have maintained a continuity of modern dance education in Germany to this day.[14]

On the basis of this example of pre-war development in Germany, the question arises whether the victorious stance of centralistic totalitarianism was more an idealized projection than a functional instrument: it did not challenge the independence of its various outposts ('satellites'), thus opening the floodgates to arbitrary rule – which, of course, could have negative as well as positive consequences. The National Socialist Party members in charge were fighting for their jurisdictions, and the members of the dance scene used these rivalries to their advantage, just as they themselves were used by the party. Moreover, the representatives of the 'free' dance scene lacked a clear concept of what National Socialist dance was supposed to be. Two contrasting tendencies coexisted: the tendency toward individualization, and the tendency toward unification and standardization. Both claimed – as vaguely as they did emphatically – to represent the only system that had final victory as a premise. The established members of the ballet held back politically, probably because they were more or less safe, protected by the institutional theatre and less exposed to the vagaries of survival than the 'individually' working freelancers. In any event, a national idea of dance was, ironically, not produced either by the dictatorship of the National Socialists nor by the free elections during the bourgeois period.

Theatre Forms and Reforms: After the Second World War

Bourgeois control/capitalist enchantment

In Germany, as we have seen, ballet was used as a model of opposition to as well as integration with other dance forms. The German dance scene thus always reflected and reacted to the distinctive aesthetic and organizational confrontation with international classical dance, which eventually proved to be invigorating for the second half of the twentieth century. The disenchantment following the Second World War, and the division of Germany, triggered in both parts of the country a tendency towards the formal and objective, reflecting an ideological oversaturation with expressionism and expressionist dancing. Theatrical dancing in both parts became synonymous with the ballet subsidized and performed in established opera houses: as the third force behind drama and opera, which nevertheless did not receive a commensurate share of their high subsidies. Officially, the revolutionary impulses of the pre-war period were simply ignored, though their expressive potential remained implicit in the works of choreographers who were employed in the theatres before the war and continued to work in the late 1940s and 1950s. Tatjana Gsovsky (1901–93) in Berlin, for example, devoted herself to a balletic neo-expressionism, using the technical and structural elements of the ballet but blending them into a highly expressive gestural vocabulary. In the early 1960s, however, the American influence on West German life in general became prevalent, and materialized on the dance stage as ballet neoclassicism, notably through the works of George Balanchine. Its technical brilliance was soon modified by a more human, emotional and also narrative element, as practised by a number of English choreographers, such as John Cranko.

John Cranko (1927–73) became director of the Stuttgart Ballet in 1961. Without discarding the classics, he built a lively repertoire, with an emphasis on contemporary work. His narrative ballets were vivid and meaningful, typified by a joy in movement and carried both by emotional spontaneity and psychological insight. Exploiting these qualities, Cranko's choreography rendered the abstract movement code of the ballet almost translucent. Talented in the policies of programming, Cranko did not rely solely on his own imaginative choreographic reservoir, but employed other well-known British choreographers such as Peter Wright and Kenneth MacMillan to contribute works to the Stuttgart repertoire. From 1975 to 1996, Cranko's leading dancer, Marcia Haydée, safeguarded Cranko's legacy, before another former Cranko dancer, the Canadian Reid Anderson, became director of the Stuttgart Ballet. Haydée, as well as Anderson, renewed the company's repertoire by reviving the classics, expanding it through regular collaboration with established choreographers such as Maurice Béjart, John Neumeier, Jiří Kylián and David Bintley. Neumeier (born 1942) first received recognition as a choreographer while still in the ranks of Stuttgart Ballet under Cranko's reign; and Haydée has supported, as had Cranko, new generations of ballet directors and choreographers such as Uwe Scholz (in Leipzig, since 1991/2) and William Forsythe (in Frankfurt, since 1984/5).

Neumeier pursued Cranko's reform of the narrative ballet. Like Cranko, he fashioned his ballets around emotional processes. Through his talent for movement invention, his ballets became dramaturgical and choreographic games that integrated a multilayered view of his subjects. Although frequently inspired by literature and music, Neumeier did not subjugate himself to the dictum of a logical display of a story or role development. Instead, he consolidated the scenic action by constructing a complex relationship among the dancers as persons, their capacities as dancers, the inner world of the portrayed figures, the particularities of the world outside that encompasses them, and the components of the plot. On yet another level, Neumeier's ballets incorporated choreographic reflections on the uniqueness of dance and its historical and sociological development.

Tanztheater

Cranko and Neumeier decisively shaped the concept and the aesthetics of ballet in West Germany, not only by their work on stage (Neumeier celebrated twenty years of the Hamburg Ballet under his direction in 1993, and he frequently also works as a choreographer at the Semper Opera in Dresden), but also by the foundation of schools.[15] Their intense and meritorious efforts, however, did not forge a new dance identity in West Germany, which began to reform itself when *Tanztheater* emerged in the early 1970s. For although their innovations set trends, Cranko and Neumeier remained basically committed to the narrative and the particularities of movement methods rooted in the traditions of their medium: the ballet. *Tanztheater* was different. The way in which the protagonists related to the story referred less to a particular type of dancing and more to themselves as people and to the socio-psychology of corporeality. In *Tanztheater*, the course of changing circumstance took a back seat to the intuitive, physical acting out of personal responses. Implemented in the search for individual truth, the body was treated as both medium and message, as an autonomous universe with its own expressive characteristics. This attitude obviously found little use for any preordained movement codes as a theatrical means. True-to-life, everyday experience became the focal point of an attempted reconciliation of art with life: in *Tanztheater*, the actions on the stage were comparable with the real experiences of the audience members in their daily lives. The choreographic collage provided the participants (choreographers, dancers, audience members) with the essential elements of their own experience, and the seemingly 'accidental' stringing together of scenes recreated the spontaneous effect of everyday happenings. At the same time, the avoidance of narrative structure prevented the audience from directing their attention to the throes of other individual fates, and forced them personally to confront the theme at hand. In this respect, *Tanztheater* departed decisively from the notion Kurt Jooss had established with his concept of *Tanztheater* between the world wars.

An important initiator of West German post-war *Tanztheater* was the Tanzforum Köln, formed in the mid-1960s under collective leadership, which displayed multimedia spectacles that were aesthetically unfamiliar at the time.[16] This collective arrangement followed, for reasons of a cut in subsidy, the Dutchman Peter Appel who, in times of artistic stagnation, had promoted, in an exemplarily open way, choreographic work not only in the genre of ballet but of modern choreographers too. At this time, Köln, together with Stuttgart, Hamburg and Berlin, was one of the centres for new developments in dance in West Germany. The politics in the choreography of Aurel von Milloss, whose aesthetic came from the tradition of the Ballets Russes style, had brought technical proficiency, a repertory, and a general open-mindedness to Köln. Dance was also supported outside the theatre companies: in 1961, for example, the Institut für Bühnentanz was founded, which from 1966 was directed by Kurt Peters (his private library was the foundation for the Tanzarchiv Köln). In 1961, the international summer classes moved from Krefeld (where they started in 1957) to Köln. They gave many dancers the opportunity to study not only German dance, as was the case in the beginning, but also American modern dance. With their choreographic competition, initiated in 1968, the Köln summer classes have also been an international forum for the new generation of dance-makers. In this climate, Appel created the stage for the second phase of the formation of national identity in twentieth-century German dance. This second national dance identity, perpetuating the innovations of the Tanzforum Köln, was first shaped, thematically and stylistically, by Johann Kresnik, one of Appel's Köln dancers and choreographers, and by the former Gsovsky dancer, Gerhard Bohner.

The Austrian Johann Kresnik (born 1939) succeeded in pursuing democratic principles in the organizational structure of his company as well as in his collabora- tively evolved choreographies. Kresnik invents stringent, provocative and pictorial choreographic solutions for political, social and historical ills in Germany. In a world in which the body has become a commodity, Kresnik loudly defends the right of the individual to his or her own body. His central concern is to present any revolutionary coping with the power of norms and authority.

More gently, Gerhard Bohner (1936–92) invented dance collages that explored the ways in which images of the body, movement, music, speech and space interrelated and determined spatial and psychological perception. He was the first to return to the roots of German dance by attempting to re-establish a continuity in dance that had been disrupted by the Second World War. His pieces examined the principles found in the work of the Bauhaus master Oskar Schlemmer. Bohner's choreographies were uniquely uncompromising in their reflection of the tradition of theatrical imperatives, the concerns of production within an institution, the preoccupations of the dancers as well as the choreographer, and the problems and potential of the ageing dancer. Unwilling to adapt to the machinations of the established theatre system, he choreographed independently, and frequently appeared in solo performances.

Bohner's disavowal of the German theatre system at the beginning of the 1970s was symptomatic of his generation's sympathy for democratization, and of his contempt for a theatrical establishment dependent on box-office returns. In addition, the dance ensembles, trained to serve the repertory needs of the theatre establishment, were incapable of providing the creative potential required by the avant-garde choreographer. In the mid-1970s, this clash of experimental impulse with the pragmatic priorities of institutionalized theatre resulted in the formation of the first freelance dance groups in post-war West Germany. They existed at first at subsistence level. Although the interest of the general public in dance was steadily increasing, the independent groups garnered primarily regional acclaim. It took about fifteen more years to establish dance companies outside theatres as an artistic and organizational challenge to the theatre system. This development was influenced by the increasing emergence of festivals during the last two decades which allowed German audiences to become familiar with dance groups from other countries and cultures. It was also affected by a third form of organization that started to affect the dance market: the financial support of larger political and economic entities such as municipal governments, and (so far, to a much lesser degree) industry. When these sponsors began to support dance beyond the theatre system or the self-support of freelance dancers or companies by the income of their schools, the festivals gained increasing financial subsidy and were eventually able to establish alternative performance spaces, such as abandoned factories. Later, these locations became permanent stages employing regular groups. One successful example was Rui Horta's S.O.A.P. company, in an old soap factory in Frankfurt, the Mouson Turm. In the 1990s, when money had become tight in Germany due to reunification, many of these festivals had been discontinued.

The women who came to the fore of the second generation of *Tanztheater* travelled a different route to gain prominence. While their personal commitment to their environment was no less intense than that of their male colleagues, they did not focus on social and political circumstances and their effects on people. More preoccupied with the artistic expression of their own emotional experiences as women, and as commodities, they produced realistic depictions of the often painful cohabitation of the sexes in a society marked by rules and obsessions. The conditions and irritations of the relations between the sexes were brought to the stage.

Pina Bausch (born 1940) was the first and most significant artist to attain an international reputation, with her Wuppertaler Tanztheater. Rather than develop a plot in order to tell a story, or to display a dramaturgy consistently and logically, Bausch visualizes and theatricalizes her themes associatively from diverse viewpoints, and presents them as an open structure, a collage that eludes definite, objective or rational descriptions and interpretations. In her productions, movement, speech, music and scenery develop an independent dynamic, which she welcomes because they expand her (and the audience's) sensory experience and intuitive understanding.

In contrast to the choreographic procedure of Pina Bausch, which uses the creative energy of the entire ensemble, Reinhild Hoffmann (born 1943) works with preconceived scenic ideas, often based on well-known music. Her pieces also revolve around the issue of women in society. In addition to employing everyday movements, Hoffmann integrates theatrical and social dance material that adds boldness to her visionary, sometimes surrealistic and often blasphemous choreographic style.

Generally speaking, the protagonists of West German *Tanztheater* searched through their personal and professional histories in order to make them more understandable as well as bearable. Unlike Gerhard Bohner, whose professional concern extends back to the early years of the century, Susanne Linke (born 1944) has researched the 1950s and 1960s and discovered an important 'missing link' in the post-war history of German theatre dance: Dore Hoyer (1911–67/8). Exploring the mechanics of body movement and theatricality, Hoyer transformed the expressionism of *Ausdruckstanz* to a more structural, formalist approach to dance. Linke's reconstruction of Hoyer's dance cycle *Affectos Humanos* led her to formulate her own contemporary responses to the existential questions Hoyer once raised in this solo work. Linke's choreographic commentary transposed the original themes into a context of duets centring on the conflicts between men and women.

In 1992, together with her partner, the Swiss Urs Dietrich, Linke, finally found her way into the establishment, the Tanztheater Bremen, after many years of freelance work, and continues to choreograph pieces, increasingly using literary plots as a background for personal experience. Kresnik and Hoffmann are now freelancing, having departed from work with an established company; and Pina Bausch is still in Wuppertal, where the new aesthetic started, relying on her group of people (although in 1997 she gave one early, structurally choreographed work, *Le Sacre du printemps*, to the Paris Opera).

The energy behind *Tanztheater's* minimalization of traditional forms of dance has passed its peak. The emotional resources required by the archeological exploration of the psyche, society and (dance) history seem to be exhausted. Interestingly enough, this happened while social and political attention in Germany was focused on the unforeseen and overwhelming problems of reunification. In the years after 1989, the five new states absorbed a great deal of energy and money; *Tanztheater* companies, founded and established in many West German theatres, had to be closed down due to the shortage of money.

Socialist colonization, rediscovery of folk dance

In the eastern zone of Germany, the communist influence of the Soviet Union brought about, in the early 1950s, what the government called the 'realism debate', through postulating the de-Nazification of culture; in other words, its socialization according to the Soviet model. In the course of this development, everything that could be associated with Fascism was condemned, using the reproach of 'formalism', such as the individually expressive *Ausdruckstanz*. Instead, what was promoted was genuinely anti-individualistic ballet, popular in the Soviet Union too, as well as folkloric dance. Folk dances formed the vocabulary for a new communality that was adopted, activated and moulded by many dancers and choreographers trained in *Ausdruckstanz* who had been active before and during the Second World War. 'Every man is a dancer', Laban's cosmological–philosophical dictum, now underwent a socialist interpretation, and in time was transformed according to the directives of party politics in East Germany. A great number of professional as well as lay ensembles were created. Their main field of activity was the research and performance of folk dances considered to be of East German or East European origin, whereas choreographic material from the West was condemned as capitalist.

These ensembles coexisted with the heavily ballet-oriented theatre companies. Theatre repertoires only haltingly followed cultural/political dictates, and presented the obligatory fairy tales and folkloric ballets in a thoroughly bourgeois–conservative style; that is, in an entertaining and decorative aesthetic fashion. Only sporadically were officially sanctioned 'realistic' ballets produced, with socialist content portraying class struggle and sporting the appropriate scenery. These were associated with particular choreographers, for instance Jean Weidt, who had already been active during the Weimar Republic. The dance groups, while drawing on the pre-war notion of communality, generated and produced particular, in other words, socialist, images. The East German theatre aesthetic, however, was primarily characterized by a change in the manner of reading or interpreting traditional plots, which did not really alter the way of producing ballets – a reading that testified to the 'realistic' reworking of the formerly bourgeois theatre institutions in the GDR. Both dance scenes, ballet and folkloric, were highly influential in their respective cultural attitudes towards lay movement and aesthetics until the reunification of the two Germanies in 1989; then they lost their social and political justification.

The development of dance according to socialist standards led, also in East Germany, to the establishment of a so-called 'realistic' *Tanztheater*, following Walter Felsenstein's demand for a 'realistic' musical theatre in the early 1970s. West German *Tanztheater* espoused contemporary subjects, while pointing up the fragility, the contradictions and damage sustained in human relations. East German *Tanztheater*, however, pursued the ideologically sanctioned relevance of content which was interpreted 'spiritually and intellectually' true to the written script (Köllinger 1983: 8), intending to create, educate and entertain the working class of the GDR. The choreographers employed at the state theatres – for example the widely known Tom Schilling (born 1928), or Dietmar Seyffert (born 1943), a student of the Palucca School – tried to accommodate these conditions and to create a *Tanztheater* that translated the ideological restrictions of official dictates into artistic dimensions through the skilful selection of music and subject-matter. Thus they maintained (or at least insisted on) political independence. The Palucca School in Dresden similarly displayed elements of *double entendre*, ambivalence and ambiguity, in which the socialist regime (mis)used the work of the well-known *Ausdruckstanz* protagonist Gret Palucca. Although the school programme was mainly ballet oriented and structured according to the conservative Soviet model, the application of the name and pre-war fame of the modern dancer Palucca, as well as her active collaboration, camouflaged the school as cosmopolitan, historically continuous and artistically progressive.

Corporealities

Dance in Germany today defines corporeality traditionally in ballet choreography, as well as in compositions influenced by *Tanztheater* strategies. The struggle for the recognition of new styles of performance and means of interpretation on the dance stage is over. Everyone can do as he or she pleases now, everyone quotes the methods of others, creates imagery puzzles, resolves the fundamentals of dance technique and the concept of choreography and drama, stylizes the means of expression of dance theatre, and ends up by creating a new professional vocabulary. New styles and interpretations are flourishing. Extreme physicality, as used by American choreographers or the Belgian dance scene, is well known and well received, but remains without conceptual or aesthetic influence on the choreographers working in Germany. For the time being, there is only one intellectual and artistic phenomenon which can compete with the innovative artistic approach of the Belgians Jan Fabre, Wim Vandekeybus or Anne Teresa De Keersmaeker: the work of the American choreographer William Forsythe (born 1949). Forsythe explores the genesis of the ballet code and the laws of representational, theatrical dance, explicitly referring to Laban's space harmony as well as to Balanchine's structuralism. While the other influential American on German stages, John Neumeier, attempts to alter the structural parameters of the ballet by means of dramaturgical and narrative polyvalence and multiplicity, Forsythe considers the parametal structures themselves. His is a reflection on the mechanical premises of ballet: muscular perception, the function of internal joints, space. He explicitly refers to some of Laban's movement and space concepts and transforms them according to the structuralist rhetoric: 'deconstruction and rearrangement' (Roland Barthes). In his technically and intellectually demanding works he experiments with ballet as artifact, probing moments of instability in movement, of segmentation in space and of extension in time. In so doing, he extensively uses new technology for structural devices and aesthetic framework. Thus, Forsythe's research process amounts to fractal, digitalized choreographic solutions, 'looking for conditions that inform' us about dance (Brandstetter 1994: 48).

The German dance scene is hampered by dance–political particularism. The fact that all cultural matter in the Federal Republic of Germany is in the hands of the regional states is a major reason that a national identity has never materialized in German dance. Apart from the centralized National Socialist attempts before the Second World War and the later Socialist efforts in East Germany between 1949 and 1989, it has never been possible to establish cultural influence on the dance scene, to form a national ballet, or even to draw up unified nationwide training and regulations for the profession of dance.[17] Depending on political and historical viewpoint, Germanness in dance existed either as threat (during the democratic, federal periods), or as expectation (under the totalitarian governments).

The picture today is characterized by the dance-makers' ambivalent acceptance of the institutionalization of dance in theatres, because of its secure financial support on the one hand, and because of the constraints this institutionalization places on artistic freedom on the other. The particular cultural situation in Germany supports and contributes to the historical and still prevalent apolitical attitude in the arts due to an absence of understanding of the degree to which art is integrated into the social life of the nation as a whole. It remains to be seen whether this far-reaching political and national lack of consciousness (or, since 1989, even weariness) will produce advantages or disadvantages in the context of European integration. For even where incipient political reflection and action did begin to form – that is, in West German *Tanztheater* – hardly any of the groundbreaking spirit of the 1968 pioneers survives today. Nor is it adequate to ascribe this attitude to the creators alone: German audiences too are not trained in conceiving the critical potential of dance as a cultural and national practice.

Notes

1 The term 'political' is used in this context to describe any kind of active participation in state institutions and society. Specific research on the relationship between politics and dance is still lacking in German historical research on dance.

2 *Ausdruckstanz* is sometimes held to have begun at the end of the First World War, or even at the turn of the century, and is sometimes considered to extend after 1930, or even beyond the Second World War.

3 The teaching of François Delsarte (1811–71) played an important role in the development of modern dance. It was primarily Delsarte's attempt at categorization and systematization that was adapted in Germany, and thus also by Laban. Delsarte tried to express through his categorizations the relations between micro- and macrocosm, body and soul; he preserved the dialectic between a religious and communal system and individual and empirical observation. The mythologizing, collective approach of German dance theorists and dancers, however, functionalized movement as an image of 'natural', 'cosmic' and 'unique' laws and could later be assimilated all too easily by Nazi ideology.

4 After his emigration to Great Britain, Laban's focus of interest shifted from the psycho-physical aspects of movement, applied in a theatrical context, to a more general approach, to movement functionality, when he worked with F. C. Lawrence on the effort–shape system.

5 Their animosity was quite intense. Laban excluded Wigman from the First German Congress of Dancers in 1927. In 1928, they founded separate associations, looking for their own individual lobbies. In the same year, however, they agreed on a truce at the Second German Dancers' Congress.

6 See Manning (1993) for a possible nationalist and feminist potential in Wigman's works. The career of Gret Palucca (1902–93) can be seen as quite controversial. She characterized her artistic and political life with the statement 'I got through it pretty well' ('Hab ich ganz gut durchgehalten.') (Jarchow and Stabel, 1997: 74).

7 Also successful were the Jutta Klamt, Palucca and Berthe Trümpy schools, as well as the institutes of Rudolf Bode and Dorothee Günther.

8 On the cultural politics of Nazi Germany regarding dance, see in particular Müller, 'Tanz ins Dritte Reich' in Müller and Stöckemann, 1993: 108–17.

9 The battles of the different styles and their schools over their association with the various departments are as telling as the helplessness of the authorities in this dead-end situation. Finally, the assignment of theatrical dancing to the theatre department and of free dance to the dance department was agreed in 1934–5.

10 It is interesting that the National Socialists considered many expressionist works in the fine arts to be *entartet* (degenerate), whereas not only did they not mind expressionism in dance, they embraced *Ausdruckstanz* as a kind of Nazi avant-garde of the arts.

11 Lizzie Maudrik, ballet-mistress of the Berlin State Opera, was director of the ballet classes, while the Department for German Dance was led by Gret Palucca with

Charlotte Hübner and Marianne Vogelsang. In modification of the official opinion, the dance scene itself started to consider *Ausdruckstanz* an outdated product of the Weimar Republic. (Cf. Dahms and Schroedter 1997: 82–4.)

12 Max Terpis (1889–1958) originally worked as an architect in the 1920s, and then became a student of Wigman. He moved on to the position of ballet-master at the opera house in Hanover in 1924, and in the Berlin State Opera Unter den Linden from 1924 to 1930. For Laban's career, see Hodgson and Preston-Dunlop 1990, Kant and Karina 1996; for Jooss, see Markard and Markard 1985.

13 Thus, for example, the Tanztheater separated from the opera house in Essen again in 1932 and was continued privately under the name of Ballets Jooss. Another example: in 1953 the city of Essen cut its subsidies and the Tanztheater Jooss had to discontinue its tour. Jooss joined the opera at Düsseldorf in order to rebuild the Tanztheater, but with a new artistic director he could not pursue this project further. And in the Folkwang School there was a trend towards implementing ballet classes.

14 Among the directors of the Folkwang Dance Studio were some of the people who later became protagonists of West German *Tanztheater* such as Pina Bausch (1969–73), Reinhild Hoffmann (1975–7) and Susanne Linke (1975–85). Other schools that picked up the techniques and aesthetics of the pre-war era were the Lola Rogge School in Hamburg and the Tanzakademie Brakel in Hanover, as well as the Palucca School in Dresden.

15 The development of the John Cranko School (as it has been called since Cranko's death) has strongly relied upon the connection with existing structures such as the private and long-established Werkschule Albrecht Merz in 1965, and the city of Stuttgart, as a source of finance. The Noverre Society, founded in 1958, had also been an important factor in the patronage of ballet as an art form and in the promotion of a new generation of dancers. See Percival 1985: 202–3 on the status of ballet training in Germany, the lack of knowledge about it, and the respective merits of John Cranko. The ballet school of the Hamburg State Opera opened in 1978. It is supported by a society of Hamburg citizens that finances scholarships and any kind of equipment.

16 The democratic model survived until 1968. After that, Jochen Ulrich became the only head, and since 1985 he has directed the Tanzforum Köln independently from the theatre.

17 The body awareness that has its roots in the beginning of the century can be estimated today by the number of dance schools (1,600 at the beginning of the 1990s), even though most of them are financed privately. It is also interesting that, at least early in the 1990s, dancers at public theatre companies would like to follow the trend of the 'free' groups in going beyond traditional training methods. See Gerstmeier, Jeschke and Vettermann 1992: 55–70.

References

Andrä, H., Jeschke, C., Kittel, C., Kleßmann, U., Krause, C., Lehmann, D., Schulze, I. and Wohlgemuth, J. (compilers) (1996) *Zwischen Idealismus und Ideologie. Tanz in der DDR 1949–1956*, unpublished manuscript, Tanzarchiv Leipzig e.V.

Bohner, G. and Akademie der Künste Berlin (1991) *Gerhard Bohner: Tänzer und Choreograph*, Berlin: Hentrich.

Brandstetter, G. (1994) 'Neue Formen der Repräsentation. Grenzgänger zwischen Tanz, Theater, Performance und bildender Kunst', *Ballett International/Tanz Aktuell*, 8(9): 44–8.

Dahms, S. and Schroedter, S. (eds) (1997) *Der Tanz – ein Leben. In Memoriam Friderica Derra de Moroda*, Salzburg: Selke.

Dauber, A. (ed.) (1995) *20 Jahre John Neumeier in Hamburg*, Hamburg: Intendanz der Hamburgischen Staatsoper.

Delahaye, G. (ed. and photos), Gubernatis, R. de and Bentivoglio, L. (text) (1986) *Pina Bausch*, Malakoff: Solin.

Fischer, L. (1984) *Anita Berber: Tanz zwischen Rausch und Tod*, Berlin: Haude und Spener.

Gerstmeier, J., Jeschke, C. and Vettermann, G. (1992) 'Die Berufssituation: Tanz in Deutschland', *Tanz Aktuell*, Sonderheft: 55–70.

Hodgson, J. and Preston-Dunlop, V. (1990) *Rudolf Laban*, London: Northcote House.

Hoghe, R. (1986) *Tanztheatergeschichten*, Frankfurt am Main: Suhrkamp.

Jarchow, P. and Stabel, R. (1997) *Palucca: Aus ihrem Leben, Über ihre Kunst*, Berlin: Henschel.

Kant, M. and Karina, L. (1996) *Tanz unterm Hakenkreuz*. Berlin: Henschel.

Koegler, H. (1974) 'In the Shadow of the Swastika: Dance in Germany 1929–1936', *Dance Perspectives* 57, spring.

Köllinger, B. (1983) *Tanztheater*, Berlin: Henschel.

Kraus, H. (1990) *Johann Kresnik*, Frankfurt am Main: Fischer.

Lewitan, J. (1927) 'Tanzabende im Oktober', *Der Tanz*, 2, November: 26–8.

Manning, S. (1993) *Ecstasy and the Demon: Feminism and Nationalism in the Dances of Mary Wigman*, Berkeley: University of California Press.

Markard, A., and Markard, H. (1985) *Kurt Jooss*, Köln: Ballett-Bühnen-Verlag Rolf Garske.

Müller, H. (1986) *Mary Wigman: Leben und Werk der großen Tänzerin*, Weinheim: Quadriga.

Müller, H., Peter, F.-M. and Schuldt, G. (1992) *Dore Hoyer: Tänzerin*, Berlin: Hentrich.

Müller, H. and Stöckemann, P. (1993) '. . . jeder Mensch ist ein Tänzer.' *Ausdruckstanz in Deutschland zwischen 1900 und 1945*, Gießen: Anabas.

Oberzaucher-Schüller, G. (1992) *Ausdruckstanz*, Wilhelmshaven: Noetzel/ Heinrichshofen.

Percival, J. (1985) *John Cranko: Biographie*, Stuttgart: Belser.

Regitz, H. (ed.) (1984) *Tanz in Deutschland: Ballett seit 1945*, Berlin: Quadriga.

Schlicher, S. (1987) *Tanztheater: Traditionen und Freiheiten*, Reinbek: rororo.

Schmidt, J. (1992) *Tanztheater in Deutschland*, Berlin: Propyläen.

Servos, N. (1996) *Pina Bausch: Wuppertaler Tanztheater oder die Kunst einen Goldfisch zu dressieren*, Seelze-Velber: Kallmeyer.

Städtische Bühnen Frankfurt, Ballett Frankfurt and Forsythe, W. (eds) (1989) *Parallax*, November.

Key Texts

Kant, M. and Karina, L. (1996) *Tanz unterm Hakenkreuz*. Berlin: Henschel.

Koegler, H. (1974) 'In the Shadow of the Swastika: Dance in Germany 1929–1936', *Dance Perspectives* 57, Spring.

Manning, S. (1993) *Ecstasy and the Demon: Feminism and Nationalism in the Dances of Mary Wigman*, Berkeley: University of California Press.

Müller, H. and Stöckemann, P. (1993) '. . . *jeder Mensch ist ein Tänzer.' Ausdruckstanz in Deutschland zwischen 1900 und 1945*, Gießen: Anabas.

Oberzaucher-Schüller, G. (1992), *Ausdruckstanz*, Wilhelmshaven: Noetzel/Heinrichshofen.

Schlicher, S. (1987) *Tanztheater: Traditionen und Freiheiten*, Reinbek: rororo.

Schmidt, J. (1992) *Tanztheater in Deutschland*, Berlin: Propyläen.

Table 4 Important dance and political events in Germany (1900 to present)

Year	Dance: artists, works, events	Dance: institutions	Arts scene	Sociocultural and political events
1900			Monte Verità, Ascona, meeting of artists and intellectuals International Arts Exhibition, Dresden	Wandervogel Ausschuß für Schülerfährten
1901	*Loie Fuller tours Germany			
1902	*Isadora Duncan (Munich)			
1904		I. and E. Duncan school, Berlin		
1906	*Ruth St Denis tours Europe			
1907	*Anna Pavlova (Berlin)			
1908				Prussia allows women to study at universities
1910	*Ballets Russes (Berlin)	Bildungsanstalt Jaques-Dalcroze (Dresden)		
1911		Dalcroze moves to Hellerau E. Duncan opens school, Darmstadt (South) American dances become popular	First congress of Vereinigte Kinematographen-besitzer-Verbände	
1913		Laban Schule für Kunst, Monte Verità, and Schule für Tanz–Ton–Wort, Munich	Anthroposoph. Gesellschaft, Berlin (R. Steiner)	
1914	Hexentanz I (Wigman)			First World War
1915				
1916		Bildungsanstalt bankrupt	Dadaists open Cabaret Voltaire, Zürich	
1917				Russian Revolution; USA enters war
1919			Staatliches Bauhaus	Wilhem II abdicates; end of First World War

Table 4 continued

Year	Dance: artists, works, events	Dance: institutions	Arts scene	Sociocultural and political events
1920		Labanschule, Stuttgart Wigmanschule, Dresden	Theatrical innovations in Essen (Jooss, Heckroth, Cohen)	
1922	*Triadisches Ballet* (Schlemmer)			Mussolini marches to Rome; agreement of Rapallo
1923		Wigman's first group		Hitler's riot
1924	*Szenen aus einem Tanzdrama* (Wigman)			
1925	*Don Juan* (Laban)	Major European tour of Tanzbühne Laban, disbands in Yugoslavia Palucca opens Fachschule für modernen Tanz, Dresden Performances of Kammertanzbühne Laban		Hindenburg elected
1926	*Hexentanz II* (Wigman)	Choreographisches Institut Laban Charleston becomes modern		
1927		Folkwangschule First Dancers' Congress *Der Tanz*		
1928		Folkwang Tanztheater Studio Second Dancers' Congress Deutsche Gesellschaft für Schrifttanz Wigman's group disbanded		
1929	*Pavane on the Death of an Infanta* (Jooss)	Labanzentralschule and Folkwangschule united under Jooss Kreutzberg tours USA with Georgi		Stresemann dies Great Depression
1930	Ted Shawn performs in Central Europe *Tannhäuser Bacchanal* (Laban)	Folkwang Tanztheater Studio permanent ensemble of Essen Opera Ballet		Emergency Decree

Table 4 continued

Year			
1930 continued	Third Dancers' Congress Wigman tours USA Laban becomes ballet director of Berlin State Opera		
1931	Serenata (Palucca)		
1932	The Green Table (Jooss), First prize at Concours de Chorégraphie, Paris Folkwang–Tanzbühne becomes private, named Ballets Jooss	The Theatre of Cruelty (Artaud)	Hindenburg re-elected
1933	Ballets Jooss tours Europe and USA, but not Germany; then homeless	Public burning of books Reichstheaterkammer	Hitler becomes Chancellor
1934	Frauentänze (Wigman) First German Dance Festival Jooss emigrates to England		
1935	Second German Dance Festival Reichsbund für Gemeinschaftsbund		Nurenberg laws
1936	Laban runs International Dance Competition Die Deutsche Tanz-Zeitschrift Reichsfachschaft für Tanz Meisterwerkstätten für Tanz (Laban)	Olympic Games, Berlin	
1938	Laban emigrates to England		Reichskristallnacht
1939			Germany declares war
1940	Palucca school closed		First gas chambers in Auschwitz
1941	KdF-Ballett and school, dir. Derra de Moroda Collaboration of Der Tanz with Die Deutsche Tanz-Zeitschrift		USA declares war
1945	Wigman reopens school, Leipzig Palucca reopens school, Dresden		Germany surrenders Hitler's suicide Potsdam conference
1949	Wigman reopens school, Berlin		Foundation of FRG and GDR
1950	Moiseyev group tours GDR		

Table 4 continued

Year	Dance: artists, works, events	Dance: institutions	Arts scene	Sociocultural and political events
1951		Jooss returns to Folkwangschule, Essen Folkwang Tanztheater der Stadt Essen	Formalism debate in GDR; rejection of capitalist art	
1952		Staatliche Volkskunst Ensemble, GDR		
1953		Folkwang Tanztheater tours Europe, then disbands Dance Conference in GDR against formalism *Das Tanzarchiv*		Stalin's death Revolt in GDR
1954	*Polowetzer Tänze* (Weidt)	Jooss director of Düsseldorf Opera		USSR acknowledges GDR East integration of GDR, West integration of FRG FRG becomes sovereign
1955	*Gajaneh* (Lilo Gruber)	European–American summer courses established at Folkwangschule		Warsaw pact; politics of relaxation
1956		*Der Volkstanz*		
1957		Tanzarchiv Köln and Leipzig		
1958		*Der Tanz*		
1960		Soviet classical dance teachers at Palucca school	Innovative theatre developments, Bremen	Foundation of EEC
1961		State subsidies for masterclasses at Folkwangschule, promotes experimental choreography		
1962	Graham company (Köln) NYCB (Hamburg)	Twist and disco become popular		Berlin Wall built
1964		Folkwangballett first West German company to tour GDR		
1965		*Ballett*		

Table 4 continued

1966		*Tanzbibliographie*		New constitution in GDR
1968		Folkwangballett becomes Folkwang Studio; Kresnik choreographer at Bremen Theater		Emergency laws in FRG
1969	*Der Widerspenstigen Zähmung* (Cranko)			
1970				Brand–Stroph meeting; Russo-German negotiations on renunciation of power; Berlin agreement
1971	*Schwanensee AG* (Kresnik); *Die Folterungen der Beatrice Cenci* (Bohner); Cunningham lecture tour	Tanz-Forum, Köln		
1972		Tanztheater Darmstadt (Bohner)		Fundamental treaty of GDR and FRG
1973		Bausch directs Wuppertaler Tanztheater	*Angst essen Seele auf* (Fassbinder)	UN accepts FRG and GDR; Honecker becomes head of SED
1975		*Documenta Choreologica*		
1976				Bierman exiled; many artists leave GDR
1977	Bohner reconstructs *Triadisches Ballett*; *Solo mit Sofa* (Hoffmann)			
1978	*Café Müller* (Bausch); *Kameliendame* (Neumeier)	Bohner and Hoffmann direct Bremer Tanztheater; *Ballett International*; Tanzfabrik Berlin		
1980	*Im Bade wannen* (Linke); *Familiendialog* (Kresnik)		*Berlin Alexanderplatz* (Fassbinder); Awards for female film directors Trotta and Sanders	

Table 4 continued

Year	Dance: artists, works, events	Dance: institutions	Arts scene	Sociocultural and political events
1980 continued				
1982	*Matthäuspassion* (Neumeier)		'Neue Wilde', grafitti art	Beginning of Kohl era
1983	*Wahlverwandschaften* (Schilling)	Deutscher Tanzpreis	*Paris, Texas* (Wenders) *CIVILwarS* (R. Wilson) in Köln	Green Party participates in Federal Diet
1984				
1986		Gesellschaft für Tanzforschung *TanzAktuell* *Tanzdrama*		
1987				
1988		Dance Festival, North Rhine Westfalia		
1989	*Im (Goldenen) Schnitt* (Bohner)		Hebbel-Theater, Berlin	Unification process of Germany
1990	*Limb's Theorem* (Forsythe)	*Tanzforschung*	*Die Klage der Kaiserin* (film, dir. Bausch) Fitness studios emerge	
1991		Tanzwerkstatt Europa S.O.A.P.		
1992		Linke and Dietrich direct Tanztheater Bremen		
1994		*TanzAktuell* merges with *Ballett International*		
1995	*Travelog* (Sasha Waltz) *Hautnah* (Felix Ruckert)			
1996	*xyz-Bewegtes Opfer* (Wölfl, Wanda Golonka)			
1998	*Allee der Kosmonauten* (Waltz) *Small Void* (Forsythe) *Opus 13* (Forsythe)	Tanzhaus NRW (North Rhine Westfalia)		

*First visit

5

HUNGARY

On Hungarian dance

Lívia Fuchs

Geographically, Hungary is located in the Carpathian basin. From a historical point of view, however, it is on a borderline reflecting both 'eastern' and 'western' streams of development. Politically, until the end of the First World War, the kingdom of Hungary was the easternmost country of the Austro-Hungarian Empire. Having gained its independence, Hungary then became the eastern border of German influence and remained so for several decades. After 1945, Hungary became yet again an important demarcation line, this time of Soviet influence. Although this, historically, stormy border situation has been at the root of numerous social and human dramas, it did offer unique material for artists. It resulted in a unique, multifaceted cultural life, creating a space where conservatism and desire for innovation co-existed, where avant-garde and traditional trends engaged in dialogues and challenged each other.

At the turn of the century, theatre dance was solely represented by the Hungarian Royal Opera, which opened in 1884. Lacking any romantic ballet traditions of its own, the ballet company not only followed the Vienna Opera in its choice of programmes but was also traditionally led by Italian ballet-masters who signed contracts with the Hungarian Opera after leaving the Viennese Opera. In addition to taking over the romantic ballets which were highly popular throughout Europe, the Budapest ensemble also performed Smeraldi's *Excelsior* (1887), the spectacular piece of the period, and presented *Puppenfee* (*Fairy Doll – Babatündér*, choreography by Hassreiter 1888), a typical 'Viennese' choreography, in the year of its creation. The most successful works among the original world premières, however, were 'pseudo-Hungarian' dance plays. These adopted popular themes such as weddings, outlaws and gypsy camps. Choreographies, such as Mazzantini's *Csárdás* (1890) and *Viora* (1891) for example, drew from the national ballroom dances and café gypsy music of the period and reinforced the audience's national identity through their allegorical and romantic nature.

It is difficult to pinpoint the exact moment in history when a new dance movement was formed. It would be nice if we could declare, for example, that as early as 1902 movements towards new dance styles could be seen, when Isadora Duncan, the priestess with a strong vocation, made her début before the Budapest audience. The truth, however, is that few in Hungary regarded her as a revolutionary of dance art. Indeed, the bourgeoisie was probably more interested in her provocative 'nakedness' than in her choreography, and for some time she had no followers. In contrast, a decade later, Émile Jaques-Dalcroze's new rhythmic methods, when demonstrated at the Academy of Music, had an immense impact on the young musicians of the time. Many veered away from their careers as musicians towards *Bewegungskunst* (movement culture/art), the up-and-coming modern dance trend of the period. These musicians were enchanted by the possibilities of connecting rhythm and kinetic art in a new way.

Another important influence from outside Hungary was undoubtedly the 1912–13 seasons of Diaghilev's Ballets Russes. Their dazzling performances highlighted the fact that the repertoire of Hungary's only official ensemble, the Opera Ballet, was outdated. Even Nicola Guerra, probably the most outstanding Italian ballet-master ever employed by the company, had failed to change the repertoire. Furthermore, it was not Guerra but Sándor Hevesi, the director of the theatre, who insisted on the need to modernize ballet. Hevesi directed three short dance pieces on an updated script inspired by Fokine's ballets. Unfortunately, however, he did this without a creative choreographer of Fokine's stature. Another significant work presented before the end of the First World War was Béla Bartók's dance drama, *A fából faragott királyfi* (*The Wooden Prince*, choreography by Otto Zöbisch, Ede Brada and Béla Balázs, the last also the librettist, 1917), which was staged at the Opera. Balázs directed the drama, which was unworthy of Béla Bartók's music, lacking in choreographic talent and sensitivity.

Until the second half of the 1920s it seemed as if time had come to a halt at the Hungarian Royal Opera. There was a change of personnel, Otto Zöbisch (from Sweden) replacing Guerra, yet the repertoire was not updated. Zöbisch, who had started his career at the Berlin Opera, tried to merge Dalcroze's method with classical dance technique, but his choreographies were accepted neither by the audience nor by the press. In compliance with the taste of the period, the programmes continued to consist mainly of pseudo-Hungarian character ballets.

In the late 1920s, however, certain experimental and innovative efforts made themselves felt within ballet, alongside all the new attempts that were getting underway worldwide as a result of the splitting-up of Diaghilev's company. There seemed to be a chance, at last, for dance to extend and, as a result of the spreading of Hungarian modern dance trends and the extensive folklore research works carried out at the time, there was also much hope that folk dance would survive on stage. Following the Diaghilev company's return guest appearance at the Opera in 1927, the 'Russian' artistic example influenced the company's policy. First, Albert Gaubier, from Poland, who had danced character roles with the Diaghilev company, was offered a contract. Next it was the turn of Rudolf Kölling from Germany, who, after training in ballet, had studied with Rudolf Laban and with Mary Wigman. They both taught the company an 'original' Fokine as well as

Massine choreography (*Three-Cornered Hat*, *A háromszögletü kalap* by Gaubier, 1928 and *Sheherazade* by Kölling, 1930).

In 1931, Jan Cieplinski from Poland was offered a permanent contract with the Opera. Cieplinski had first danced with the Warsaw Opera ballet and had later been a member of both the Pavlova and the Diaghilev companies. He was an exceptionally talented pedagogue as well as a choreographer with great foresight. He not only recomposed the character pieces and dance dramas of the 'Russian' repertoire (*The Legend of Joseph*, *József legendája*, 1934; *Petrushka*, 1946) but created symphonic ballets (*Seasons*, *Évszakok*, 1931). Furthermore, he responded to the great challenges of the 1930s and composed national ballets, just as was happening both in Europe and America. He staged works from Hungarian literature, set to the music of Hungarian composers. While doing so, he tried to include in his choreographies original Hungarian peasant dances, which he and his contemporaries had got to know through the performances organized by the so called *Gyöngyösbokréta (Pearly Bouquet)* movement which had taken place throughout Hungary. This movement, led by Béla Paulini, aimed to unite and mobilize the peasant ensembles to collect and preserve their own local traditions. Paulini took great care in staging these still living traditions in as authentic a way as was ethnographically possible in the circumstances, since by the second half of the 1930s, they had turned into large-scale and spectacular shows catering mainly for tourists.

Cieplinski was a member of the Hungarian Opera for more than fifteen years, although he also had several foreign engagements and spent occasional lengthy periods abroad (Warsaw and Argentina). In 1936, during one of his absences, Gyula Harangozó, a young dancer, made his début as a choreographer with *Csárdajelenet* (*The Village Inn Scene*), becoming the first major native choreographer. He too presented Hungarian character ballets, with overwhelming success. Together with Cieplinski's *Magyar ábrándok* (*Hungarian Fantasies*, 1933), *The Village Inn Scene* was used abroad until 1945 as the emblem of the Hungarian nature of the company. Harangozó also adapted one-act pieces from the 'Russian' repertoire such as the *Polovtsian Dances* (*Polovec táncok*, 1938). From this he drew inspiration to develop his own talent for dramatization and characterization.

Harangozó followed in the footsteps of Fokine and, perhaps more emphatically, those of Massine. In addition, he was also influenced by the now flourishing expressionist movement, although he himself only once experimented with these modern means of expression when he choreographed *A csodálatos mandarin* (*The Miraculous Mandarin*) in 1941. For the general taste of the period, this modern choreography seemed so immoral and the music so incomprehensible for the times that the work did not get beyond rehearsal stage.

By this time, the Opera could no longer disregard endeavours for creating modern works and developing modern techniques. This led to the recruitment of Aurel von Milloss, who was attempting to merge classical and modern dances (which were then in a fierce battle with each other) mainly on German stages (Augsburg). The conservative opera ballet company of the 1930s, however, thought his efforts somewhat eccentric. He directed only the 'Russian' *Petrushka* before being commissioned to choreograph a Hungarian dance play. For this reason, his further choreographic attempts, drawing from expressionist dance, came out not at the Opera but were pursued in drama theatres as well as in his own studio. With Antal Németh (in the footsteps of Reinhardt), the director of the National Theatre, Milloss experimented with an individual synthesis of movement and speech and the organic integration of expressive dance interludes into dramas. Milloss also founded *Magyar Csupajáték (The Hungarian Fullplay Ensemble)* with the participation of artists, composers and actors as well as dancers. He staged dance plays and dances with scenes inspired by Hungarian folklore.

Alongside the development of modern dance, the inner reform of classical ballet and the rediscovery and staging of folk traditions, were also among the ambitions of the period. The aforementioned *Gyöngyösbokréta* movement saw its responsibility as preserving and presenting tradition rather than dealing with artistic interpretation. Its members were all peasants, primarily interested in exploring their own traditions. The artists of the stage, however, turned to folklore as their source of inspiration, regardless of whether their careers had started off in the direction of ballet or modern dance.

By the 1930s, the representatives of the first generation of Hungarian modern dance (also referred to as *Bewegungskunst*) had matured. As representatives of a new type of aesthetic, they were opposed to the official and professional dance ideal of the period. In addition, as far as politics was concerned, their links to the left-wing politicians were obvious. As a consequence of the pedagogical and artistic achievements, their outstanding representatives had close connections with the expressionist trends, which were then unfolding on German territories. As early as the 1910s, Valéria Dienes had started to elaborate her system of theory of movement which she called *orchestics*, in which she examined the domain of kinetics, rhythm, dynamics and semiotics, inspired by Raymond Duncan's artistic concepts (relying on the *contrapposto* positions of Greek sculpture) as well as on Isadora Duncan's revolutionary innovations.

Dienes's theoretical findings – whose main concern was movement itself, especially from a philosophical point of view (with this she could be seen as having been a forerunner of semiotics) – can only be compared with the theoretical achievements of Rudolf Laban, who was also Hungarian but worked first in German- and then English-speaking countries. Up until 1944, Dienes presented large-scale movement compositions 'movement dramas' (miracle plays and fairytale plays) with the participation of her Orchestics School. Her pedagogical work became popular among the daughters of upper-middle-class families.

By the 1930s, Alice Madzsar, the other outstanding representative of 'movement culture', had also infiltrated theatrical work with the popularization of new ways of using the body in art. Together with her most talented students – Magda Róna, Ödön Palasovszky and Ágnes Kövesházy – she participated in elaborating a new and total theatrical language in the course of the avant-garde theatrical experiments of the time. On these evenings (mostly banned by the official cultural politicians), movement, dance and acrobatics were mixed with poems and light, sound and music, special scenery and occasionally with puppet shows.

The third leading figure in Hungarian modern dance was Olga Szentpál, a former student of Dalcroze who, like her colleagues, founded a school and an ensemble, and worked out her own movement method. Among the movement culture artists, she was the first to have turned to folk dance traditions and, at the same time, like Dienes, to the music of Bartók. Not only did she learn the steps by watching the *Gyöngyösbokréta* performances, but she also tried to stage folk ballads and folk customs, mixing the modern dance vocabulary of the time with folk dance motifs, somehow bringing about a reconciliation between European modernity and Hungarian tradition, just as Bartók had been doing. For him, nationalism and modernism belonged together.

Aurel von Milloss too tried to bring together nationalism and modernism, though in a different way. Already an established artist of the Rome Opera, he tried to return home as a choreographer. In 1942, he showed another of his facets as a modernist classicist in staging *The Creatures of Prometheus* (*Prométeusz teremtményei*), to music by Beethoven. This, however, seemed rather recondite for the audience who expected to see plot, colourful commotion, and character dances in the conservative Opera.

In 1944, after the German troops had marched into Hungary, Hungarian dance life collapsed. The theatres closed in December because of the siege and 'life' only started again in April 1945. The Second World War caused impossible conditions for everybody, which, for many, culminated in the artistic annihilation after 1948 when a new political situation developed and the Soviet influence became dominant. During the three years after the war, there was once again a revival of cultural life which allowed diverse and often contrasting artistic values to co-exist for a certain time. Tradition and innovation, national and international, conservative and avant-garde co-existed in a maelstrom never seen before. In 1945, *The Miraculous Mandarin* (by Harangozó), Bartók's 'pantomime' was finally premièred at the Opera, though the plot was transferred from the modern city into a Far Eastern setting to make it somewhat 'tamer'.

Cieplinski might have felt that in the post-war euphoria, the time had come for the public to understand plotless ballets; that the audience might be able to watch the former gypsy–romantic pseudo-Hungarian works with a sense of irony, and might at last accept the presence of modern city life – as reflected in the pulsating music of *Divertimento* composed by Sándor Jemnitz, a student of Schönberg's – rhythm and dance on the ballet stage; but they did not. During this period, for example, Janine Charrat taught some of her works to the Hungarian Opera company, but her initiative was not continued.

A new feature in Hungarian balletic life was the foundation of the second ballet company in Szeged in 1946, which for two years operated as a provincial branch of the Opera Ballet. From 1948–49 there was a new artistic director to lead the company: György Lőrinc, a former student of Olga Szentpál. Having pursued his training in movement culture as well as classical ballet, it was a matter of course for him to merge the two dance vocabularies, first seen in his staging of *The Miraculous Mandarin*. In Hungary, this Lőrinc choreography was the first to set the piece in its original milieu of a modern city.

The Szeged Company, however, along with all the movement culture art schools which had reopened after the war, was silenced in 1949 at a stroke. Following the Communist Party's takeover, cultural politics came to a standstill. Anything that had any link to the West was forbidden. Modern art was regarded as 'shallow' and 'formalist' and training and education in movement culture was banned by order of the Minister of the Interior. Its representatives could retrain themselves: they could either enrol into the Vaganova method courses run by Soviet ballet-masters, who first came to Hungary in 1949; or they could find work with the folk dance ensembles of certain factories if they were able to teach them some simple folk dances. What they were not allowed to do was teach the material that they themselves had conceived during the past decades or what they had learned from their masters.

The cultural politics of the period destroyed the basis of modern dance education. Throughout the following decades, dance life in Hungary lacked a concept of appreciating individual initiatives or emphasizing the importance of creativity as well as freedom of expression. Canonical and standardized forms, systematic quality and hierarchy were the things that counted. Innovation and experiment were rather risky. They had to withdraw from a dance life which was being restructured according to the Soviet example. In certain cases – as will be seen later – the innovations were pushed aside and could work only under the circumstances which characterized amateur ensembles.

Although the Soviet influence on ballet was the enemy of any kind of modernity – as proved by the repeated banning of Harangozó's *Miraculous Mandarin*, as well as by the removal of the 'emigrant' Stravinsky's works from the repertoire (e.g. Cieplinski's *Petrushka* and Charrat's *Jeu de cartes*) – it was, despite this, a fruitful one. One could argue that the most brilliant tradition in classical ballet was – and still is – the Russian one. Consequently, through the Soviet mediators, the Hungarian State Opera Ballet was in a prestigious situation in which it could obtain and make its own the fundamental works of the international romantic and classical repertoire.

Besides the traditional choreographies, the company also performed 'realistic' works originated in the Soviet Union in the 1930s. These followed strict require-ments: they had to be based on literary works to enable better understanding, and the theme had to be heroic and 'progressive', emotive in tone and powerful in acting. In addition, it was required that classical and character dances be merged together. These schematic, full-length works slowly replaced the repertoire of the company, which had consisted, as was shown earlier, of one-act pieces emerging from the 'Diaghilev' inheritance. The Hungarian national themes and formations, however, did not fall victim to this sweeping change. Harangozó continued his choreographic work although, from then on, he had to create full-length ballets.

There was also the Soviet example for the former amateur folk dance movements to follow, and professional folk dance ensembles were born, first that of the Hungarian Army, then the representative State Folk Ensemble. Their artistic leaders – Iván Szabó (once a dancer in Milloss's Hungarian Fullplay), and Miklós Rábai, who, as a teacher, had carried out fieldwork as well as directed amateur student groups – did not consider it their task, however, to take over an artistic model from their Soviet colleagues. Folk dance tradition in Hungary was still very much alive and there had been scientific research works in this regard for decades. Musicologists and folklore researchers had collected dances and published their findings from the 1940s. As a result, stage work could get nearer to its origin than the Soviet type of adaptation, which was a balletic-virtuoso character dance developed especially by the ballet dancer Moiseyev. What could not be ignored, however, was the obligation to meet the artistic–political expectations of the state, which declared that folk dance should be the artistic expression of a people coming to power, who believed in socialism and who trusted in a happy future. For this reason all the state and political celebrations included not only simpler folk dance adaptations but also political themes in dance.

The 1949 and 1950 seasons were also milestones in Hungarian ballet pedagogy. Alongside the nationalization of the factories, fields and theatres, the State Ballet Institute was founded, the predecessor of which had been Ferenc Nádasi's outstanding private school. Nádasi had been a student and follower of Cecchetti and had also been the ballet master at Hungarian Opera from 1936. At the State Ballet Institute the training followed the Vaganova system.

The first signs of changes to this rather isolated dance life could be felt in the years of consolidation following the 1956 revolution, alongside the renewal of dance art throughout Europe. Following the revolution, the one-act pieces were performed again and new choreographers had the chance to introduce themselves. The three-word slogan of artistic policy – 'prohibit, endure and support' – had practically prohibited experimental trends, although in the countryside, far from the capital, the policy was not as stringent and in the case of amateur artistic ensembles the government in power even gave subsidies, enduring a 'different character' and not suspecting anything revolutionary behind it. The government thought that there were two things deserving support: professional folk dance, which also undertook representative tasks, and the art of ballet, which represented both classical and socialist–realist values.

The first important event of the 1960s was the decentralization of ballet life. The Szeged ensemble was reborn and a new company was founded in Pécs creating a situation in which, far from the capital, new trends could develop. This was in addition to the Opera, which was pleased with its repertoire of romantic and classical-style pieces, works by Harangozó and Soviet choreographers. Nevertheless, the cultural politicians paid attention exclusively to the Pécs Ballet (Ballet Sophiane): the company was founded not only because the state subsidized its members but also because it was the will of the central power – young dancers had to sign contracts with the Pécs Theatre. The company there was led by Imre

Eck, a young dancer at the Hungarian Opera where he had made his début in 1959.

Eck attempted to put contemporary themes onto the dance stage in Pécs. Like his contemporaries all over the world, he also tried to break with everything rooted in classical ballet. First of all, he tried to shatter the classical dance vocabulary. Being unfamiliar with modern dance performed in the West, which was so different from the aesthetics of ballet, he could only draw from the expressive dance of pre-war times and from his own creativity. He broke the span of classical poses and lines and made the dance-flow turn into a series of poses. He also rejected pointe shoes and mingled the dance vocabulary with everyday movements like walking, standing about and barely stylized gestures. He made every effort to make good use of the expressiveness of poses, gestures and glances instead of presenting purely dance technique. Most of his choreographies included one-act pieces which, at the beginning of his choreographic career, had real plots from beginning to end. In his works, Eck introduced either common characters showing their everyday feelings like happiness or tragedy, as in *Variációk egy találkozásra* (*Variations on an Encounter*, 1961) or presented political, particularly anti-war themes, as in *Az iszonyat balladája* (*The Ballad of Repulsion*, 1961) and *A parancs* (*The Command*, 1962), which were very characteristic of the period.

Eck also reconceived pieces choreographed to Bartók's music in addition to choreographing ballets on the themes of common concern, to music by young Hungarian composers. This idea is represented by *The Miraculous Mandarin* (1965), which he staged as a pantomime and by doing so, followed Bartók's original instructions. In his version, the parts of the old cavalier and the student were taken by actors. Soon, however, Eck abandoned narrative ballets and turned to universal themes like fighting, power, love and loneliness. Very often, his choreographies were crammed with mysterious props and symbolic gestures and his enigmatic works (with *Requiem*, 1976, as his highest achievement) were ambiguous. Hungarian dance innovations on stage in the 1970s could have gone no further.

The Szeged Ballet became a serious rival to the Pécs Ballet, if only for a short time, and despite its disadvantageous conditions compared with the Pécs company (it did not receive any distinguished financial, moral or political support). What is more, it did not have a resident choreographer. During the Szeged Ballet's second period, the company performed one-act pieces borrowed from the Hungarian Opera alongside preserving the 'updated' values of the past decades. However, no company can exist for a long period without new works. Such was the case of the Szeged Ballet, which only became significant when Zoltán Imre became the company's resident choreographer. He endeavoured to reform ballet, partly following in the footsteps of Eck, whom he regarded as his choreographic example, and partly inspired by the young Maurice Béjart, who meant so much to Eck as well, and whose work could be seen in just one film (*Symphonie pour un homme seul* in the film *'Paris Ballet'* directed by Louis Cuny).

Imre had a different approach. Since he had an original sense of musicality – entirely missing in Eck, and took a great interest in fine arts – he abandoned ballets with plot and turned to choreographing those with an abstract subject. In his one-act pieces, he built on the musical, scenic and thematic contrasts between classical and contemporary dance. His strivings, however, were too daring for the time. His choreography to the first Hungarian dodecaphonic composition by Szervánszky, *Six Orchestral Pieces* (*Hat zenekari darab*, 1966) for example, which was conceived in a socialist–realist milieu, was only appreciated by representatives of the profession. The audience, used to choreographies with a plot featuring heroes, demanded works that were familiar in structure and easy to understand, and was at a complete loss with his new ideas.

Unable to get replacements for his company from the State Ballet Institute – the only official ballet school – Imre and his small troupe gave up the struggle in 1969. When one of his *pas de deux* won a competition in Cologne, he decided to continue his career as a dancer and choreographer in western Europe. He danced in Düsseldorf, Stuttgart, Cologne, Darmstadt and finally with Ballet Rambert in London. By this decision, the fate of the Szeged Ballet was sealed: it was no longer a company that performed individual pieces, but now could only dance in ballet inserts of operas and operettas.

In the 1960s and 1970s the Hungarian Opera company, which was very keen to preserve tradition, could no longer resist the new trends. Although one or two Eck pieces were performed at the Opera as well, the real breakthrough came with the première of the first full-length ballet by young choreographer László Seregi. Seregi has never gone as far as Eck in denying classical aesthetic values, yet he can be considered a real reformer in the light of Hungarian choreographic traditions. Having started his career as a folk dancer with the Ensemble of the Army, Seregi was able to synthesize the achievements of the previous epochs: the swing momentum, theatrical character and heated atmosphere of the Soviet ballets, with the vividness and humour of the Harangozó's pieces, as well as the non-linear dramaturgy adopted from new films. His very first work was *Spartacus* (1968), a grand ballet demonstrating his musicality and sense of theatre. In it, the dancers are not schematic heroes from posters, but real, suffering people with whom the audience can sympathize. Excluding *Cedar* (*Cédrus*, 1975), a ballet with no linear plot, Seregi has since been the great master of storytelling choreographies. From time to time, though, he plays with making one-act pieces, and even more, he occasionally entered the world of musicals, just as Jerome Robbins did in the US. Yet at the same time, he was the master of *Spartacus*-like works, preserving tradition while using new composing methods, in works such as the extremely witty *Sylvia* or the later pieces of his Shakespeare series, *Romeo and Juliet* (*Rómeó és Julia*, 1985), *A Midsummer Night's Dream* (*Szentivánéji álom*, 1989) and *The Taming of the Shrew* (*Makrancos Kata*, 1994).

There was one more vital characteristic of these years which followed Seregi's early period and made the panorama complete: a slow change into liberalism. During this phase, after years of hermetic isolation, there began sporadic guest performances, and the Opera company started to take in some of the basic works from the twentieth-century western European and American ballet repertoire.

These pieces updated the repertoire and brought the audience, and of course the profession, face to face with all those innovations that had already taken place elsewhere more than several decades earlier. The greatest impact, a real explosion of a success was achieved by Maurice Béjart's triple bill of *Firebird*, *Op. 5* and *Le Sacre du printemps*, because their emotional character was so familiar. The more abstract choreographies – George Balanchine's *Symphony in C* and *Agon*, and Hans van Manen's *Adagio Hammerklavier* – found a more muted response since the general taste had been formed by the more 'understandable' ballets that had a plot.

In this period, innovative efforts also showed themselves in the field of folk dance. Yet no new ensemble was founded, and the impulse did not come from abroad. By this time, a new generation of choreographers had emerged from the many hundreds of amateur ensembles whose members had revolted against the artistic concept represented by the professional companies, which had to represent the continuous high spirits of the working class – the cliché of 'perky lads and modest lasses' – using the artistic means of folklore. It was not vital to present real human feelings and relationships.

The question asked by this generation in revolt in the second half of the century was: how could folk dance material be staged and be simultaneously 'authentic' and 'contemporary'? By raising this question, even if heading in different artistic directions, the members of this generation were referring back to the Bartók model. There were two types of approach, one based on the original folklore material and the other on free, artistic interpretation. One of the groups, headed by Sándor Tímár, declared the importance of turning from stage back to folklore, to the 'clear source', which was still alive. This new folkloristic trend in the second half of the 1960s tried to recreate the original folk dance proceedings on stage, and hence the main concern became the dance language itself. But this time, it was not just treated as a motif taken out of context, but as a complex integration of dance phrase, music accompaniment and interpretation. According to this concept, the creator is a recreator, who almost impersonally draws from the original source; the subject-matter of his choreography is the authentic dance proceedings and the customs themselves.

For the creator, folklore was not a source of inspiration but a perfect example to be followed to such an extent that – in accordance with Hungarian ethnographers' findings, that the main characteristics of Hungarian folk dances rely on their improvisational character – a new composing method was born. Prior to this, the folk dance artists had set the folklore material in theatrical forms borrowed from ballet. Using the new composing method, they conceived the counterpart of these characteristics for the stage by moving the groups next to one another concurrently and thus recreating the spontaneous improvisational character of the dances. This kind of 'disorder' was to give back the preserved freedom and variations of the original peasant dances.

There could not be anything more 'modern' than the rediscovery of the 'archaic' during a time when the political regime tended towards standardization and resistance to the desire for personal freedom. This is why the *Dance-House Movement (Táncház mozgalom)*, which was getting under way in the 1970s, contained some political undertones: through this, the youth of the towns could use the same century-old folk dances, including music and costumes, for their own pleasure and not only for the stage, and they could do it freely and creatively, finding their identity.

The other group representing the other approach to folk dance, a group which included Katalin Györgyfalvay, Károly Szigeti, Ferenc Novák and Antal Kricskovics, tried to synthesize a new, updated theatrical language based on the vocabulary and spirituality of folklore, following in Bartók's footsteps (in this case, we refer to him as a contemporary composer and not as a folk music collector, if, that is, it is possible to speak of two different Bartóks). Their idea was not to recreate the ancient but to create something new. That is why they considered the folklore material of the Carpathian basin, which preserved the dance material of old and new styles, as a rich language in which to address their own epoch. What had been the aim of the former group became, for this group, the means. In works of this type, tradition survived with faithless faith. Creators come into the foreground to conceive their reflections and their own world-view.

This choreographic trend resulted in two new individual composing methods. One of them is the so-called 'collage' method, in which two decisively different dances are arranged next to each other in order to represent two types of human behaviour. The fruitfulness of this method was demonstrated by the series of choreographies such as *Cain and Abel* (*Káin és Ábel*, 1972 by Györgyfalvay), in which the *verbunk*, a slow, graceful dance with a heavy stressed beat, is contrasted with the lads' dance (*legényes*), which is quick and contains little airy jumps. This type of dance includes some of special note, such as *Carmina Burana* (1977), in which Kricskovics, the choreographer, mingled the collective dance material of girls' dances in the Balkan with the beginnings of the Graham technique.

Katalin Györgyfalvay was the representative of the other so-called 'montage' method, who experimented with assembling different dance layers: music and text on top of and beneath one another. As a consequence, multi-layered choreographies were born, the complexity and domain of association of which can only be compared to the Miklós Jancsó's films of the period. The four movements of *Montage* (*Montázs*, 1973) – the foremost work of this trend – were not built up in a linear way, and the choreography did not have a plot or any typical characters. The pictures of the movements – consisting of children's games, rhymes, laments, marching and popular songs from the Second World War, weddings and mourning songs – assembled on top of one another offered an astounding, contemporary and non-verbal theatrical experience, while the dance vocabulary of the piece was genuine folk dance. In the 1980s, working with a short-lived professional state ensemble, Györgyfalvay choreographed pure dance pieces to the music of contemporary composers, using folk dance material but without any ethnic reference, as if considering her material as something neutral.

In this flourishing period in the second half of the 1970s, there was another so called 'dance theatre range' in folk dance art developing within this trend, using plots and traditional dramaturgy. Among the narrative compositions – in most cases mythological, such as *Paris's Apple* (*Páris almája*, 1981, by Kricskovics), biblical, such as *The Prodigal Son* (*A tékozló fiú*, 1975, by Kricskovics) and *Passion* (*Passió*, 1981) and literary themes *Hungarian Electra* (*Magyar Elektra*, 1984) and *Kelemen Kőmüves* (*Kőmüves Kelemen*, 1974) – all of them by Novák – were elaborated. In these one-act pieces – stories were told in dance using the folk dance vocabulary.

This, we can say, completed the Hungarian folk dance 'school', which from the 1970s stood in total contrast to its Soviet counterpart that had been the example for the official Hungarian folk dance art from its birth. There were real experiments in theatrical and dance language going on in the amateur Hungarian folk dance workshops, which were quite out of reach of the representatives of official art policy. As a result, a rich and modern folk dance repertoire has developed, with no match elsewhere in Europe.

Hungarian ballet and folk dance art entered the 1980s without any staggering changes. Fundamental changes in Hungarian dance life had taken place long before the political ones – almost, one could say, as precursors to what was to come later politically. First, a new generation of choreographers entered the scene in the 1980s. They did not even try to meet official aesthetic expectations, and did not try to acquire official positions in order to become leaders of ensembles. They were the first to have the opportunity of artistic and individual independence, thanks to the support of certain foundations (mainly the Soros Foundation). Earlier, artistic policy had tolerated the amateur ensembles, while in the 1980s alternative culture, without the support of the state, began to flourish even in smaller theatres, university clubs and culture houses, with, initially, small audiences.

The first of these to open was the Kreatív Mozgás Stúdió (Creative Movement Studio) in Budapest in 1983. It was a private school where, at last, internationally known pedagogues, such as Matt Mattox and Bruce Taylor, came to teach modern and contemporary dance techniques and philosophies, at first during summer schools, later more frequently. This studio had such a liberating impact, that from 1984 and 1985 a great many independent ensembles started to form comprising pantomime artists, actors and gymnasts as well as dancers. It was because of this varied background – where dance *per se* was rather scarce – that these new ensembles were most able to immerse themselves in contact improvisation, promoting the movement theatre so that it became the strongest trend at that time.

The greatest talent of this genre, the so-called 'movement theatre', was Josef Nadj, who had started his career in Budapest. He won the New Dance Competition organized by the Creative Movement Studio in 1984 and, after returning to Budapest from Paris, he premièred his first group choreography *Peking Duck* (*Pekingi kacsa*, 1986). His other colleagues – Gábor Goda, László Rókás and László Hudi – have since been working at declaring the permeability of diverse artistic

90

trends and languages to the extent that they sometimes find it difficult to classify themselves, regarding themselves variously as representatives of theatre or movement theatre, or even dance ensembles.

There were very few representatives of established dance (which even in the 1980s mostly included ballet and folk dance), who had turned to experimental work, in this case partly because they lacked a living model and roots, and being involved in alternative art meant an insecure existence. Yvette Bozsik, for example, danced with the Operetta Theatre for years after graduating from the classical ballet faculty of the Hungarian Dance Academy (earlier, Hungarian State Ballet Institute). With artist György Árvay, she experimented with elaborating a new theatrical language. As one of the co-founders, along with Árvay, of Natural Disasters (Temészetes Vészek, 1986), for years Bozsik travelled the world, from Edinburgh to Beijing, giving guest performances with great success, while she hardly had the opportunity to perform in Hungary. The reason for this was that she had radically chosen to deny tradition and to discard the concept and technique of classical ballet. Bozsik and Árvay achieved a new theatrical language, which had its roots in fine art rather than in narrative theatre. In these works, using the scenic potentials of space, Bozsik did not appear as a dancer but rather as a kind of living plastic element. In order to achieve this, she had to rid herself of all the techniques she had learned and absorbed in order that she might discover possible, rather 'inarticulate' ways of elemental human self-expression. In her solo performances *Living Space* (*Eleven tér*, 1987), *Originator* (1989), and *The Yesterday of Victory* (*A győzelem tegnapja*, 1986) she presented human beings' pre-conscious state, the pulling and pottering of sexless embryos, mother earth hatching a world egg, animated beings immersing themselves in the first principle – metaphysical experiences presented in sensual forms.

Bozsik's second creative period dates back to 1987, the time of the Szeged Ballet's second rebirth. Zoltán Imre, on his return from Great Britain, became the artistic director of the company, gave young talent the chance to create, and so Bozsik had the opportunity to make her first group choreographies, *The Little Ladies' Parlour* (*Kis női szalon*, 1992) and *Waiting* (*A várakozás*, 1992), inspired by Genet and Kafka, and a little later *Wilis* (*A villik*, 1993), in which she alluded to her years studying ballet. In these one-act pieces, the young choreographer elaborated on her individual dance language, consisting mainly of movement fragments and their repetition, the vibrating movements of the body as well as everyday gestures. However, there were no narrative signs in her works later, either.

Since she founded her own company in 1993, Bozsik's greatest venture so far has been the staging of *The Miraculous Mandarin* (1996). Bozsik's version is not only radically harsh and elementally expressive, but offers a totally new angle, presenting the magic and cathartic ecstasy of carnal desire, disregarding customs and rules. Bozsik's suggestive performing style and the eclectic character of her works – regardless of whether we consider her solo pieces or any of her theatrical works that mingle projected pictures and words, as in *The Yellow Wallpaper* (*Sárga tapéta*, 1995) – have won a new, relatively young audience for contemporary dance, especially since 1994, when her independent ensemble was admitted to one of the leading theatres in the capital, the Katona József Theatre.

In contrast, the TranzDanz company, led by Péter Gerzson Kovács and founded in 1992 by dancers whose standpoint was to reject previously accepted dance values, has not been so lucky. Kovács did not turn his back on classical ballet but on the new folklorist trend in which he had truly believed and actively participated during the 1970s. After a time, the imposing richness of the original dance material and the 'authentic' peasant way of presentation had become a barrier for him, preventing him from expressing his personal response. This is why he turned to jazz music since his ability to improvise, which originated from folk dance, could easily mingle with jazz improvisation, namely with the music of Mihály Dresch, who was, conversely, just turning to folk music to find a new source of inspiration. The result of this encounter was Kovács's first solo, *Tranz Dance* (*Transz tánc*, 1988), a base that might not have been built upon had Kovács not been offered a contract with Ballet du Fargistan, a French contemporary dance ensemble.

Kovács's two years there allowed him to find his own artistic way, even though he did not adapt any existing contemporary dance techniques or characteristic compositional methods from his time in France. In this foreign environment, he suddenly realized that anything could be done and that it is not ethnographic but artistic originality and authenticity that count. With this new awareness, he founded his ensemble, which, even today, has neither a permanent seat nor permanent members. Nevertheless, the choreographer being so distinctive, the ensemble's style is coherent. His one-act pieces do not build on narration, but rather bear signs of suggestion, and occasionally we can feel the presence of a magically strong performer, in its richness of rhythm and dynamics, the dance language fragmented in its elements, and the music alive and breathing with the performers. Kovács's works radiate a specific ritual atmosphere, as if transporting the audience into the domains of eternity, and dealing with archetypal situations in works such as *Astral Years* (*Asztrál évek*, 1993), *Profana* (1994) and *In Sol* (1996). In his works, even the most recent present can be detected alongside the past, which is also permanently present: the demolished world with only words and snatches of music whirling around, where entirety no longer exists but scarcity, with the roughest instincts and tempers training against each other. This is the atmosphere felt in *Temporary Title* (*Ideiglenes cim*, 1992), a work that won the Bagnolet Prize. Although Kovács built on folklore, this agent from folklore has disappeared. He does not even try to recreate the past on stage but 'speaks' this archaic language in his role as a contemporary choreographer.

Tamás Juronics has similarly turned to contemporary dance from folk dance. He has been the artistic director of the Szeged Contemporary Ballet since 1993, the year Zoltán Imre left. Juronics, a member of a younger generation, joined the Szeged Ballet after graduating from the folk dance faculty of the State Ballet Institute. Imre had regularly invited guest teachers and choreographers (Jorma Uotinen, Matthew Hawkins and Roberto Galvan) to the company, which was being reorganized at the time. Such was Imre's background that it was a matter of course that the company's young members could experiment within its studio; which is how Juronics started choreographing. His early works clearly show the signs of his wide-ranging experiences gained by acquiring various dance techniques and styles over the years. Although his very first choreography was a grotesque folk dance study, his later pieces no longer contain folkloristic elements.

Juronics's movement language mingles contact and Limón techniques with acrobatic elements. His one-act pieces are a set of loosely linked independent studies, imbued with melancholy or humour. In most cases, these independent episodes reveal the human relations residing in the chosen dance form – concurrently presenting their positive and negative sides. Juronics considers his subjects in a grotesque way, questioning each existing form and convention. His work *Arena* (*A porond*, 1994), which conjures up the world of the circus, uses a thick sponge to cover the stage, reminding us of a trampoline, which always makes the dancers stumble, even in the most solemn moments. In *Homo Ludens* (1996) continual bizarre and humorous undertones are attached to everyday situations. Sentimentalism turns to ridicule, rudeness to poetry and playfulness mingles with tragedy.

In his latest works, Juronics is no longer concerned with episodic composition but tries to experiment with musical and spatial dramaturgy, and in these works scenic questions acquire a more prominent role. *Sacre du printemps* (*Tavaszi áldozat*, 1995) pries into the question of the victim's responsibility, possibility and impossibility, and is set in the uninhabited outskirts of a town that is flooded with water, simultaneously both dirty and purifying. In the tripartite space of *Mudman* (*Sárember*, 1996) water appears again, as well as sand, which dries as mud on the hero's body after he has rolled in slushy dirt: destruction and birth turn into each other. In *Splinters* (*Szilánkok*, 1997), his most recent work, it is not only the bottles that break into splinters in a mysterious pub but also human lives and relations. In this work about the human condition (although not in story format), Juronics uses space not only in a traditional, horizontal way but also puts it on a vertical level: his dancers also dance on the wall. Juronics seems to be able to absorb all the elements of contemporary dance from the past decades. He sifts his experiences through his own personal past and that of a dancer, and immediately refracts it through his sense of irony.

The gates which have opened from and led to the West over the past decades are too recent for us to be able properly to judge their effects on the present. From this present perspective, Hungarian dance life seems to care for its past, so that it can be part of the global dance stream by respecting the characteristics of its roots, namely the creators' and audience's compulsion to convey artistic messages, an aversion to abstract subjects and a concern for living folk dance culture. It can only adapt influences in accordance with its artistic aspect, which simultaneously tolerates tradition and reform. What Hungarian dance life is able to offer is something that is presented by its own relationship to the traditions of national and universal dance art, be they positive or negative.

Key texts

Dienes, G. and Fuchs, L. (eds) (1989), *A színpadi tánc története Magyarországon*, Budapest: Múzsák Kiadó.

Fuchs, L. (1994) *Félúton. A kortárs tánc egy évtizede* [*A mi-chemin: dix ans de danse contemporaine en France et en Hongrie*], Budapest: French Institute.

Lenkei, J. (ed.) (1993) *Mozdulatművészet*, Budapest: Magvető Kiadó–T-Twins.

Várszegi T. (ed.) (1994) *Félúton*, Budapest: Foundation for New Theatre.

Várszegi, T. and Sándor, L. I. (eds) (1992) *Fordulatok*, Budapest: private edition.

Table 5 Important dance and political events in Hungary (1900 to present)

Year	Dance: artists, works, events	Dance: institutions	Arts scene	Sociocultural and political events
1901		*A tánc* (*The Dance*) was the first Hungarian motion picture		
1902	*Isadora Duncan			
1907	*Ruth St Denis *Maud Allan			
1910		Madzsar school	Folk Opera House	
1911				
1912	*Ballets Russes *Jaques-Dalcroze	Dienes school		
1914	Pavlova company			
1917	*The Wooden Prince* (Zöbisch, Brada and Balázs)			
1918				Proclamation of Hungarian Republic
1919		Szentpál school	Operetta Theatre	Proletarian dictatorship
1922			Green Donkey Theatre,	
1925			First avant-garde theatre company	
1926		*A tánc* (*The Dance*) was the first Hungarian dance magazine		
1928	*The Three-Cornered Hat* (Gaubier)	Hungarian Soc. of Movement Culture		
1930	*Csongor and Tünde* (Cieplinski)			
1931		Pearly Bouquet	Szeged Open Air Theatre	
1933	*Petrushka* (Milloss) *Hungarian Fantasies* (Cieplinski) *Ballets Jooss	*Mozdulatkultura* (*Movement Culture*) was a magazine on movement culture/modern dance		
1936	*Village Inn Scene* (Harangozó)	Nádasi school		

Table 5 continued

Year	Dance: artists, works, events	Dance: institutions	Arts scene	Sociocultural and political events
1938		Hungarian Fullplay		First resolution of borders, Vienna
1940				Second resolution on borders, Vienna
1941	The Miraculous Mandarin (Harangozó, dress rehearsal)			
1942	The Creatures of Prometheus (Milloss)			
1943	Bolero (Cieplinski)			
1944				German occupation
1945	The Miraculous Mandarin (Harangozó)			
1946	*Moiseyev company	Szeged Ballet		Proclamation of Hungarian Republic, re-establishes 1938 borders
1948				Nationalizations
1949	The Miraculous Mandarin (Lőrinc)	Folk Dance Co. Hungarian Army		New constitution Hungarian People's Republic
1950	The Nutcracker (Voinonen)	Association of Hungarian Dancers State Folk Dance Company State Ballet Institute		
1951		SZOT Folk Dance Company Táncművészet (The Art of Dance) monthly magazine on dance until 1956		
1952	The Fountain of Bakhiserai (Zakharov)			
1953	Coppélia (Harangozó)		Museum and Institute for Theatre Research	

Table 5 *continued*

1956	*The Miraculous Mandarin* (Harangozó, modern version)			Revolution, put down by Soviets
1958	*Giselle* (Lavrovsky), *Kirov Ballet	Szeged Ballet refounded Budapest Folk Dance Company (formerly SZOT)		
1960	*Comediants* (Eck)			
1961	*Bolshoi Ballet	Ballet Sophiane (Pécs Ballet)		
1962	*London Festival Ballet			
1963	*Le Sacre du printemps* (Eck)			
1964		*Eternal Dance* (dir. Tamás Banovich), first full-length dance film		
1965	*The Miraculous Mandarin* (Eck)			
1966	*Metamorphosis* (Imre)			
1968	*Spartacus* (Seregi) *Combat of Forms* (Imre)	First Hungarian Dance Week		
1969	*Alwin Nikolais company		Institute for Musicology	
1970	*Antonio Gades company		25. Theatre, first experimental theatre *Red Psalm* (dir. Jancsó)	
1971		Folk dance faculty at State Ballet Inst.		
1972	Soloists from Béjart's Ballet du XXe Siècle *Cain and Abel* (Györgyfalvay)			
1973	*The Firebird, Sacre, Op. 5* (Béjart) *Montage* (Györgyfalvay)			
1974	*Alvin Ailey company			
1975	*The Cedar* (Seregi)			
1976	*Requiem* (Eck)	*Táncművészet* magazine was re-funded		
1977	*Serenade, Symphony in C* (Balanchine) *Carmina Burana* (Kricskovics)			
1978		Dance Company of Folk Theatre		

Table 5 continued

Year	Dance: artists, works, events	Dance: institutions	Arts scene	Sociocultural and political events
1979	The Lovers of the Sun (Markó)	Györ Ballet International Movement Theatre Festival Interballet Festival		
1980	Salome (Eck) *Het Nationale Ballet			
1981	The Miraculous Mandarin (Markó)			
1982			Rock Theatre, first independent musical theatre	
1983	*Théâtre de Arche/Marin Co.	Creative Movement Studio		
1984	Five (Gyula Berger) Hungarian Electra (Novák)	Berger Company Artus Company Natural Disaster International New Dance Competition		
1985	Romeo and Juliet (Seregi) *The Royal Ballet			
1986	Yesterday of Victory (Bozsik) Living Space (Bozsik) Commedia Senza Parole (Györgyfalvay)	Petöfi Csarnok, first contemporary dance venue		
1987	Peking Duck (Nadj)	Szeged Ballet refounded Tranz Danz		New political parties founded
1988	Stabat Mater (Imre)			
1989	A Midsummer Night's Dream (Seregi)			Iron Curtain on Austro-Hungarian border broken Proclamation of Republic First free election since
1990	The Miraculous Mandarin (Milloss) Memories of a Hardly Used Drying Rope (Juronics)			1947

Table 5 continued

1991	*Temporary Title* (Kovács)	Central Europe Dance Theatre (formerly Dance Company of Folk Theatre)
		Association of Contemporary Dancers
1992		Association of Dance Research
		Budapest Dance School (formerly Creative Movement Studio)
1993	*Soirée* (Bozsik)	Yvette Bozsik Company
	*Paul Taylor company	Szeged Contemporary Ballet (formerly Szeged Ballet)
	*Rosas	*Inspiration*, young choreographers competition
		Interfolkdance Festival
1994	*The Taming of the Shrew* (Seregi)	International Ballet Competition
	*Trisha Brown company	
1995	*Le Sacre du printemps* (Juronics)	
	The Miraculous Mandarin (Bozsik)	
	*Wuppertal Tanztheater	
1996	*Mud Man* (Juronics)	Hungarian Festival Ballet
	*Martha Graham company	*Off Light: (Ellenfény)* is a review on contemporary dance and theatre
1998	*DV8 Physical Theatre	

*First visit

6

ITALY

The Cinderella of the arts

Giannandrea Poesio

Unlike the nineteenth-century Italian ballet, twentieth-century Italian theatre dance has seldom attracted the interest of dance scholars and thus remains a grey area. Indeed, this particular epoch lacks the aura of artistic splendour that underscored the continuous choreographic outpouring and surrounded the internationally celebrated personalities of the previous century, among whom are dancers and pedagogues such as Carlotta Grisi, Fanny Cerrito, Carlotta Brianza, Pierina Legnani, Carlo Blasis, Giovanni Lepri and Enrico Cecchetti. During the first decades of this century, a complex series of reasons (examined later) led to a rapid demise of both Italian theatre dance and its popularity; ballet failed to renew itself while contemporary dance originated mainly as an élitist phenomenon destined for a long time to be appreciated only by a selected national intelligentsia.

Inevitably, the decline of public interest in theatre dance also affected the way this art form was administered and regulated. It was the lack of suitable legislation that prompted the revealing definition 'Cinderella of the arts', still in use among Italian dance writers, dance experts and dance-goers. Even when, at the end of the Fascist regime, new legislation was promulgated to regulate the theatre unions (1944), the *sindacato tersicorei* or 'terpsichoreans' union' (the adjective *tersicorei* still echoing the pompous Fascist vocabulary) was the last in the hierarchical list, immediately after that protecting stage equestrians. It is not surprising, therefore, that this negative image has often prevented an in-depth analysis of theatre dance. Still, twentieth-century Italian theatre dance offers some interesting possibilities for research, particularly when the seldom-acknowledged richness of the current dance scene, as well as its historical origins and other informing factors, are taken into account.

In 1997, the appointment of a committee of dance experts in charge of the distribution of government funds to dance companies was hailed as the first step towards a new political and administrative regulation of Italian theatre dance. The creation of the Commissione Danza, as the committee is officially called, has led to hope for further beneficial changes, such as a forthcoming, yet still not promulgated decree that should determine the end of dance's discriminatory subjugation to music, ratified in the 1967 *legge 800* (named after the number of the act or *legge*). In addition, the new committee can be considered the first governmental and administrative dance-regulating institution to be formed by non-politicians (in the past decades no dancers, choreographers or 'dance experts' had any role in the administration and organization of the dance scene). It would appear that by entrusting the administration of dance funds to a group of specialists such as dance critics, dance scholars and dance organizers – and, more recently, one choreographer – the Italian government has finally decided to recognize the particular status theatre dance enjoys today within Italian culture.

Indeed, it was the so-called 'dance-boom' of the mid-1970s that redeemed Italian dance from its inferior position and prompted an unexpected proliferation of dance events and companies, since when a more fitting legislation has been called for. The full significance of both the reforms mentioned above and their foreseeable consequences, however, can be appreciated only once the complex and multifaceted state-of-the-art form in Italy is examined and contextualized. Still, the aim of the ensuing paragraphs is not to provide the reader with an exhaustive discussion of twentieth-century Italian theatre dance – a rather ambitious task – but to examine only some of its most distinctive features, thus establishing the premises for further discussion and analysis.

Fortunately, the complexity and the vastness of the argument do not prevent a critical analysis of the most significant facets of twentieth-century Italian dance, for these can easily be singled out. The different nature of each facet, whether political, social, cultural or historical, is what has prompted and allowed the schematic discussion that follows, chosen also for the sake of clarity.

Italian Twentieth-Century Ballet

Despite critical acclaim and the enthusiastic response of some well-respected intellectuals of the time, Diaghilev's Ballets Russes did not have a strong impact on Italian ballet and did not prompt the renewal of pre-existing choreographic canons, as it did in other European countries. The Italian dance scene, in fact, was not at the time an artistically fertile ground for any kind of renovation or revolution. The demise of the Italian ballet had started at the turn of the century, when new cultural and artistic trends could no longer accommodate or justify the phantasmagorical allegories on which works such as the 1881 *Excelsior*, a choreographic extravaganza celebrating scientific progress, had successfully thrived. While the other Italian performing arts gradually adhered to the new canons, Italian ballet remained steeped in the conventions of the nineteenth-century Italian *ballo*, a unique genre that had little in common with the more widespread French Romantic ballet and its subsequent Russian derivations.

The superficial spectacular grandeur, the overwhelming amount of circus-like bravura numbers, and the futility of the subject matter that still celebrated the unrealistic aura of bourgeois prosperity that had characterized the first years of the newly unified Italian kingdom, were hardly suited to the new social awareness and its corresponding artistic trends prompted by the moderate left-oriented politics of the beginning of the century. Yet those remained the characteristic components of works such as Giovanni Pratesi's *Bacco e Gambrinus* (1904) and *Vecchia Milano* (1928), or Rosa Piovella Ansaldo's *La Taglioni*, created as late as 1945 and based, not unlike Pratesi's 1904 creation, on a nostalgic look at a much-idealised bygone era.

Even the independent all-Italian ballet companies that tried to emulate Diaghilev's enterprise proposed a repertory lacking in innovation and perpetuated a lifeless tradition. An example of this was the short-lived 1915 Balli Italiani di Nicola Guerra, named after the celebrated dancer and ballet-master Nicola Guerra, who was also the principal choreographer of the company and an inveterate representative and supporter of the nineteenth-century Italian school. Within this context, the closure of the Dance Academy attached to La Scala Theatre in Milan, between 1917 and 1921, was clearly symptomatic of a crisis. Interestingly, it was in 1917, one year before the end of World War One and five years before the Fascist party took over the Italian political life, that the Futurists published their *Manifesto della Danza Futurista* (*Manifesto of Futurist Dance*), advocating the rejection of ballet's conventions and a total re-birth of the old art.

There is also little doubt that the frequent visits and the presence in Italy of companies and personalities such as Diaghilev's Ballets Russes, Isadora Duncan, Ida Rubinstein, Bella Hutter, Mary Wigman and Jia Ruskaja, channelled the interest of Italian theatre-goers away from such a culturally sterile form of national choreography. Some of those 'innovative' foreign inputs, moreover, were soon destined to become official manifestations of the Fascist regime's politically pre-determined culture. The allegedly negative effect of Fascist culture on the Italian ballet tradition is much debated among Italian dance scholars and has yet to be fully ascertained. Some claim that, by supporting other forms of dance such as the 'free' and neo-classically inspired style promoted by Jia Ruskaja, and by forcing eminent supporters of the ballet to move abroad, Mussolini's regime gave a deadly blow to what was left of the once-acclaimed art form. Others point out that it was under the Fascist regime that two important ballet institutions were created in Rome, such as the Opera Ballet School (1928) and the Regia Scuola di Danza (Royal School of Dance) (1940). Still, an examination of the reasons that prevented the development of an identifiable twentieth-century Italian choreographic style needs also to take other factors into account.

Unlike other European countries, Italy never had a single performing space unanimously regarded as the institutionalized centre for ballet – as with the Paris Opéra or the Marynsky Theatre in St Petersburg. Similarly, it never had an institutionalized 'national' ballet company that epitomized the Italian ballet tradition, although most scholars identify such an institution with the ballet company of La Scala in Milan, thus overlooking other and equally significant companies such as the ballet of the San Carlo theatre in Naples. The geographical and historical division of the country prior to the proclamation of the unified Italian kingdom in 1861 impinged culturally and politically on the creation of such a 'national' company that so many twentieth-century Italian dance personalities have dreamed of. Almost every capital of the pre-unification states, ruled by non-Italian leaders and regimes, boasted an opera house which often had its own ballet company as well as its own ballet school or academy. Interestingly, the artistic individuality of each theatre was maintained after the geographical and political unification of the country was achieved.

It would be erroneous, however, to consider those institutions as surviving exponents of a well-rooted and glorious nineteenth-century tradition. The early twentieth-century demise of the Italian ballet led to a considerable decrease in the choreographic activities of the regional theatres, which in the previous century had hosted dance and opera performances in almost equal numbers. In most cases, the resident ballet companies were kept merely for ornamental purposes, namely to be used in artistically undemanding operatic *divertissements* to be found in the works of Verdi, Rossini, Donizetti, Ponchielli, Meyerbeer, Gounod and Bizet. These companies, therefore, neither benefited from a regularly planned dance season, nor were they able to tour. In spite of some sporadic exceptions – notably the ballet company attached to La Scala – this constraining relationship with the opera houses has remained a distinctive feature of the Italian ballet until recent times and, in some instances, is still an unfortunate reality.

Because of the different nature of these companies, an in-depth analysis of twentieth-century Italian ballet should look at each ballet company separately, a task that can only be achieved by devoting an entire publication to each, such as the monographs by Luigi Rossi (1970) for the ballet at La Scala or Stelio Felici (1977) for the dance activities at the Maggio Musicale in Florence. There are also, however, some significant commonalities that are worth taking into consideration. Despite a well-defined historical tradition, supported in some instances by the existence of a ballet school that feeds into the *corps de ballet*, each major Italian ballet company lacks the individual stylistic unity that characterizes their European counterparts. This phenomenon can be mostly attributed to the continual changes of directorship that have affected and still affect the administratively troubled life of both the theatres and the ballet companies. It is also worth noting that many of the frequently changing ballet directors were (and still are) foreign artists, who inevitably bring with them the aesthetic and stylistic canons with which they are familiar. Finally, one should not overlook the fact that the repertories of each major ballet company never had the stylistic imprint determined by the more or less constant presence of a choreographer, as in the cases of Frederick Ashton and Kenneth MacMillan for Britain's Royal Ballet, John Cranko for the Stuttgart Ballet, or Serge Lifar for the Paris Opera Ballet, the reason being that no choreographer managed to spend enough time with the same institution, given the changes mentioned above.

The only foreign personality who could be said to have contributed considerably to the development of the Italian ballet, particularly from the end of the Second World War, was the Hungarian Aurel Milloss. Following Diaghilev's artistic policy, Milloss created spectacular performances in which the collaboration between various arts was the core element. However, although between 1936 and 1970 he worked for La Scala, the Rome Opera Ballet, the Biennale Festival in Venice, and the Maggio Musicale Fiorentino in Florence, his artistic principles – which encompassed the expressionist teachings of Rudolf Von Laban and the more classical ones expounded by Enrico Cecchetti and Viktor Gsovsky – did not stand the test of time. Unlike Frederick Ashton, Antony Tudor or Kenneth MacMillan in Britain, George Balanchine in the United States, John Cranko in Stuttgart or Serge Lifar in Paris, Milloss neither created a clearly identifiable style nor did he leave a surviving repertoire behind him.

Apart from Milloss, the other eminent foreign dance personalities to work in Italy, such as Vera Volkova, Anton Dolin, Léonide Massine, and, more recently, Egon Madsen, Vladimir Vasiliev, Maya Plisetskaya, can be considered passing meteors who, in the end, did not leave a significant stylistic imprint. The same could be said of the Italian ballet directors. It should also be remembered that the artistic director of the ballet company attached to an opera house seldom has any organisational freedom. Although this particular situation is not exclusively Italian, the way theatre politics have always neglected the dance has determined the still-scarce ballet production in the country. Until the early 1980s only two ballet companies (those of La Scala in Milan and the Rome Opera) out of six (the others being from the opera theatres in Florence, Venice, Naples and Verona) could boast a standard repertoire of the so-called 'classics' from both the nineteenth and the twentieth centuries, or a proper annual dance season.

This constraining situation has often led to the creation of small independent groups of professional dancers who left the secure but restrictive life of the opera house to create a ballet company, or who asked permission to perform outside it. It is interesting to note that the two major independent ballet companies – where the adjective 'independent' refers to their not being part of an opera house – both started as groups of professional dancers willing to expand their repertoire and to experiment with new dance techniques. The Aterballetto, originally formed in 1977 by the classically trained Vittorio Biagi, soon became one of the most interesting Italian companies. Funded by the regional administration of Emilia Romagna, the company, which only acquired its name in 1979, gained considerable repute by inviting foreign choreographers and dancers to build up an international repertoire that encompassed different types of contemporary ballet. On the one hand, dance-makers such as Glen Tetley, Alvin Ailey and, later, William Forsythe restaged or created some of their successful works for the company. On the other, artists such as the Danish dancer Peter Schaufuss were invited to work with the company as both performers and *répétiteurs* of still 'unknown' ballets, such as those by August Bournonville. Thanks to these varied cultural inputs, some company members, including the artistic director Amedeo Amodio, who succeeded Vittorio Biagi in 1979, started to experiment with choreography, thus promoting new forms of what has been perceived, by both Italian dance-goers and the specialized press, as the first examples of a national form of choreography. Today, the company, under the direction of Mauro Bigonzetti, who succeeded Amodio in 1998, retains its balletic connotations, although the focus is more on a contemporary-oriented repertoire which includes works by Bigonzetti, whose choreographic style has been compared to that of Forsythe.

Similarly, the Balletto di Toscana originated in Florence from the reaction of some dancers from the local ballet of the Teatro Comunale to its limited dance activities. In 1975 they formed the Collettivo di Danza Contemporanea, which soon attracted the attention of critics as well as international choreographers by promoting a constant experimentation with techniques other than ballet. The group's fame, however, reached its apex when the director of the Teatro Comunale's ballet company, the Russian ballet-master Evgheny Polyakov, also started to work for the alternative/independent group as choreographer. His presence prompted the arrival of other eminent personalities, such as the Belgian Micha Van Hoecke, a former artist of Maurice Béjart's Ballet du XXeme Siècle, who contributed considerably to the development of the group's repertoire and who, eventually, created in 1981 his own contemporary dance company, L' Ensemble, currently based in Pisa. Finally, in 1985, the popularity that the Collettivo had gained – also promoting a series of events aimed at improving the knowledge of the dance among the general public – allowed the creation of an independent 'ballet' company, the Balletto di Toscana, with its own dancers. Since then the company has toured extensively – it was in the United States in the spring of 1998 – and boasts a varied repertoire that includes works by Hans van Manen, Ed Wubbe, Nils Christe, as well as Italian choreographers such as Mauro Bigonzetti, Fabrizio Monteverde and Virgilio Sieni. Still, not unlike the Aterballetto, the Balletto di Toscana can hardly be classified as a repertoire company, where the term 'repertoire' refers to a repertory of ballet classics from both the nineteenth and twentieth centuries. The term 'balletto', or 'ballet', in fact refers more to the way company's dancers are trained than to the actual stylistic connotation of the institution, not to mention the fact that in Italian (as in French) the term 'ballet' is also used to indicate a dance company and not just a particular choreographic genre. In recent years, in fact, the company has been the ideal springboard for the representatives of the Italian 'new dance', such as the choreography by aforementioned Sieni and Monteverde.

Danza Libera, 'New Dance', *Teatro-Danza* and *Danza d'autore*

Not unlike ballet, the Italian 'new dance' – as it is often referred to in English by some Italian dance writers – stems from a discontinuous development started during the 1920s, and largely informed by foreign inputs, such as those by Bella Hutter and Jia Ruskaya. Unlike ballet, however, the Italian 'new dance' relies today on some stylistic constants that confer a 'national' uniqueness on it. Although few Italian choreographers of the new generation have been able to test the outcome of their creativity abroad, the informed dance viewer can easily identify the distinctive traits and components of the Italian 'new dance' by comparing them with those of other European and non-European countries.

105

The distinctiveness of this form of theatre dance is acknowledged also by the different choreographers, who reckon that their works contain, to some extent, choreographic commonalities, even though the artistic background of each dance-maker differs considerably from that of the others. The continuous exploration of the possibilities offered by the interaction between a given movement vocabulary and other artistic means of expression, is, arguably, the most evident of these commonalities. Each work stands for the theoretically unrepeatable and non-reproducible approach of the creator to the chosen subject, which, in turn, determines the choice of the diverse choreographic, visual and theatrical solutions adopted in each instance. It is in relation to these principles that an Italian journalist coined the untranslatable definition *danza d'autore*, which stresses the unique imprint conferred on the dance by its author (or *autore*) and stems more or less appropriately from the notion of the 'pure artist's product' expounded by conceptual art exponent Piero Manzoni.

Terminological appropriateness notwithstanding, the *danza d'autore* summarizes the latest trends and findings within an exclusively Italian choreo-graphic experimentation, which, when compared with other European situations, stand out for being a unique blend of diverse forms of artistic expression, whether purely theatrical or not. The uniqueness of this particular movement, in fact, cannot be understood by looking solely at the evolution of contemporary Italian dance through the twentieth century, for the *danza d'autore* encompasses artistic factors that have little to do with dance.

The dependence on art forms other than dance has always been, to a greater or lesser extent, one of the distinctive features of Italian 'new dance'. In an enlight-ening article on the *danza libera* or 'free dance' – as it was called in the 1920s – the Italian dance scholar Elena Grillo demonstrates how much that choreographic genre owed its success to the interest manifested by both intellectuals and artists who had little or nothing to do with dance (1993: 98–105). It can be safely affirmed that the concept of a new form of dance was made socially and culturally acceptable mainly thanks to the theories of the Futurists. Not all the existing forms of free dance, however, garnered their favour: Isadora Duncan's creations, for instance, were heavily criticized and even bitterly caricatured. Indeed, the rediscovery of a much idealized 'natural' movement stemming from classical antiquity did not greatly impress the Italians who, for obvious historical and geographical reasons, grew up surrounded by the tangible remains of the classical purism Duncan had decided to reinvent. The interest of the Futurists in a new form of dance, however, never led to the creation of a specific dance genre. The only choreographic attempts they managed to stage, in collaboration with the classically trained ballerina Giannina Censi, were mainly provocative experiments aimed at showing different ways to make dances.

The actual introduction into Italian culture of choreographic forms other than ballet, therefore, should be credited, as Grillo reports, to Riccardo Gualino, a wealthy patron of the arts who supported and funded another group of visual artists known as I Sei (The Six). It was Gualino, in fact, who invited foreign artists such as Bella Hutter and Mary Wigman, in 1923 and 1925 respectively, to perform in Turin, both in his private theatre and in the Teatro di Torino, which he owned. Indeed, the fact that the *danza libera* had the full support of the leading artists of the country made it far more fashionable than any other form of theatre dance, first within the various cultural circles and then, by reflection, among a less artistically oriented public. In 1927, for example, Wigman's recital in Florence was preferred to Diaghilev's Ballets Russes. Still, an in-depth analysis of the few existing sources on the subject, such as the reviews of the time, reveals that the *danza libera* always remained an elitist phenomenon, enjoyed only by a select number of adepts. This is also true for the *danza libera* imported to Italy by the Russian-born Eugenia Borisenko, known as Jia Ruskaya (an 'art' name derived from the Italian transliteration of the words 'I am Russian'). Although her artistic contribution to Italian dance culture is still the subject of scholarly controversy, her 'free' dancing gained immense popularity mainly thanks to the support of intellectuals such as the drama historian, playwright and critic Anton Giulio Bragaglia, the man credited with the creation of her new name, and his circle, known as the Teatro degli Indipendenti (or Theatre of the Independents). Some political choices, as well as the innovative didactic policy she pursued as director of the Regia Scuola di Danza (Royal School of Dance), helped Ruskaya to become a leading dance personality in Italy, a role that she continued to hold after the demise of the Fascist regime. In 1948, in fact, she was reconfirmed director of the Accademia Nazionale di Danza (National Academy of Dance) in Rome, the institution born out of the Regia Scuola di Danza.

Apart from Ruskaya and Hutter (who settled in Turin to open a school in which, later in the century, were to be trained some of the forerunners of the *danza d'autore*), the other eminent modern dance representatives from abroad, such as Mary Wigman, Clothilde and Alexandre Sakharoff, Kurt Jooss, Rosalia Chladek and Harald Kreutzberg, left little or no imprint on the Italian *danza libera*. That dance genre, therefore, went through a long period of stagnation, lacking national input on the one hand, and having to endure, from the late 1930s onward, the political restrictions concerning 'foreign cultures' imposed by Fascist ideology on the other, which vetoed everything that came from the Anglo-American world.

With the exception of the performances of some independent dance groups that boasted a mixed repertoire of ballet and more contemporary oriented works, the next major move towards a further development of the Italian new dance was the 1972 creation of both a school and a dance company, the Teatrodanza Contemporanea di Roma. One of the two founders and directors, Elsa Piperno, had been trained at the London Contemporary Dance School, while the other, Joseph Fontano, had been a student of Graham in New York and a dancer with Alwin Nikolais. As it has been noted by the dance historian and critic Alberto Testa, although the Graham company had made its first appearance in Italy in 1954, the two artists were the first to introduce the Graham technique into the country, although filtering its principles through a more 'Mediterranean perspective'

(1994:200), where the adjective 'Mediterranean' hints at less austere application of Graham's principles.

It is worth noticing that the creation of an exclusively contemporary dance-based company coincided with the beginning of the so-called 'dance boom', the surge of a renewed interest in dance. What is more interesting, though, is the fact that the 'dance boom' prompted a sudden discovery of American contemporary techniques, including Steve Paxton's contact improvisation. At the same time, the creation of a contemporary dance company prompted a subsequent proliferation of similar groups which started delving into choreographic experimentation. The Italian dance scene of the late 1970s and early 1980s, therefore, looked both creatively rich and stylistically chaotic. The various appearances of foreign contemporary groups, either on 'official' stages such as those of the various opera houses, or in fringe theatres, promoted continual and overlapping changes in choreographic taste and fashion. The rudiments of one technique were soon to be combined with those from another school according to the experiences of both the choreographers and the dancers they worked with, thus leading rapidly to the creation of choreographic hybrids that stood out as 'new' ways of making dance.

To retrace the origins of the Italian 'new dance' thus entails mapping out all the major dance groups that came into being during those years as well as their stylistic contribution, a task that can be achieved only by special publications such as that compiled by Laura Delfini (1996) which does justice to a complex and varied situation. The continuous changes that affected the life of each group make it almost impossible to number the various dance companies that existed, especially considering that, according to Italian law, it does not take that long to 'institutionalize' a small group into an official dance company. In other words, the number of active dance groups is constantly fluctuating, making difficult any attempt to evaluate and to map the situation.

Not unlike the *danza libera* of the 1920s, both the 'new dance' and the *danza d'autore* did not and do not derive exclusively from a revisitation of pre-existing dance techniques and styles. The experimentation mentioned above, in fact, mirrored and to a certain extent derived from the parallel experimentation that had informed Italian drama since the late 1960s. The so-called *teatro di ricerca* (research theatre) can be seen as the first example of an Italian performing art moving towards new solutions via a constant exploration of diverse means of expression, a feature later to be found in the Italian *teatro-danza* (dance-theatre). Although a comparative analysis of the two theatre genres has never been undertaken, there is hardly any doubt that the findings of the former influenced and prompted those of the latter. Indeed, when Pina Bausch's *Tanztheater* was first introduced to Italy in 1981, the germs of its Italian equivalent were already part of the culture.

Dance writers and dance scholars, however, tend to overlook the significant influence of the *teatro di ricerca* and ascribe the move towards the Italian *teatro-danza* almost exclusively to the prompting of the American-born artist Carolyn Carlson. In 1980, Carlson, who had already made a series of successful appearances in Italy while still working in Paris, was invited to work as resident choreographer at La Fenice theatre in Venice. It was there that she worked with a group of Italian dancers who, once her Venetian engagement ended, gathered together to form the dance group Sosta Palmizi, historically considered as the first exponent of the Italian *teatro-danza*. Their first creation, *Il Cortile (The Courtyard)* (1984), was a theatrically powerful composite performance where dance and everyday movements interacted with words, utterances and sounds. Curiously, it was in the same year that two representatives of the *danza d'autore* made their debut as choreographers, Virgilio Sieni with his company Parco Butterfly in *Momenti d'ozio*, and Fabrizio Monteverde, still a member of Piperno's Teatrodanza Contemporanea di Roma, with *Bene Mobile*. The year 1984 can thus be regarded as marking new beginnings for a national form of choreography in Italy that has remained the same thus far.

It is difficult, however, to distinguish what constituted then, and still constitutes today, the difference between Sosta Palmizi's *teatro-danza* and Sieni's or Monteverde's stylistic canons. As a matter of fact, the *danza d'autore* can include characteristic components of the *teatro-danza*, for, as mentioned above, it draws upon the choreographer's individual and artistic experiences which are likely to include distinctive *teatro-danza* elements. Indeed, a powerful, vivid and multilayered theatricality, a prerequisite of the *teatro-danza*, informs most of the current creations by Italian choreographers. The stylistic eclecticism offered by the *danza d'autore* solutions, moreover, also allows a constant swapping between choreographic genres and techniques. As mentioned above, choreographers such as Sieni and Monteverde have successfully worked for independent ballet companies such as the Balletto di Toscana as well as for 'official' ballet companies annexed to major opera houses. It is difficult, therefore, to classify the *danza d'autore*, for it encompasses diverse styles and genres.

Other Aspects of Italian Dance Culture

An overview of the current Italian dance scene would not be complete without taking into consideration some 'complementary' circumstances that inform contemporary Italian dance culture. In spite of the rather critical condition of Italian ballet, the country boasts an overwhelming number of vocational dance schools that play a significant role in keeping alive the interest of the public. Most of these institutions – which according to some statistics number several thousands – came into being during the 1970s as a result of the 'dance boom'. Yet private training (where 'private' implies total independence from institutions such as opera houses as well as any form of government funding) was already part of a well-rooted tradition. It was in the early nineteenth century, in fact, that ballet-masters were granted permission to 'open' their own studios in order to coach their favourite students outside the bureaucratic restrictions of the institutionalized academies where they worked.

Illustrious dance personalities, including foreign ones, have operated in this way in different parts of the country throughout the century. In Florence, for instance,

Kyra Nijinsky taught a method she claimed to be her father's in her own school just before the Second World War. In the same town, the celebrated Dutch dancer Darja Collin opened a studio in 1952, where some of the finest Italian artists were trained. Finally, it was in Florence that the former Ballet Rambert artist Brenda Hamlyn opened the first Cecchetti-based centre in Italy in 1962. The proliferation of dance schools that followed the 'dance boom', however, generated an interesting phenomenon, considerably changing attitudes towards training. Specific methods often imported from abroad, such as the Royal Academy of Dancing syllabus, supplanted the reputation of celebrated artists in providing schools with the necessary credentials. In other words, the cult of personalities – still a distinctive feature of Italian ballet – changed into a cult of 'schools', methods and syllabi. The results of such a change were not entirely positive, for Italy witnessed the rapid growth of a market in diplomas, which diminished the artistic value of theatre dance by lowering its standards, and, above all, lowering the general perception of it to an equivalent of fashionable gymnastics.

The 'war of the syllabi', as it was called by some dance people of the time, posed a serious threat to the hegemony of the Accademia Nazionale di Danza in Rome, the sole 'state' dance school in the country. According to a 1951 decree, in fact, only those whose reputation had been acknowledged by the national academy, or who had graduated from it, could 'become dance teachers and work as such' (Bocca 1960:183). Despite its verbal strictness, the 1951 decree had limited power, for it did not prevent any form of private initiative, thus leaving ample freedom to all those who did not mind not being 'officially' recognized as 'dance teachers'. In spite of several teachers associations, a separate law regulating the teaching of dance was never ratified and no drastic measures were ever enforced. The charter of dance schools and dance teachers created by the Accademia di Danza thus ended up having the same value as the Italian branches of foreign institutions. Neither the national nor the international qualifications, in fact, could guarantee the artistic standards of both the teachers and their students.

Indeed, the role and the contribution of the Accademia Nazionale di Danza to the Italian dance culture have often been debated and heavily criticized. Much of the controversy stemmed from a misinterpretation of Ruskaya's intentions. Although people expected the institution to be the Italian equivalent of the great foreign dance academies, the original aim of the Accademia in Rome was, paradoxical as it may sound, to prepare knowledgeable teachers but not to forge dancers. On the other hand, the way chartering certificates have been granted has often raised doubts about the competence and the seriousness of the awarding panels. In more recent times, however, the entire institution has undergone beneficial changes that have improved its pedagogic function. It is worth mentioning that some of today's lecturers at the Academy are leading dance scholars, whose expertise encompasses a wide range of disciplines. Similarly, the training standards have been improved and updated, as demonstrated by some fine ex-graduates who have embarked on successful performing careers both in Italy and abroad. The fact that the National Academy is the sole state dance institution in

Italy does not impinge significantly on the reputation of historically famous dance schools such as those annexed to La Scala Theatre in Milan, the Rome Opera, or the San Carlo Theatre in Naples – which lack the same governmental support as the National Academy – or of some well-established vocational centres from which the majority of Italian dancers still comes.

Another interesting aspect of Italian dance training, whether it be ballet or other techniques, is the annual proliferation of summer courses or *stages* (pronounced in the French way) that might be organized either as private enterprises by the director of a vocational school, or receive financial support from more public institutions such as the administration of a particular town or region. When it is well organized, in fact, the *stage* draws a considerable number of people to a particular location, thus boosting the tourism of that particular resort. The aim of the *stage* is to provide its participants with a unique opportunity to expand their practical knowledge of the art of dancing, confronting them with techniques or ways to approach those techniques that are not normally on offer in the country. Needless to say, through the years the organization of the *stages* has become an industry aimed more at easy money-making – the subscription fees are often expensive – than at an actual improvement of the national dance culture. Still, there are some *stages* that, in the long run, have acquired a reputation both for outstanding quality – the course is largely taught by foreign teachers – and for the way the entire enterprise is logically and artistically organized. In some instances, the *stage* constitutes part of a broader context, namely one of the many dance festivals that materialize each year all over the country.

Although dance has always been a major attraction at events such as the Arena of Verona summer festival (which relies mainly on operatic performances) or the internationally renowned Maggio Musicale Fiorentino in Florence, there is little doubt that the Festival dei Due Mondi (or Festival of the Two Worlds) in Spoleto and the Nervi Dance Festival – named after the Nervi parks in Genoa where it takes place in summer – constitute the two most interesting and significant events of the Italian dance scene. The brainchild of composer Giancarlo Menotti, the Festival dei Due Mondi has been, since its inception in 1958, an exceptionally rich and stimulating showcase of international dance, which allowed and still allows Italian dance-goers to be in touch with the foreign dance scene and its latest trends. On the other hand, the slightly older and less adventurous – that is in terms of artistic choices – Nervi Festival, created in 1955, has mostly been the showcase for major international ballet companies, even though in more recent times it has also started to host contemporary and post-modern dance performances.

The 'dance boom' favoured the creation of many similar events. Every summer, Italy witnesses an explosion of dance activities that considerably enhance the choreographic culture of the country, either by showing national products and companies or by confronting the public with foreign companies. As in the case of the various *stages*, dance festivals too prove successful in boosting local tourism. It is not surprising, therefore, that every year the map of the various events changes and enlarges considerably. It is interesting to note that it is customary to entrust the organization of these events to a dance critic, an 'expert' able to secure an interesting, varied and, as far as funds allow, unique programme.

While dance activities may appear rather scarce, with the exception of the summer explosion, dance critics are numerous. There is hardly a daily paper, in fact, whether national, regional or local, that does not have a regular dance column. Specialized magazines, however, do not abound and the ones that exist have often had a troubled life. Only the monthly *Danza & Danza*, which stands out for its newspaper format, has been in continuous publication since 1981. Other publications worth mentioning are *Balletto 2000*, formerly *Balletto Oggi*, and the two scholarly publications *La Danza Italiana* and *Chorègraphie*.

Finally a considerable input in boosting dance culture is provided by the television dance programme *Maratona d'estate* (*Summer Marathon*), which began in 1978. The uniqueness of this programme, which underwent several changes of format but never failed to attract the interest of viewers, consists mainly in the fact that dance works were and still are broadcast in their entirety after having been presented, contextualized and explained by the creator of the programme, dance critic Vittoria Ottolenghi. It is worth noting this dance programme is broadcast weekly only during the summer months – June to September – during hours normally devoted to more prosaic holiday activities. And yet the *Maratona d'estate* is still one of the most popular televised events in a country that does not seem to care that much for dance

Conclusion

From what has been said, it is apparent that twentieth-century Italian dance stands out for its intricate web of contrasts. In spite of the popularity gained since the mid-1970s 'dance-boom' and the cultural campaign promoted by the media as well as by numerous initiatives such as the dance festivals and the summer *stages*, Italian theatre dance remains, in the eyes of those who administer culture, a lesser art. It is difficult to predict how the Italian dance scene will change when and if the promised new decree is promulgated. For the time being, the future of Italian ballet does not look exciting. The deinstitutionalization of the major opera houses began in 1997, thus depriving those institutions of government administrative support and forcing them to rely on private sponsors, a fact that has been seen as a serious threat to the already precarious position of the annexed ballet companies. Whether the funds will be better administered following the creation of the Commissione Danza remains to be seen. After all, as reported by many papers, one of its original members happened to be a leading dance critic as well as the artistic consultant for La Scala ballet, a fact that raised some doubts about the objectivity with which the funds might be assigned – although new members took over during the 1998/99 season.

The problem, however, is not a new one, for many eminent dance critics have long been responsible for the organization of dance festivals and dance seasons. Whether the new decree will settle the question concerning the indiscriminate proliferation of dance schools, also remains to be seen. The creation of an institutionalized committee assessing the quality of teaching stirs up a myriad problems encompassing the quality of the assessors, their biases towards or lack of knowledge of particular methods and techniques, and whether the committee will be a non-viable monopoly, similar to the one proposed by the National Academy of Dance in Rome. Furthermore, improving the quality of the technical training does not necessarily guarantee an amelioration of the general dance culture, which would benefit considerably from the institution of academic courses at university level. It is worth noticing that, in spite of a considerable number of excellent dance scholars and scholarly courses offered either in university-related centres or institutions such as the Accademia Nazionale di Danza, dance research has not yet become an officially recognized academic discipline taught, like Music and Theatre Studies, in the universities of the country. Yet, the number of university students who decide to embark on research in dance as part of their music or drama studies has been on the increase since the end of the 1970s.

Indeed, both the Commissione Danza and the announced decree should prevent, or at least decrease, the indiscriminate proliferation of dance companies often created for the sole purpose of enhancing the artistic reputation of a ballet school. But then, what would happen to those small yet artistically sound dance groups which strive towards new forms of choreographic experimentation? Complex and new as it might look, the current situation of the Italian dance scene remains nonetheless linked to the modes and conventions of the nineteenth-century tradition. The popularity of ballet still relies more on the often blinkered fanaticism for various stars than on a serious appreciation of the choreography. In addition, Italy remains a nation that constantly forges a wealth of talents who then have to emigrate abroad because of the unsatisfactory artistic conditions offered in their own country, as in the case of Viviana Durante, now with the Royal Ballet in London, or Giuseppe Picone, now with American Ballet Theatre.

As far as contemporary dance is concerned, the situation does not look that much better. The lack of administrative support that most independent companies have to endure does not allow an exchange or a comparison with the situation in other European countries, thus creating a hypertrophic indulgence in choreographic formulae and artistic canons that inevitably grow stale and might end up alienating any possible interest and, consequently, support. In spite of the presence of thousands of schools, moreover, only a few centres can boast a proper contemporary training, and even fewer are able to pass on the principles of fundamental techniques such as those of Cunningham, Limon or Graham. It is worth remembering that the project of creating a Graham centre in Florence, promoted by Martha Graham herself during the 1980s, sank mainly because of political interference after only three years in which the Tuscan capital hosted teachers and artists from the Graham company to train local artists. Still, considering that new political reforms now seem to be in the pipeline to renew the entire sector of the Italian arts after so many years of total darkness, it is possible that more appropriate measures will also be gradually introduced into the Italian dance world, following these first hopeful but uncertain steps.

References

Bentivoglio, L. (1985) *La danza contemporanea*, Milano: Longanesi.

Bocca, G. (1960) *I Ballerini*, Firenze: Vallecchi.

Delfini, L. (ed.) (1996) *Coreografie Contemporanee*, Roma: CIDIM Comitato Nazionale Italiano Musica.

Felici, S. (1977) *II Balletto e l'Opera di Milloss al Maggio Musicale Fiorentino*, Firenze: Salani.

Grillo, E. (1993) 'La Danza Libera in Italia negli Anni Venti', *Chorègraphie*, 1, 1, Primavera.

Guatterini, M. & M. Porzio (1992) *Milloss, Busoni e Scelsi – Neoclassico Danza e Musica Nell' Italia del Novecento*, Milano: Electa.

Ottolenghi, V. (1981) *I Casi della Danza*, Roma: Di Giacomo.

Piccione, C. (1989) 'Gli Italiani e i Ballets Russes', *La Danza Italiana*, 7, primavera.

Rossi, L. (1970) *Il Ballo alla Scala 1778–1970*, Milano: Edizioni della Scala.

Tani, G. (1954) 'Il Balletto in Italia', in Gatti, G. (ed.) *Cinquant'anni di Opera e Balletto in Italia*, Roma: Bestetti.

Testa, A. (1985) 'Diaghilev e l'Italia', *La Danza Italiana*, 2, primavera.

Testa, A. (1994) *Storia della Danza e del Balletto*, Roma: Gremese.

Veroli, P. (1996) *Milloss, un Maestro della Coreografia tra Espressionismo e Classicità*, Lucca: Libreria Musicale Italiana.

Key Texts

Delfini, L. (ed.) (1996) *Coreografie Contemporanee*, Roma: CIDIM Comitato Nazionale Italiano Musica.

Vaccarino, E., *et al.* (1999) 'l999 Nuova Italia', *Ballett International/ Tanz Aktuell* 2 (February) pp. 24–39.

Table 6 Important dance and political events in Italy (1900 to present)

Year	Dance: artists, works, events	Dance: institutions	Arts scene	Sociocultural and political events
1900			*Il Fuoco* (D'Annunzio); *Come le foglie* (Giacosa); *Tosca* (Puccini)	Umberto I assassinated
1904	*Bacco e Gambrinus* (Pratesi)		*Il fu Mattia Pascal* (Pirandello); *La figlia di Iorio* (D'Annunzio); *Madama Butterfly* (Puccini)	
1905	*Luce* (Pratesi)		*La fiaccola sotto il moggio* (D'Annunzio) 1st Italian film studios, Rome	
1909			*Manifesto of Futurism* (Marinetti); Manifesto of Futurist Theatre	
1911	*Ballets Russes		*Il codice di Perelà* (Palazzeschi); *I funerali dell' anarchico Galli* (Carrà)	
1914			*Canti orfici* (Campana); *Francesca da Rimini* (Zandonai); *Manifesto dell' architettura futurista* (Sant'Elia); *Cabiria* (Pastrone & D'Annunzio)	
1915		Balli Italiani di Nicola Guerra	*Fedra* (Pizzetti)	Italy enters First World War

Table 6 continued

Year	Dance: artists, works, events	Dance: institutions	Arts scene	Sociocultural and political events
1917	*Manifesto della danza futurista* (Balla)	La Scala Ballet School closed		
1921		La Scala Ballet School reopened, directed by Preobrajenska		Communist Party National Fascist Party
1922	*Il carillon magico* (Cellini), first ballet at Arena di Verona		*Enrico IV* (Pirandello); Exhibition of 'Valori Plastici' movement, Florence	Fascist regime
1925	*Vecchia Milano* (Pratesi) Wigman in Turin	Cecchetti directs La Scala Ballet School		
1933			*Sentimento del tempo* (Ungaretti); *Teatro totale per le masse* (Prampolini); Maggio Musicale Fiorentino	
1937	*Aeneas* (Milloss)		*I giganti della montagna* (Pirandello); Cinecittà studios *Il signor Max* (Camerini)	
1940		Ruskaja director of Regia Scuola di Danza		Italy enters Second World War
1942	*Il mandarino meraviglioso* (Milloss)		*Ed è subito sera* (Quasimodo); *Ossessione* (Visconti)	
1945			*Cristo si è fermato a Eboli*	Mussolini dies

Table 6 continued

Year			
1945 continued			(Levi); *Napoli milionaria* (De Filippo); Mascagni dies; *Roma città aperta* (Rossellini)
			Italy liberated
1946			*Filumena Marturano* (De Filippo); *Sciuscià* (De Sica); *Paisà* (Rossellini)
			Italian Republic; Women vote for the first time
1948		Accademia Nazionale di Danza	*Menzogna e sortilegio* (Morante); Movimento Arte Concreta; *Ladri di biciclette* (De Sica); *La terra trema* (Visconti)
1952		*Foyer de danse* (Egri), first televised ballet; New York City Ballet at La Scala	*Il visconte dimezzato* (Calvino); *Musica su due dimensioni* (Maderna); *Lo sceicco bianco* (Fellini)
1954		*Martha Graham	
1955		Nervi Festival	*Metello* (Pratolini); *Ragazza di vita* (Pasolini); Studio di Fonolgia Musicale; Arte Programmata; Arte Informale
			Italy joins UNO and EEC
1958		Ballets USA at Spoleto Festival	*Il Gattopardo* (Tomasi di Lampedusa)
1960		Paul Taylor at Spoleto Festival; Massine director of Nervi Festival	*La noia* (Moravia); Arte Concettuale after British Art and Language; *La dolce vita* (Fellini); *Accattone* (Pasolini)

Table 6 *continued*

Year	Dance: artists, works, events	Dance: institutions	Arts scene	Sociocultural and political events
1969			*Mistero Buffo* (Fo); *Rara Requiem* (Bussotti)	Terrorist attack at Piazza Fontana, Milan
1972		Teatrodanza Contemporanea di Roma		
1974			*Todo Modo* (Sciascia); *La Storia* (Morante); *Gli esami non finiscono mai* (De Filippo)	Divorce legalized 'Brigate Rosse' terrorism
1975		Collettivo di Danza Contemporanea di Firenze	*Tratatto di semiotica generale* (Eco); Montale, Nobel Prize; *Il gran sole carico d'amore* (Nono); Pasolini murdered	
1978		Maratona d'Estate		
1980	Carolyn Carlson in Venice	Aterballetto	*Il nome della rosa* (Eco); *La Transavanguardia italiana* (Bonito Oliva)	
1984	*Il cortile* (Palmizi)		*Semiotica e filosofia del linguaggio* (Eco)	*Ballando Ballando*
1985	*Bagni acerbi* (Monteverde)	Balletto di Toscana		
1988	*Victor* (Bausch)			
1990	*Palermo Palermo* (Bausch)			
1992				Lega Nord–Lega Lombarda 'Tangentopoli' scandal
1995				Governo dei tecnici
1997			Fo, Nobel Prize	

*First visit

7

THE NETHERLANDS
The Dutch don't dance

Anna Aalten and Mirjam van der Linden

Introduction

In 1997, the English choreographer Thom Stuart formed The Dutch Don't Dance Division, one of the many small *ad hoc* dance companies in The Netherlands. Twenty years earlier, the famous Dutch writer Annie M. G. Schmidt had composed a song for her musical *Foxtrot*, entitled 'The Dutch Don't Dance'. The song begins, in English, with a complaint about the Dutch who 'don't dance/can't dance/won't dance'. In the following couplets, written in Dutch, explanations are given for these statements in the form of widely accepted clichés: the Dutch are pessimists and Calvinists, marked by religious quarrels; they are stuck with their feet in the mud, unable to move let alone dance.

In a way it is true that the Dutch don't dance. They don't dance at weddings or funerals, or at national gatherings, or spontaneously in the streets. Although they have a national anthem, a national flag and several national symbols (like the tulip and the windmill), they do not have a national dance. The so-called clog-dance is at best preserved by some specialist regional folk dance groups; or it is used as a joke, as in *De Klompendans*, made in 1959 by the well-known choreographer Hans van Manen, a geometric dance in which all the dancers wore wooden shoes, making the danced patterns not only visible, but audible too. This ballet was performed again (and broadcast) by a large group of dancers to honour Van Manen and celebrate his sixtieth birthday in 1992.

Of course, social dance and theatre dance are two different fields, which cannot be related unproblematically. Nevertheless, set against the poor climate for social dancing, the present-day flourishing state of theatre dance in The Netherlands is striking. For that matter, Stuart's The Dutch Don't Dance Division should not be understood too literally: in the theatre, the Dutch definitely do dance, but they have not been doing so for long. It is not that the Dutch totally lack any dance tradition, for Dutch theatres presented dance performances as early as the seventeenth century. But without a royal court to favour dance, this was mainly a middle-class matter. The lower middle classes enjoyed realistic, comical dance plays, and the upper middle classes appreciated classicist, allegorical and (later) romantic ballets, all of which were often presented or influenced by foreign ballet-masters and groups (Rebling 1950). After 1870, ballet in The Netherlands, as elsewhere in western Europe, lost its respect and popularity as an art form. The romantic ballet had become empty of meaning, a display of technical virtuosity and cheap drama. The art of dancing became stigmatized as a vulgar, immoral, and amateurish public amusement. The moral taboo against dance, influenced by Calvinism and Catholicism, had been going on for ages; but now it was manifested even more strongly. Dance became associated with scantily clad ladies performing acrobatic tricks. Around 1900, ballet was more or less banished from the official bourgeois theatre world. In 1940, the first year of the Second World War (Germany occupied The Netherlands in May 1940), a national ballet company was established, closing down again within a year.[1]

Among Dutch dance historians and scholars it is generally accepted that 1945 marks the starting point of the Dutch theatre dance tradition (Van Schaik 1981; Utrecht 1987). But, having just come out of a war, and with no established dance tradition to speak of, The Netherlands had hardly any dance to offer at all. Dutch dancers had to start from scratch. Now, only fifty or so years later, dance is a respected and highly vital art form in The Netherlands, with an enormous diversity of classical and modern, big and small, structurally subsidized and *ad hoc* financed groups and initiatives. In 1996–7 around 250 new productions were premièred. The latest statistics on audience research, from 1995–6, show 937,000 visitors for theatre dance.[2] The four-yearly state *Kunstenplan* (arts plan) for the arts subsidies, which has been functioning since 1989, has reserved about *f*35 million for theatre dance for 1997–2000 (the total state budget for the performing arts is about *f*200 million). Additionally, the *Fonds voor de Podiumkunsten* (fund for the performing arts) has a yearly average of *f*1,750,000 to spend on (experimental) theatre dance projects. National and international works are presented at several dance festivals, such as Springdance, Julidans, the Holland Dance Festival and the Cadance Festival, and an international contest for choreographers takes place in Groningen every two years. Both artistically and financially, the Dutch seem to have created a stimulating climate for dance and dance practitioners.

It is only during the past five decades that dance has become more generally known and accepted as a valuable art form, that the audience for dance has grown, and that dance productions have increased both in quantity and in diversity. In short, a prominent and enduring dance culture and climate has been born. How was it possible for this flourishing and diverse dance scene to come into existence in such a short time? What cultural and social factors have contributed to the contemporary situation? In this chapter we will answer these questions by paying attention to four specific features of the Dutch dance scene: its non-nationalist character, its commitment to democratic principles, its inclination towards levelling and its desire for innovation.

Non-nationalism

Sonia Gaskell, founder of Het Nationale Ballet and one of the major forces behind the development of dance in The Netherlands, remarked in 1954 that 'the way the Netherlands are situated geographically does not only define the national character, but also the culture. The sea forced its boundaries upon the people, but it also offered possibilities for foreign cultures to find their way in. The Dutch developed a richer taste and an understanding and tolerance towards other races, religions and cultures. The Netherlands have been at the crossroads of Latin, Anglo-Saxon and German influences'.[3] This general attitude, together with the lack of a long dance tradition in The Netherlands, may be at the root of the absence of overt nationalism in dance. Without a strong Dutch national drive for dance, dance in The Netherlands can be characterized as non-nationalist.

Although the absence of national pride can be seen as a negative result of this non-nationalist profile, there is also a positive and productive side to it: it frees dancers and choreographers from the obligation either to fit into or to reject a specific tradition, thereby giving them room to create their own styles. It creates an atmosphere of artistic openness. Another result of the non-nationalist character of Dutch dance is its international orientation: Dutch dancers and choreographers tend to look across their borders for inspiration and ideas.

This attitude is not specific to the post-war period, but has roots in earlier times, and is partly explained by the absence of a royal court tradition. We have already stated that, in the nineteenth century, ballet was a middle-class affair, which was banished from the Dutch theatre stages around 1900. At the beginning of the twentieth century there was a slight turn of the tide. Although its morality was still suspect, dance regained a little of its status as an accepted art form. Isadora Duncan's first visit to The Netherlands, in 1905, introduced the Dutch to early modern dance. Dutch critics were extremely enthusiastic about her natural and poetic dance, which they regarded as real art.[4] She inspired the Dutch pioneers Jacoba van der Plas, who gave solo performances and started her own school in The Hague, and Lili Green, who performed solo and with her own groups, and founded several schools in The Hague and in Amsterdam.[5] It was Green who in 1945 helped Sonia Gaskell start her first company in The Netherlands, Studio '45, and it was Green's own studios in The Hague that welcomed mutineers from Gaskell's later company the Nederlands Ballet in 1959, where they founded the Nederlands Danstheater. In the 1920s, the Ballets Russes and Anna Pavlova made the Dutch audiences aware, if sporadically, of the latest developments in ballet.

But the main influence came from European expressionism and modern dance. In the inter-war period, Mary Wigman's *Ausdruckstanz* inspired several Dutch women who had a lasting influence on the development of Dutch dance, such as Corrie Hartong, Florrie Rodrigo and Yvonne Georgi, to create their own performances and start private dance schools. Hartong was the director of the dance academy in Rotterdam between 1934 and 1967 and initiator of the valuable dance library at the Theater Instituut Nederland in Amsterdam. Rodrigo performed, choreographed and taught numerous dancers between 1920 and 1980, the German Georgi choreographed and staged many modern ballets, founding the Yvonne Georgi Ballet in 1932, a company that would set the standard for many years (Van Schaik 1981: 52).

During the Second World War these developments came to a standstill, and when the war ended in 1945 there was a great aversion to anything German, making *Ausdruckstanz* a 'genre *non grata*'. It was classical ballet that Hans Snoek, Mascha ter Weeme, Françoise Adret and Sonia Gaskell – the four women who would become the 'leading ladies' of Dutch dance – took on to conquer the audience. Going abroad – at this stage from sheer necessity – was a way to get in touch with dance developments. The big traditional ballet companies in Paris and London became the main models. In the late 1950s and 1960s those dancers interested in dance other than classical ballet (such as Koert and Bart Stuyf, Pauline de Groot and Bianca van Dillen) left The Netherlands for the United States, to study with Graham, Hawkins, Cunningham, Limón, Tudor and postmodern dance heroes (ibid: 116). In the late 1970s, Pina Bausch's *Tanztheater* was the next important source of inspiration, followed in the late 1980s by the Flemish variety of this neo-expressionism.

In addition to going abroad themselves, Dutch dancers and artistic leaders welcomed dance, dancers and choreographers from abroad: a large number of foreign dance companies have visited The Netherlands since 1945. Dance from abroad was welcomed, and it did not present a threat to Dutch companies, who, for a long time, could not compete with them in any case, because in the first few years after the Second World War the Dutch companies that existed did not have high technical standards. Thus the highly prestigious Holland Festival invited more dance companies from abroad than from The Netherlands itself (Voeten 1997). This trend has increased, but Dutch audiences can still go and see many dance performances from all over the world. Furthermore, many Dutch companies invite choreographers from abroad to stage ballets with them. Het Nationale Ballet, for example, has a great number of Balanchine ballets in its repertoire, and Nederlands Dans Theater often presents work by William Forsythe, Nacho Duato, Mats Ek and other foreign choreographers.

Dutch dance companies often were, and for the most part still are, led by non-Dutch artistic leaders. Two out of the four biggest companies that were responsible for the rapid development of dance in the 1950s were founded by foreign women. The French Françoise Adret took over the Ballet van de Nederlandse Opera in 1952 from Darja Collin, and Russian-born Sonia Gaskell started the Nederlands Ballet in 1954. Gaskell was also responsible for another company that has been dominating Dutch dance until now, Het Nationale Ballet, the result of a fusion of the Nederlands Ballet and the Amsterdams Ballet in 1961. Gaskell did not find it easy to leave her company to others. In 1965, she invited Rudi van Dantzig and Robert Kaesen, the second resident choreographer, to join her as artistic directors of HNB. The artistic triumvirate was not a success, and Gaskell left two years later. Van Dantzig and Kaesen continued as co-directors, but Kaesen did not enjoy the work and left after six months. Van Dantzig was reluctant to lead the company alone and asked Benjamin Harkavy, co-artistic director of the Harkness Ballet, to team up with him. Harkavy agreed, but left after a year. Then, in 1971, Van Dantzig became sole artistic director of HNB, succeeded in 1992 by the British Wayne Eagling. The other major Dutch dance company, Nederlands Dans Theater, came into being as a result of a dancers' mutiny within the Nederlands Ballet in 1959, and has been led to international fame by the Czech Jiří Kylián since 1978.

Among the smaller companies more Dutch faces appear, but there are still a fair number of foreigners active as artistic leaders and choreographers: the Hungarian Krisztina de Châtel, the Israeli Itzik Galili, the Japanese Shusaku Takeuchi, the Belgian Piet Rogie, the Americans Ron Bunzl and Arthur Rosenfeld, the Spanish Ana Teixidó and the French Désirée Delauney, to name just a few. The absence of a protection policy for Dutch dancers is remarkable; nationalistic feelings do not seem to make themselves felt here either. Non-Dutch dancers abound, in many companies exceeding the number of Dutch dancers. This has been the situation since the late 1960s.

The young, non-nationalist, open and internationally oriented character of dance in The Netherlands makes it difficult to define a typically Dutch dance style. When asked whether such a style exists, most people will answer 'no'. Dutch choreography brings together a great variety of styles and as such cannot be recognized as typically Dutch. Or is this its Dutchness – the openness to different influences and traditions, the shameless use of different techniques and styles, without having to bow to a specific tradition or explicitly to reject one? To this question most people will answer 'yes'.[6] 'The Dutch are the leeches of dance', Marc Jonkers, former director of Springdance and the Holland Dance Festival once said. 'We are like parasites. We suck others for ideas and use them in our own ways' (cited in Wessels 1995). Francine van der Wiel, a major Dutch dance critic, put it a little more positively: 'There is no such thing as a Dutch dance, meaning there is not one specific, recognizable "Dutch" style. Dutch choreographers have picked and chosen elements of their liking from the international dance scene and every now and then succeeded in putting them together, mixing and combining them into new, fresh forms. So beware of Dutch choreographers. They can be very intelligent thieves'.[7] We would like to put it even more positively: no matter what its influences, Dutch dance has never followed them slavishly.

Considering the absence of strong national feelings, and the long tradition of international orientation, the absence of non-western influences in Dutch dance is striking. Dutch dancers and choreographers have stolen from everywhere, but not from the dances of their former colonies Surinam and Indonesia, nor from other dance traditions in the East or in the South. This is not to say that dance from non-western cultures is not performed on Dutch stages. The Internationaal Danstheater, the biggest folklore dance company of Europe, founded in 1961 and one of the companies that is structurally financed by the Dutch state, presents dances from all over the world. Other companies from abroad, bringing traditional dances from the former Indonesian courts, flamenco, tango, African dance, *butoh* and many other non-western dance forms can be seen regularly all over The Netherlands. But these performances are usually staged at the theatre of the Tropenmuseum, where artefacts from the former colonies are housed, or at other centres for non-western art. The dance scene in The Netherlands is characterized by a sharp separation between companies, theatres and individuals who present ballet and contemporary dance and those practising non-western dance forms.[8]

Dutch dancers, companies and choreographers may not be able to rely on a very long and rich tradition, but they are not bothered or hampered by one either, which has created a stimulating openness. In our opinion, this is exactly why dance in The Netherlands has not only survived but artistically flourished. Dutch choreographies have become well known abroad, and the number of foreign companies staging Dutch choreography is increasing. Work by Jiří Kylián, Hans van Manen and Rudi van Dantzig has been popular for some time, but now younger choreographers from The Netherlands are also invited to present their work at international dance festivals or to create new works for companies abroad. Dutch dance was the central theme of the prestigious Festival de la Nouvelle Danse in Montreal in 1995. According to Chantal Pontbriand, organizer of the Festival, young choreographers like Angelika Oei, Paul Selwyn Norton, Maria Voortman and Roberto de Jonge, Suzy Blok and Christopher Steel, and Harijono Roebana and Andrea Leine – not all of whom are of Dutch origin – were invited because of their development of an idiosyncratic dance vocabulary (Mallems 1995: 27). An increasing number of Dutch choreographers, or choreographers who began their careers in The Netherlands, now work as artistic leaders all over the world: Nacho Duato (NDT) went to Madrid, Jan Linkens (HNB) to Berlin, Krzysztof Pastor (HNB) to Washington and Ted Brandsen (HNB) to Perth, Australia.

Borrowed, stolen or leeched, the Dutch dance scene is unmistakably non-national in character. But it is also characterized by a very Dutch political, social and cultural setting which centres, among other things, around a truthfulness to democratic principles and a less positive inclination to levelling. These social and political characteristics will be discussed next.

Democracy

The Dutch are proud of their democracy. Since the formation of a constitutional monarchy in 1814–15, there have been three main political movements: confessional, liberal and socialist. Typical of the Dutch so-called consociational democracy is – on a national level – the tradition of coalition government, which suppresses radical revolution and cherishes compromise. At the same time, society itself has for a long time been organized according to a system called *verzuiling*, a typically Dutch phenomenon couched in a typically Dutch word, which can best be translated as the formation of political parties on denominational grounds. From 1917 until at least the early 1960s, the population was split into different denominational groups, each with its own schools, sports clubs, broadcaster, and so on.

In our opinion, the anti-revolutionary pacification democracy and the system of separation have influenced the development of theatre dance as well. The dominant idea of both concepts is that every Dutch citizen has the right to develop his or her potential. Security, development, justice and solidarity are key to all the big political programmes, confessional, liberal or socialist, regardless of their differences. Dutch dance reflects this attitude in three different ways: the many ways in which it can rely on financial support, the relatively large number of different academies spread over the country and last but not least a democratic variety of companies and styles.

The financial climate for the arts in general is fairly positive in The Netherlands, at least compared with other European countries. The Netherlands has a typical welfare state with an extended system of subsidies. The national government has three means of subsidy: structural, multiannual and incidental. Structural subsidy is given to companies considered to be of a national significance, like Het Nationale Ballet and Nederlands Dans Theater. Multiannual subsidy is granted for a period of four years, the *Kunstenplan* period, without a guarantee that it will be renewed after that. On a national level, applications for money by thirteen out of twenty-five companies have been taken up for the 1997–2000 *Kunstenplan*, some of which also receive structural financing. In the big cities like Amsterdam, Rotterdam and The Hague, state subsidies are often complemented by municipal subsidies. The third form of state subsidy is intended for incidental projects, for which individuals and groups may apply for one-off projects (Bronkhorst 1997: 5–8). Recently, the Fonds voor de Podiumkunsten, the committee that awards incidental subsidies, began using some of its budget for longer-term projects, in some cases financing projects for two years instead of the usual one year.[9]

One important note should be made here. The field of dance has always lagged behind the other arts. Dance became structurally financed by the government quite late compared with other art forms. When a special Department for Arts and Sciences was set up in 1874, money was at first only spent on visual arts and monuments. Besides, dance could not even rely on bourgeois lobbyists to get into the system. Between 1940 and 1954 the first incidental subsidies for dance were handed out. Local authorities took care of dance companies, although opera dance could rely on some government support. It took until 1954 for dance to gain a separate vote on the state budget for the arts. The budget for dance was only 2 per cent, much smaller than what was available for the other performing arts (Cannegieter 1989). When the national expenditure on the arts, which was set up on an incidental basis after the Second World War, increased during the 1950s and 1960s, Dutch dance was still too young to benefit from this growth.

In general, the decade from 1975 to 1985 is regarded as the period of the definitive breakthrough of Dutch theatre dance, when many groups and initiatives put themselves on the map. In financial terms, however, the dance world has never managed to catch up with the other performing arts. Since the general economic depression of the 1980s, the arts in The Netherlands have had to face stagnation and even backsliding, a double problem for dance, with no chance at all of extra money (although everybody agreed something should be done about the backlog), and with no reserves from the budget, precisely because dance was such a flourishing art form. Nevertheless, the democratic and tolerant system of subsidy regulation aims to offer opportunities to all artists, young and old, experienced and just beginning, whether in dance or in the other arts.

For Dutch dancers seeking a professional dance education, The Netherlands has several possibilities on offer. Shortly after the war there were hardly any professional schools, but nowadays there are five state-subsidized academies, besides several private schools, where one can train to become a professional dancer. The school in The Hague, as well as one department of the academy in Amsterdam, concentrate on classical ballet. The other departments in Amsterdam and the academies in Rotterdam, Tilburg and Arnhem offer all kinds of modern and postmodern dance. Although they also offer classical ballet specializations, students from these three academies usually aim for a career with one of the contemporary dance companies.

The next and probably most convincing and interesting indication of the importance of democratic principles and diversification in the development of dance in The Netherlands is the wide variety of companies and styles. To give a necessarily brief idea of the Dutch dance scene, we will present an overview of the most important companies and choreographers today.[10]

The so-called first circuit of dance companies in The Netherlands consists of three large- and two medium-sized companies: Het Nationale Ballet (HNB) in Amsterdam, Nederlands Dans Theater (NDT) in The Hague, Scapino Rotterdam, Introdans in Arnhem and De Rotterdamse Dansgroep (DRD) in Rotterdam. HNB is the only Dutch company that is hierarchically organized, with first and second principals, *grands sujets*, *coryphées*, a corps de ballet and *élèves*. All the other companies have either never used ranks or have done away with them long ago. HNB is also the only company that preserves nineteenth-century ballets.

Since its foundation in 1961, HNB has never diverged from its original policy of trying to be, in the words of its founder Sonia Gaskell, a 'dance museum' (Van de Weetering and Utrecht 1976). By this she meant that HNB had to build a repertoire of new work of contemporary choreographers, but also to respect the traditions of both ballet and modern dance. Each year, HNB presents three series of classical ballets, like *Swan Lake* or *Giselle*. They also stage important and influential neoclassical and modern ballets of the twentieth century, for example works by Balanchine, Graham, Jooss, Massine, Nijinska, and other modern classics. The third pillar of HNB's repertoire is new, contemporary work. In the 1970s and 1980s, the company was a fertile breeding ground for Dutch choreographers such as Hans van Manen, Toer van Schayk and Rudi van Dantzig (Utrecht 1987). In the 1990s, it has continued to present work by young choreographers, also staging ballets by William Forsythe and Jan Fabre.

NDT was formed by dancers from Sonia Gaskell's original group who had grown dissatisfied with her artistic goals. They left Gaskell in 1959 to pursue their own ideal: the presentation of new work which reflected the spirit of that day in a daring combination of the techniques of academic ballet and modern dance (Van Schaik

1981; Versteeg 1987). Like HNB, NDT has also stayed true to its origins. The arrival of Jiří Kylián in 1975 initiated a long period of artistic prosperity, with Kylián creating more than fifty ballets for NDT (Lanz 1995). NDT presents ballets that combine a strong academic base with expressionism and contemporary speed. An interesting development is the founding of NDT2 and NDT3, the first a company of young dancers who lack the stage experience required to be part of the main group, the second a small group of dancers who are over 40 years old and who present work that fits their artistic maturity.

Scapino Rotterdam, the third big company in The Netherlands, has been around since 1945 (Voeten 1985). Originally founded by Hans Snoek as a company for children, Scapino has gone through many artistic changes, and is now a modern dance company dedicated to presenting new choreography. Founder and first artistic director of Scapino, Hans Snoek, one of the leading ladies of post-war dance in The Netherlands, wanted her company to educate the public. She presented work that was to be accessible, like pantomimic ballets and informative ballets about current topics. After she left in 1970, Scapino's artistic course under Armando Navarro started to meander, until Ed Wubbe took firm control in 1993. Under Wubbe, Scapino became Scapino Rotterdam, identifying with the cosmopolitan city that had had to rebuild itself after being destroyed by German bombs in the Second World War. Wubbe stages original choreography and new, contemporary interpretations of old classics like *Romeo and Juliet*, using African and Asian music, and mixing classical ballet technique and contemporary dance. He also invites young choreographers to create work for his company, and he aims to attract a young audience.

The two medium-sized, established repertory companies are Introdans in Arnhem and De Rotterdamse Dansgroep in Rotterdam. Introdans is a modern ballet company with a classical ballet foundation. The artistic directors Ton Wiggers and Roel Voorintholt present accessible triple bills for adults and children's performances. They stand for an approach to dance that is contemporary and free of extremes. In Rotterdam, Ton Simons is the successful artistic director and choreographer-in-residence of De Rotterdamse Dansgroep (DRD). Although work of many more, especially young, choreographers is presented, his style, which is strongly based on Cunningham, has more or less come to represent DRD.

This first circuit is complemented by a great number of smaller dance groups and individuals that present a wide variety of contemporary dance, too numerous to discuss fully in this article. To give an idea of the broad variety of styles nowadays, a selection of a few representatives will do. Some of the small companies or individuals occupy a relatively established position within the Dutch dance scene, both financially and in their styles. A fair number of people who caused the boom of the 1970s and 1980s are still actively involved in dance. We have already mentioned Pauline de Groot, one of the pioneers of the late 1950s and 1960s, who opposed classical ballet and explored (post)modern dance in the States. Her dance idiom is rooted in the American avant-garde and allied to the improvisation principles of the Judson Church generation. Krisztina de Châtel and Truus Bronkhorst have, in their own ways, marked Dutch dance for a long time. The Hungarian De Châtel founded her company in 1978, and is particularly known for her severe minimalism and her cooperation with contemporary artists. For the last couple of years her style has become a little more theatrical and emotional, without losing its formal characteristics. Film (as part of performances, as well as dance films) is her latest passion. In 1977, Bronkhorst was one of the founding members of Dansproduktie, an all-female collective of dancers and choreographers that existed between 1977 and 1993. During her later career she was very successful with her solo performances. More recently she has concentrated on ensemble works. Bronkhorst is a typical example of a choreographer who constantly redefines her dance, by working together with artists from different disciplines. Her work skirts the borders between dance and theatre, in often provocative and humorous ways. Another pioneer who is still active is Beppie Blankert, also a former member of Dansproduktie. Blankert stayed true to the anti-expressionism of Dansproduktie, with its preference for conceptual and formal dance. Nowadays, she presents dance concerts in which she incorporates spoken text, singing and film. Of the above, only De Châtel and Bronkhorst are honoured by the 1997–2000 *Kunstenplan*; the others work with incidental money for *ad hoc* projects.

Two choreographers and artistic leaders of their own companies who have been around for some time but still have to work with project-funding are Shusaku Takeuchi and Piet Rogie. Audiences interested in dance that has links to *butoh*, mime and theatre, can count on the Shusaku and Dormu Dance Theatre of the Japanese Shusaku, who has been working in The Netherlands since 1974. The Flemish Piet Rogie trained as a visual artist before he became a dancer and a choreographer. He worked with Werkcentrum Dans (later De Rotterdamse Dansgroep) and with Stift and Het Penta Theater, until he founded his own company, Compagnie Peter Bulcaen, in 1989. At first he worked along two different lines, literary and abstract; more recently, his narrative choreography (often based on literary themes) has given way to more pure dance pieces.

Among the youngest generation, eclecticism comes naturally. These choreo-graphers do and take whatever they like, from ballet to contemporary dance, music, theatre, visual and video arts. The influence of William Forsythe is too obvious not to mention here. Following in his tracks, they develop their own dance vocabularies. Andrea Leine and Harijono Roebana, Paul Selwyn Norton, Karin Post, Arthur Rosenfeld and Ana Teixidó, Maria Voortman and Roberto de Jonge, Angelika Oei, and Suzy Blok and Christopher Steel are examples of this younger generation. Most of them started choreographing in the early 1990s. Leine and Roebana explicitly question music in their dance. In their search for a new dance vocabulary they explore deconstruction principles, both in regard to structure and movement. But their use of isolation technique does not exclude a smooth, sometimes even lyrical dance style. Karin Post often works with contemporary (video)artists and musicians, although dance is always her starting point. Rosenfeld and Teixidó create funny theatrical dance performances for audiences of all ages. Voortman and De

Jonge explore the possibilities and limitations of the body in a radical redefinition of classical ballet technique. A couple of years ago, their work was much discussed because of their sensational use of pointe shoes in modern dance. Oei performs more abroad (especially at festivals) than in The Netherlands itself. In her dance she often experiments with other arts, especially video and film. Blok and Steel are especially known for their highly vital, almost acrobatic dance. Of all the individuals and small companies mentioned here, only dance company Leine and Roebana and Karin Post are to receive a subsidy in the 1997–2000 *Kunstenplan*.

Commitment to democratic principles ('every Dutch citizen has the right to develop his or her potential') and a tendency towards diversification created a firm basis for the structure and development of Dutch dance. But the way dance in The Netherlands has developed has also been formed by another feature: the Dutch inclination towards levelling.

Levelling

The lack of a strong Dutch national drive in dance, allowing an openness towards new ideas and experiments from many different directions, together with the systematic tendency towards diversification, have shaped the field of dance in The Netherlands, where there is now a great variety of companies and styles. The positive financial climate has also been an important factor, and because of the social security system and the accessible, although certainly not abundant, subsidies available (especially the possibility of receiving subsidies for individual projects), a certain amount of uncontrolled growth of small dance companies took place in the 1980s. Since 1965 there has also been the *Algemene Bijstandswet*, a system of social security which guarantees financial support to all Dutch citizens who are not able to support themselves. This system has become an important though not officially accepted way of financing the arts. By offering a basic income, the Bijstand makes it possible to dance and to create choreography even without subsidy. But the relatively easy means of getting money to create choreography and set up small productions has its drawbacks, and by accepting too many applicants ('everybody should be able to express him or herself') Dutch arts policy runs the risk of giving space to mediocrity (Van den Berg and Van Gemert 1989). This risk is increased by the inclination towards levelling that has been a central feature in Dutch culture and in policy-making. We will illustrate this statement by elaborating on the position of the dance academies and the *danswerkplaatsen*.

Ever since Sonia Gaskell managed to make the training and education of professional dancers part of the officially recognized and subsidized conservatory in The Hague in 1956, there have been complaints about the level of dance education. We have already mentioned that The Netherlands has five officially recognized academies where one can train to become a professional dancer. Schools that train young people to become classical ballet-dancers have been particularly vulnerable to the criticism that their education is not up to international standards. The main problem is that the education of professional dancers is not concentrated

129

enough to create the atmosphere of excellence and healthy competition required to train good ballet-dancers. There are too many schools, and they are too spread out across the country. Also, because each school needs pupils, the selection process for prospective ballet-dancers is said to be not severe enough.

Another criticism is that there is no official connection between the dance academies and the ballet companies. Unlike in many other countries, dance companies in The Netherlands, even the large ones, do not have their own schools. There is some cooperation between the academy in The Hague and NDT, and between the ballet academy in Amsterdam and HNB, but the schools are completely independent. This peculiar situation is a consequence of the lack of dance tradition on the one hand, and the Dutch educational system on the other. When dance education started to develop after the war, there were no companies and no schools. The new dance academies that were founded had to fit into the existing educational system, and the possibility of aligning them with the dance companies (also new) was the least of the worries of the Dutch government. As a result of this situation, graduates from Dutch dance academies do not blend easily into the big Dutch companies, whose artistic directors claim they have to go abroad to find the dancers they need – and given the international job situation for dancers, they have few problems in finding good foreign dancers, despite the fact that until very recently salaries for dancers in The Netherlands were much lower than in other European countries.[11]

In 1979, a national committee of dance experts reported that the education of professional ballet-dancers needed to be concentrated in one school. Twelve years later, in 1991, an international committee reached the same conclusion. As yet, though, nothing has changed. Although the dance academies themselves agree on this need, they resist it out of sheer self-interest and through fear of losing jobs and established positions. The several Dutch governments that have been confronted with the problem did not take responsibility: while acknowledging the problematic situation and the resultant loss, no government has dared to take the step of closing down schools. Even in arts education it seems to be more important to avoid conflict and to give many people a fair chance than to spot and stimulate the highly talented. Moreover, young dance students and their parents oppose reducing the number of schools. Children who aspire to a career in ballet have to start very young, preferably around the age of ten, and the Dutch, who never had a boarding-school tradition, are not comfortable with the idea of their children leaving home at an early age; so with several dance academies available, many more children can live at home while they finish their education.

The missing link between educational and professional worlds is a problem not only for ballet-dancers. The many young dancers and choreographers who study modern and new dance often do not manage to get a job with a company either. They form the so-called open field of freelancers who try to stay in the dance scene by creating their own work and staging their own small productions. For some, this is a deliberate choice, because they prefer to work independently; but for many it is sheer necessity. Often graduates do not have enough stage experience to join a company right away; and besides, especially with the considerable number of foreigners who try to set up a career in The Netherlands, there are too many people for the available jobs. To give an idea of the numbers involved: in 1997 there were approximately 500 professional dancers in The Netherlands, only half of whom were employed by a dance company. Since the mid-1980s more and more people dance unpaid, living on social welfare, or trying to get money for their own independent projects. The pressure on project subsidies and rehearsal and performing spaces has risen considerably. Several independent, scarcely financed dance workshops – some of which have existed since 1979 – offer space and production assistance, but not sufficiently, and in a somewhat amateurish way.

The Dutch would not be the Dutch if they did not look for a solution to this problem. When it became obvious that the numbers of unaffiliated dancers was continuing to grow, Dutch politics became interested in dance work-shops. After some discussion they became an official part of the arts policy as *danswerkplaatsen* (dance workshops), and consequently were subsidized. In 1986 a report was published in which the government officially defined the tasks of the *danswerkplaatsen*: to stimulate the flow of young choreographers to the regular professional field, to form a link between academies and professional companies, and to offer training and performance opportunities to dancers. They would also offer production and artistic assistance (Zellerer 1994). In all fairness, we should add that, in the eyes of the policy-makers, giving everybody a chance to dance was not the only objective of the *danswerkplaatsen*; they were also asked to be selective, and the ideal *danswerkplaats* should also function as a kind of screen. Now, after more than ten years and many discussions, definitions and reports, three main *danswerkplaatsen* are left: Dansateliers (Rotterdam), DWA (Amsterdam) and Korzo (The Hague). Dansateliers functions as a laboratory, DWA has two programmes, one for inexperienced and another one for more experienced choreographers and Korzo specializes as a production house for advanced young choreographers. Nowadays, it is thought that although the *danswerkplaatsen* fulfilled their promise as a fertile breeding ground for new choreographic talent, they allowed too much space for mediocrity; they should be far more selective and only the best choreo-graphers should be rewarded. In the context of the Dutch commitment to democratic principles and the inclination towards levelling, it is not surprising that this has apparently been the hardest task for the *danswerkplaatsen*.

Innovation

One of the striking features of the Dutch dance scene has been the constant call for innovation, which has been loud throughout its development (Van Schaik 1993). This continuous call for innovation is not exclusive to dance; yet more than for the other arts, it is woven into the historical origins of dance. Dance in The Netherlands started to develop in the 1950s, a period of reconstruction and rebuilding, and in the 1960s, when revolution was the catchword of the day. The general atmosphere, in society and the arts, was one of change, and it was in this climate that the new art form of dance came onto the scene.

An aversion to following well-trodden paths is still strong in all Dutch dance companies, big and small. Tradition is an ugly word with which no artistic director wants to be associated. Even HNB, the most traditional of Dutch dance companies, had innovation at its roots from the beginning. Although Gaskell clearly saw the importance of tradition, one of the three cornerstones of her company's artistic policy was the encouragement of young choreographers to create new work for her company. This policy continued under Rudi van Dantzig's leadership, when HNB housed three young Dutch choreographers – Van Dantzig himself, Hans van Manen and Toer van Schayk – who presented the company with new, experimental work. Since 1978, HNB has also stimulated young talent by organizing choreography workshops in which dancers can develop their choreographic skills. Choreographers like Ted Brandsen, Jan Linkens and Krzysztof Pastor, who have found their way to major companies all over the world, started their careers in the HNB workshops. In 1987, the company moved from the Amsterdam city theatre to the much bigger and more costly Muziektheater, and since then it has chosen to present more classical ballet because it is easier to get full houses with nineteenth-century classics than with new choreography. Van Manen and Van Dantzig have left the company, and have not been replaced by young choreographers in residence. In the last few years, the company, under Wayne Eagling, has been heavily criticized for its policy, accused of conservatism and lack of daring (Van de Graaf 1995; Kottman 1996).

The other big Dutch company, NDT, has had innovation as its *raison d'être* since it started as a group of revolutionaries in the late 1950s. The dancers experimented with a combination of ballet and modern dance that was extremely revolutionary for the time. The presentation of new work has been one of NDT's aims ever since. The company also organizes yearly choreography workshops to enable dancers to create their own works. Acclaimed choreographers like Nacho Duato, Nils Christe and Ed Wubbe developed their skills in these workshops. As for the third big company, Scapino Rotterdam, the arrival of Ed Wubbe as artistic director in 1993 meant a change in artistic policy. Wubbe did away with the traditional roots of the company, even cancelling the Nutcracker performance at Christmas, Scapino's best moneymaker. Under his leadership Scapino Rotterdam became a modern dance company that only presents original choreography.

This striving for artistic innovation, which seems to be central, is enabled and strengthened by governmental policies which favour innovation above tradition. Of course, the buzzwords of government arts policy have changed over the past decades: in the 1950s and 1960s it was all 'decency' and 'beauty'; in the 1970s, art was supposed to implicate 'cultural diversity' and 'social relevance'; and since the 1980s the main criteria are 'professionalism', 'internationalism' and, importantly, 'quality' – with quality largely (and explicitly) defined in terms of innovation and originality.

The broad field of contemporary dance outside the big companies is, not surprisingly, innovative by nature. But its innovative character is encouraged by its means of funding. We have already mentioned that only a few of the groups or individuals outside the first circuit receive money from the *Kunstenplan*. Most are dependent on incidental subsidies, which means they have to apply for money for each new dance project. There are two main consequences. First, incidental subsidy in itself offers no basis for continuity, let alone for building a tradition. Second, as government policies favour innovation above tradition, the usual way for an applicant to impress the funding committees is by being innovative – and it is unsurprising that in funding applications a high number of people describe their next dance piece as a form of research. This may be largely a form of words to suit the funders; but it nevertheless reinforces the idea that being innovative is the only way to survive.

Conclusion

The Netherlands may have a poor social climate for dancing and no dance tradition to speak of, but, at the end of the twentieth century, dance in the theatre was a flourishing art form. One of the central features of dance in The Netherlands is its diversity. With only 15 million inhabitants, The Netherlands has produced three large, two medium-sized, and over thirty small companies, who together present hundreds of new dance productions each year. How was it possible for this flourishing and diverse dance scene to become established within only fifty years?

We have discerned four key elements to explain the development and the structure of dance in The Netherlands over the last fifty years: its non-nationalist character, its commitment to democratic principles, its inclination towards levelling, and its desire for innovation. The absence of a national tradition in dance, freed dancers and choreographers working in The Netherlands from the obligation to fit into traditions, and has given them room to experiment and to create their own styles. Of necessity, they have looked across their borders for examples and for inspiration, borrowing and stealing whatever they liked. The commitment to democratic principles led to a financial climate that favoured many, and the tendency to segregate into separate groups generated many different dance initiatives. The inclination towards levelling that has been a central feature of Dutch culture and policy-making brought forth an extensive dance education system and the *danswerkplaatsen*. The constant call for innovation has been both a result and a cause of the lack of tradition of dance in The Netherlands.[12]

Within fifty years, dance in The Netherlands has become a respected art form, characterized by originality and diversity, and recognized as such by policy-makers and critics.[13] The Dutch may not dance in the streets, but many of them certainly dance on stage in the theatres.

Acknowledgement

Many thanks to Wouter Hos for valuable comments and to Britt Fontaine for superb editing. Any remaining faults in the final text are our own.

Notes

1 The reasons for the closing down are too complex to go into here. One of the reasons lay, obviously, in the German occupation. In 1941 the Germans founded the Kulturkammer. Only artists who were members were allowed to perform or create. But membership was – of course – regarded as an act of collaboration, so many did not subscribe. This made it hard for dancers to continue working (see also Van Schaik 1981).
2 According to the CBS, the Central Office for Statistics in the Hague.
3 'De geografische ligging van Nederland heeft niet alleen het karakter van zijn bevolking bepaald, maar ook zijn cultuur . . . Waar de zee aan de ene kant tot begrenzing dwong, bood hij tegelijkertijd de mogelijkheid aan vreemde culturen zich een weg te vinden naar Nederland. Op deze manier verrijkte de smaak van de bewoners zich en ontwikkelden zij begrip en verdraagzaamheid voor andere rassen, godsdiensten en culturen. Nederland was het trefpunt van Latijnse, Angelsaksische en Germaanse invloeden' (Gaskell in *Algemeen Handelsblad*, cited in Van Schaik 1981: 93).
4 Their positive attitude may also have been influenced by the fact that Duncan had been enormously successful in Paris, which in those days was considered to be the cultural capital of Europe.
5 In 1995, dancer–writer Yoka van Brummelen published a book on Lili Green. She also dedicated a series of performances to this Dutch dance pioneer, with reconstructions of Green's choreography and with new dances that were inspired by Green.
6 The youngest dance generation occupies a special place in this discussion. They grew up in this internationally oriented Dutch dance world, and, more than any former generation, they are used to the world as a 'global village'. We believe that 'national' and 'international' are completely interchangeable terms for them; and they are probably least aware of, and most down to earth about, the question of whether their work is 'typically Dutch' or not.
7 Lecture at the Festival International de Nouvelle Danse in Montréal, 1995, where special attention was paid to dance from The Netherlands.
8 Only one Dutch choreographer has admitted to non-western influences in his work, the Indonesian-born Glenn van der Hoff. In 1983 Van der Hoff founded Djazzex, a modern jazz dance company that was immensely popular but lost its state subsidy with the new *Kunstenplan* in 1997.
9 More information on the cultural policy of Dutch governments can be found in the Cultural Policy Memorandum produced every four years, and in other publications by the state secretary of education, science and cultural affairs. For this chapter we have made extensive use of the following two texts: Ministerie van WVC/Raad van Europa, *Cultuurbeleid in Nederland* (Zoetermeer: Stafdirectie Cultuurbeleid van het Directoraat-Generaal voor Culturele Zaken, 1993), and Raad voor Cultuur, *Een Cultuur van Verandering – Adviescultuurnota 1997–2000* (deel 11 Dans, Den Haag: SDU, 1996).
10 Much of the information on present-day groups and choreographers is derived from the *Dansjaarboeken* (dance yearbooks) published in 1957 by Gottmer, Haarlem, and between 1984 and 1993 by the Theater Instituut Nederland. Before 1984 and after 1993 recent developments in dance were covered by the *Theaterjaarboeken* (theatre yearbooks), published by the same institute.
11 It was not until 1993 that it was decided and confirmed in the *Kunstenplan* that Dutch companies would have to raise their salaries up to the European level by 1997.
12 In 1993, when Marc Jonkers, director of the Holland Dance Festival, invited several modern dance choreographers to reconstruct a few of their works from the 1970s, he was heavily criticized by the dance critic of one of the country's major newspapers (Korteweg 1993).

13 Acknowledgement for the high quality of Dutch dance also comes from the European committee for the Erasmus Prize. The committee decided to give the Erasmus Prize for the year 2000 to dance in The Netherlands, and specifically to choreographer Hans van Manen. Dutch dance receives this reward for the high quality of its choreographers, its dancers, and its educational and financial system. The £100,000 Erasmus Prize is awarded annually to a person or institution that has made a special contribution to European culture.

References

Berg, H. O. van den and Gemert, M. van (1989) *Nederlands cultuurbeleid en Europese eenwording – Muziek en dans*, Rijswijk: Ministerie van WVC, Directoraal-Generaal Culturele Zaken.

Bronkhorst, P. (1997) 'Cultural Policy in the Netherlands', *Theatre and Dance from The Netherlands*, Amsterdam: Theater Instituut Nederland.

Brummelen, Y. van (1995) *Lili Green 1885–1977*, Amsterdam: Uitgeverij International Theatre and Film Books.

Cannegieter, F. (1989) *Principe versus pragmatisme – dans-en mimebeleid in Nederland*, Amsterdam: Boekmanstichting.

Graaf, R. van de (1995) 'Geen plaats meer voor experiment en avontuur', *de Volkskrant*, 25 August.

Korteweg, A. (1993) 'Berichten uit de Bermuda-driehoek', *de Volkskrant*, 15 October.

Kottman, P. (1996) 'Oude getrouwen', *NRC Handelsblad*, 11 October.

Lanz, I. (1995) *A Garden of Dance: A Monograph on the Work of Jiří Kylián, 20 Years at Nederlands Dans Theater*, Amsterdam: Theater Instituut Nederland and Nederlands Dans Theater.

Mallems, A. (1995) 'Chantal Pontbriand, Verantwoordelijk voor open klimaat', *Notes – Maandblad over Theaterdans en Mime*, November: 25–8.

Rebling, E. (1950) *Een Eeuw Danskunst in Nederland*, Amsterdam: Querido.

Schaik, E. van (1981) *Op gespannen voet – Geschiedenis van de Nederlandse theaterdans vanaf 1900*, Haarlem: De Haan.

Schaik, E. van (1993) 'Wegwerpkunst – het geheugenverlies van de dans', *De Groene Amsterdammer*, 13 October.

Utrecht, L. (1987) *Het Nationale Ballet 25 jaar: de geschiedenis van Het Nationale Ballet van 1961 tot 1986*, Amsterdam: De Lange and Het Nationale Ballet.

Utrecht, L. (1988) *Van Hofballet tot Postmoderne-dans: de geschiedenis van het akademische ballet en de moderne dans*, Zutphen: Walburg Pers.

Versteeg, C. (1987) *Nederlands Dans Theater, een revolutionaire geschiedenis*, Amsterdam: Balans.

Voeten, J. (1985) *Scapino*, Zutphen: Walburg Pers.

Voeten, J. (1997) *50 jaar Holland Festival – een Nederlands wonder*, Zutphen: Walburg Pers/Stichting Holland Festival.

Weetering, C. van de and Utrecht, L. (1976) *Sonia Gaskell. Geloof in wat je danst*, Zutphen: Walburg Pers.

Wessels, P. (1995) 'Het publiek als getuige', *De Groene Amsterdammer*, 4 October.

Zellerer, Y. (1994) *Danswerkplaatsen – een nieuw profiel*, Amsterdam: Boekmanstichting.

Key Texts

Bilder, E. and E. van Schaik (1987) 'Dutch Theatre Dance. A Strange Bird in the Lake', *Ballett International* 9/10: 40–52.

Korteweg, A. (ed) (1989) *Made in Holland*, promotion magazine on dance in The Netherlands, Amsterdam: Theater Instituut Nederland.

Rebling, E. (1950) *Een Eeuw Danskunst in Nederland*, Amsterdam: Querido.

Schaik, E. van (1981) *Op Gespannen Voet: de geschiedenis van de Nederlandse theaterdans vanaf 1900*, Haarlem: De Haan.

Schaik, E. van (1997) *Hans van Manen: Leven & Werk*, Amsterdam: Arena.

Schmidt, J. (1987) *Der Zeitgenosse als Klassiker, über den Holländische Choreographen Hans van Manen*, Keulen.

Utrecht, L. (1992) *Rudi van Dantzig: a Controversial Idealist in Ballet*, Zutphen: Walburg Pers.

Table 7 Important dance and political events in The Netherlands (1900 to present)

Year	Dance: artists, works, events	Dance: institutions	Arts scene	Sociocultural and political events
1901				Queen Wilhelmina marries Hendrik
1905	*Isadora Duncan			
1906				NVV founded (first Dutch labour union)
1908			*Molen bij zonlicht* (Mondriaan)	
1909				Princess Juliana born
1914				The Netherlands neutral in First World War
1916			Nederlandse Opera (first performance)	
1917				Universal suffrage for men
1918			*De Stijl* manifesto Govt department for Education, Arts and Sciences	Troelstra's failed revolution
1919	Florrie Rodrigo solo performance	Lili Green opens studio and school in The Hague Dutch Dalcroze Society		Women get the vote
1920			First city council subsidies for theatre and drama	The Netherlands member of League of Nations
1924			Amsterdam Drama School (50th anniversary)	
1925	*Ballets Russes		Museum for Drama in Amsterdam	

Table 7 continued

Year	Dance: artists, works, events	Dance: institutions	Arts scene	Sociocultural and political events
1927	*Anna Pavlova			
1928				
1929			*De Brug* (Ivens)	Stock market crash
1930				Colijn forms committee on 'the dance problem'
1931		Corrie Hartong starts dance academy as part of Rotterdam Conservatory	Pavlova dies in The Hague	
1932		Yvonne Georgi starts school and company in Mascha ter Weeme's studio		54 parties participate in general election
1933				First Jewish refugees enter The Netherlands
1934	*De Schepelingen* (Rodrigo)		Wagner Society (50th anniversary)	
1936	*Vreemd Land* (Rodrigo)			
1937		First officially recognized dance exams	Concertgebouw (40th anniversary)	
1938				Juliana's first daughter, Beatrix, is born
1939		Lili Green starts Nederlandsch Ballet	Nederlandse Dansliga	First socialists in government
1940		Dansliga takes initiative to start national company Nederlandsch Ballet in The Hague		Invasion by Germany
1941		Dancers of Nederlandsch Ballet refuse to perform in Germany Nederlandsch Ballet closes		German occupiers institute *Kulturkammer* Communists organize strike against persecution of Jews

Table 7 continued

Year	Dance	Theatre / Arts	National events
1942	Last performance Yvonne Georgi Ballet (*Coppélia*)	Second National Contest for Dance Orchestras Artists publish manifesto against *Kulturkammer* *Het uur U* (Nijhoff)	
1944			Southern part of country liberated, northern part suffers winter hunger
1945	Scapino Studio '45 Georgi's company convicted collectively for collaboration	Toneelgroep 5 mei 1945	5 May, northern part liberated, also Labour Party founded
1947	Darja Collin director of Ballet van de Nederlandse Opera Ballet der Lage Landen	Amsterdams Toneelgezelschap Haagse Comedie Rotterdams Toneel *De Avonden* (Reve) First Holland Festival	
1948			Wilhelmina abdicates, Juliana queen Indonesia independent
1949	Nel Roos takes over Georgi's school	Cobra exhibition causes scandal	
1951	Françoise Adret director of Ballet van de Nederlands Opera Scapino Dansschool	Realist painters organize exhibition in protest against abstractionism	
1953	Nederlands Ballet Rotterdamse Dansacademie		Zeeland floods
1954	*Martha Graham	Dance gains separate vote in arts budget Toneelgroep Theater performs Becket's *Waiting for Godot*	
1955	*Nachteiland* (Van Dantzig's first choreography)		Fokker Friendship (1st flight)
1956	*Het Heksenjong* (Jack Carter) First govt-subsidized dance academy in The Hague (Gaskell director) Centraal Dansberaad	TEST performs Ionesco	

Table 7 continued

Year	Dance: artists, works, events	Dance: institutions	Arts scene	Sociocultural and political events
1957	Le Sanctuaire (Adret)	First Ballet Yearbook		EEC founded
1958	Disgenoten (Van Dantzig) Ommegang (Lucas Hoving)	Adret leaves Ballet van de Ned. Opera	Fanfare (Haanstra) Film and Television Academy	
1959	Feestgericht (Van Manen's first choreography)	Nederlands Dans Theater Scapino Dansacademie Ballet van de Ned. Opera and Ballet der Lage Landen become Amsterdams Ballet	International exhibition of expressionism in Amsterdam	
1960	*Kirov Ballet, with Galina Ulanova			
1961	Jungle (Van Dantzig)	Amsterdams Ballet and remaining dancers of Nederlands Ballet become Nationale Ballet Folkloristisch Danstheater (later Internationaal Dans Theater)	Manifest tegen Niets by Nul-artists	
1964			Ik, Jan Cremer (Cremer) Nederlandse Opera	
1965	First complete Swan Lake by Dutch dancers Monument voor een gestorven jongen (Van Dantzig) Metaforen (Van Manen)	Dansacademie Tilburg Pauline de Groot opens studio		Provo founded, Amsterdam anarchists
1967	Romeo en Julia (Van Dantzig), first classic by Dutch choreographer Visibility . . . by chance (Koert Stuyf)			
1968	Mutatie (Koert Stuyf)	Rotterdams Danscentrum Dansacademie Arnhem Theaterschool Amsterdam		Mammoetwet; arts education under law on vocational training

Table 7 continued

1969		Noord Nederlandse Dansgroep	Aktie Tomaat Aktie Notenkraker	
1970	*Mutations* (Van Manen)			
1971	*Grosse Fuge* (Van Manen)			
1972	*Voor, tijdens en na het feest* (Van Schayk) *Twilight* (Van Manen)	Introdans	Mickery Theatre moves from Loenersloot to Amsterdam	Oil boycott because of sympathic attitude towards Israel
1973	*Adagio Hammerklavier* (Van Manen)	First dance history course by Corrie Hartong		
1974		Dept of contemporary dance part of Amsterdam Theaterschool		
1975		Werkcentrum Dans		
1977	*Vier Letzte Lieder* (Van Dantzig) *Vijf Tango's* (Van Manen)	Stichting Dansproduktie		
1978	*Sinfonietta* (Kylián) *Spiegels* (Bart Stuyf) *Vermiljoen* (Van Dillen)	Dansgroep Krisztina de Châtel First Springdance Festival		
1979	*Live* (Van Manen) *Lopen* (Dansproduktie) *Lines* (De Châtel)			
1980	*Soldatenmis* (Kylián)			Beatrix becomes queen
1981	*Sarcasmen* (Van Manen)			New, permissive Abortion Law
1982		Djazzex		
1983	*Jardi Tancat* (Nacho Duato) *Stamping Ground* (Kylián)	Post for dance studies at Utrecht University		
1984	*Nailed* (Käthy Gosschalk)	Nederlands Instituut voor de Dans (NID)		
1985	*Want wij weten niet wat wij doen* (Van Dantzig)			550,000 people march against Cruise missiles

Table 7 continued

Year	Dance: artists, works, events	Dance: institutions	Arts scene	Sociocultural and political events
1986	Silent Cries (Kylián)	St Omscholingsregeling Dansers Raad van Cultuur brings out 'Ruimte voor de dans' report Danswerkplaats Rotterdam	Van Dantzig publishes first book, Voor een verloren soldaat	Delta Plan finished to protect country against sea level
1987	Buigen of barsten (Van Dantzig) Before Nightfall (Christe) Staunch (De Châtel)	Fusion of Scapino Dansacademie and Nel Roos academy First Holland Dance Festival Hans van Manen offered chair at University of Nijmegen		
1988	Lood (Bronkhorst) Kaguyahime (Kylián)	Werkcentrum Dans becomes De Rotterdamse Dansgroep		
1989	Goud (Bronkhorst) Grace (Simons) Muddle (Shusaku Takeuchi) Cargo (Rogie)	Blok & Steel Leine & Roebana Compagnie Peter Bulcaen Danswerkplaats Korzo Danswerkplaats Arnhem	First Kunstenplan period	
1990		Raz		
1991	Charles (Blankert) Alind (Oei)	Itzik Galili Dance	Désirée Delauney	
1992	Johnny Panic (Norton) No Sleep till Dawn of Day (Kylián) Kathleen (Wubbe) Alcool (Delauney)	Informeel Dans Overleg (IDO)		Airplane crashed in Bijlmermeer, populated Amsterdam district
1993	The Idea of Order (Simons) Perfect Skin (Wubbe) When you see God tell him (Galili) Naakt (Rogie)	De Meekers NID becomes part of Theater Instituut Nederland Dansateliers Rotterdam Danswerkplaats Amsterdam	Second Kunstenplan period	

Table 7 continued

1994	*Pork* (Norton)		
	Softly, as I leave you (Paul Lightfoot)		
	Quest for Rest (Voortman & De Jonge)		
1995	*If we only could even if we could* (Leine & Roebana)		
1996	*Notenkraker en Muizenkoning* (Eagling & Van Schayk)		
	Naast (Rogie)		
1997	*The Fall* (Bronkhorst)	Galili Dance	
1998		First international dance studies conference on Dutch dance	Third Kunstenplan period

*First visit

8

SPAIN

Between tradition and innovation: two ways of understanding the history of dance in Spain

Nèlida Monés, Marta Carrasco, Estrella Casero-García and Delfín Colomé

Theatre in Spain expresses the course of Spanish history with both strength and originality, a history which has run against the tide of European history throughout the twentieth century – a fact which has often boosted its creative potential. Dance has faced this process in two different ways: on the one hand, with its own language represented by flamenco, the *escuela bolera* and the inaptly named 'Spanish dance'; and on the other, with styles common to other countries, such as ballet and contemporary dance, albeit with certain distinguishing characteristics.

Through dance, we can follow social, political and economic events that have taken place in Spain, because, in the final analysis, any form of art reflects what is happening in society in general. In contrast with much of Europe, Spain was neutral through the two world wars, and so attracted people with a multitude of different experiences and opinions during the inter-war period, including artists looking for an outlet for their talents, Jews escaping Nazi persecution and genocide, as well as sympathizers with National Socialism and, of course, with Franco's regime. Fortunately, with the arrival of democracy in 1978, Spain has inherited the positive aspect of these arrivals, both culturally and politically; the old guard has been left behind and has little influence nowadays, leaving the stage open for new artists and creators.

A study of dance in Spain also illuminates the question of nationalism, an issue of utmost relevance in Europe today. The Franco era promoted a centralized Spanish nationalism that smothered other forms of expression in culture, art, language and history – a nationalism exemplified in the dance world by the Coros y Danzas (Chorus and Dance Divisions) of the Sección Femenina. On the other hand, we find cultural regionalism linked to language and rooted in the historic communities of Catalonia, Galicia and the Basque country, who have struggled for their cultural rights and identity. After the introduction of democracy in 1978 this found official representation in the establishment of Estados de las Autonomías

144

(autonomous regional governments), institutions that could more easily promote regional culture and art. In the dance world, popular forms of dance that reflect different regional cultures can now be seen alongside the more artistic and creative forms, such as contemporary dance and the small amount of ballet produced here, reflecting the diversity of both artists and public, a simple fact that will enrich European culture in the future.

Spain Against the Tide

Ballet and contemporary dance: speaking the same language across Europe?

The second part of the twentieth century in Spain can be divided into two radically different periods. The first started at the end of Spanish Civil War (1936–9) and lasted until the end of the 1950s – a period of severe dictatorship and diplomatic isolation, to which was added a tenacious political and a dangerous intellectual autarchy. In this period, Spain was denied any access to the modernization process developing in other parts of the world.

Spanish society experienced a slow economic recovery during the period that followed, from the 1960s until the death of Franco in 1975, during which time, with the entry of several technocrats into the Franco government, the economy began to recover by means of three main factors. These were: a degree of liberalization in trade and industry, the mass emigration of Spanish workers abroad, and the arrival of mass tourism, all of which brought in a generous amount of foreign currency. It was clear that this economic development could not but entail a certain parallel political and social development with the outside world, and this was reflected by opposition to the ruling regime in many artistic demonstrations, characterized by the exuberant creativity that the Spanish have shown throughout history, in spite of the difficult conditions in which they have had to live.

During the period from the end of the Civil War until the arrival of democracy, traditional dance had to adapt to the centralized aesthetic, however impoverished that was, of Francoism, which was based on tradition, the exaltation of all things national, inclined to the *españolada* (a vulgar characterization of all things Spanish). Fortunately, the high cultural values of traditional dance, with flamenco as its exegesis, gave the results a certain dignity.

The second period of Spanish history in the second half of the century dates from the recovery of democracy and a system of liberty and freedom, above all from the 1978 constitution following the general election in 1977. During this time the Spanish people as a whole demonstrated a prime example of civic conscience and prudence in guiding one of the most spectacular transitions to democracy in recent times.

In the search for modernity, from which Spain had been isolated for many decades, dance, especially modern dance, represented an excellent driving force, for several reasons. One, of anthropological–cultural character, was that the

145

language of modern dance connected with the cultural feeling of the country in the process of what was called the democratic transition. A real transitional culture existed in Spain, demonstrated not so much in the number of books published, films shot, music composed or choreography premièred between 1975 and 1986 (the year in which Spain entered the European Union, which in some way seemed to close this period of transition), but in the decisive willpower of the Spanish people – a large section of them at least – to create and participate in something new, breaking with the schemes of the long period of dictatorship. This willpower gave rise to a cultural and aesthetic phenomenon of great magnitude, of which dance was a substantial part. Freedom and democracy provoked curiosity, sometimes spectacular, sometimes speculative (as with the famous *movida madrileña*, an underground arts movement in Madrid in the 1980s, its best-known protagonist being the film-maker Pedro Almodóvar); but above all they enabled vast numbers of the public to perceive art, social relations, feelings, life itself, in a new and attractively different way.

A more sociological reason for taking to modern dance was through its association with the liberalization of customs, personal attitudes and individual lifestyles. Freedom and the exercising of individual rights broadened the scope of the ambiguous (and at times manufactured) concept of permissiveness, which allowed a wider range of attitudes and behaviours, and, by extension, no longer cast them in a negative light. One focus for this, of singular importance, was how people related to their own bodies. This relation now became clearer, less distorted by the traditional repression of centuries of Judaeo-Christian civilization and dualistic tradition that had formed the foundations of Spanish society. The image of the liberated man, and above all of the liberated woman, produced an ideal of individual freedom of the body. And the liberation of the body lay at the deepest roots of modern dance. This liberation also brought with it a cult of the body, which found an excellent ally in dance because of its emphasis on fitness and health. Separately and cumulatively, these small revolutions forced a change in thinking.

A third, political reason was the democratization of state structures. The new shaping of the state, authorized in 1977, broke the previous strict centralization by creating new Estados de la Autonomías with a clearer understanding of local government politics. This brought citizens closer to the worlds of art and culture, producing a proliferation of shows, festivals, competitions and choreographic works of all types.

Finally, modern dance in Spain was able to connect quickly with the day-to-day lives of the public, with issues that really concerned them – in contrast to the fantasies of romantic ballet or the aestheticism of the academic ballet of Petipa, which were known largely through seasons at the Palacio Real in Madrid or the Liceu in Barcelona; and this may be the most important of the reasons for its flourishing after the introduction of democracy.

In the light of these general remarks, we now turn to the main landmarks on the path that Spain has taken over the last fifty years to reach its present-day choreographic modernity.

The period up until the 1940s was poor in the fields of ballet and modern dance because of the dominating and powerful influence of indigenous forms such as the *escuela bolera*, flamenco and Spanish dance. There were no big ballet companies in existence, except at the Gran Teatre del Liceu, founded in 1847; even there the *escuela bolera*, flamenco and Spanish dance were strong, with a fair sprinkling of artists of international stature, though ballet did in fact predominate.

One matriarchal figure in ballet was María de Avila. She performed a mixed repertoire of ballet and indigenous dance forms with Joan Magriñà at the Liceu in Barcelona from 1939 until 1948, and then danced with the Ballets de Barcelona in the 1950s. In 1982 she directed the Ballet de Zaragoza, a company subsidized by the city council, and from 1983 to 1986 she took control of the two national companies of ballet and Spanish dance, the Ballet Nacional de España and the Ballet Lírico Nacional. Shortly afterwards, in 1989, the Joven Ballet María de Avila was formed, a semi-professional ballet company linked to de Avila's school, which lasted until 1991. During her time as head of the school, de Avila trained some dancers who would later become established stars, such as Víctor Ullate and Ana Laguna.

Foreign companies visited Spain on regular tours, from the 1960s onwards performing mainly within the standard structure for dance in these years, such as the Festivals of Spain, a solid network of summer shows financed to a large extent by the state.

The 1960s were years of incubation, humble and hidden, before the explosion that took place after 1975. During the last days of Francoism, the progressive decomposition of the dictatorship combined with economic growth allowed more outside contact, which notably speeded up this incubation.

Modern dance broke through under the leadership of Anna Maleras in Barcelona in 1967, and later under Carmen Senra in Madrid. Anna Maleras studied under the supervision of Rosella Hightower in Cannes and with jazz teachers such as Walter Nich and Vayon Aikens. Carmen Senra, whose choreographic training was in the USA, was aided by the North American Carl Paris, who ended up living in Spain. A former dancer with Alvin Ailey, he was also an excellent teacher of the Graham technique and jazz, and the majority of contemporary Spanish dancers of the time passed through his classes.

In 1978, the Ballet Nacional de España was formed under the direction of Antonio Gades, based on indigenous dance forms. To complement this company, the Ballet Lírico Nacional was set up in 1979, led by Víctor Ullate, a dancer of solid background and a long-time member of Maurice Béjart's company Ballet du XXᵉ Siècle in Brussels. In 1983, the companies were unified for administrative purposes under the direction of María de Avila, although they continued performing independently.

The 1970s and 1980s were effervescent times, times of discovery. Courses, or *stages*, sprang up everywhere. In Palma de Mallorca, Anna Maleras and the critic and musician Delfín Colomé established the first *stage* devoted exclusively to new tendencies in contemporary dance. There was a great hunger to learn and compare styles and techniques. It was a period of tentative first steps, full of illusions, with projects often ending as mirages. Private dance studios abounded, a response to the tightly corseted programmes that remained in the official state-subsidized schools where it was only possible to study indigenous forms, ballet and traditional folk dance, markedly academic and conservative in contrast with the modern forms introduced by private schools – Graham, Nikolais, Horton, Cunningham and jazz techniques.

In 1981, the Madrid Festival of Dance was set up, and in 1983 the Autumn Festival, also in Madrid, an excellent shop window of what was on offer both at home and abroad. In 1986, the Madrid Choreography Competition was initiated (the work of a real choreographic activist, Laura Kumin), on whose honours list appeared the names of the best choreographers of recent years. A new festival was created in the same year, Madrid in Dance, with an explicit manifesto to provide 'a meeting place between dancers and spectators to celebrate together the resurgence of a dance which reflects the spirit of the end of the twentieth century and revitalizes public interest in the magic of dance'.

The 1980s were boom years, with frenetic activity giving rise to the growth of dance companies and groups everywhere, notably Vianants (Gracel Meneu, Valencia, founded in 1984), Bocanada (Maria José Ribot and Blanca Calvo, Madrid, founded in 1986) and 10 x 10 (Mónica Runde and Pedro Bedäyes, Madrid, founded in 1989). Felipe González's socialist government from 1982 substantially increased resources for cultural activities. In 1987, it adopted a coherent package of measures for dance that included a certain amount of legal regulation, created a national dance prize, included representatives of the choreographic world on the Music Council (the Dance Council was not set up until 1991), and established a system of two-year subsidy for companies that aided the development of choreography enormously, with companies receiving a substantial subsidy on the condition that they premièred a creative work each year and undertook to give a set number of performances.

Nevertheless, there was an ideological switch when, after again separating the two state companies in 1986, a year later the Ballet Lírico Nacional was entrusted to Russian ballerina Maya Plisetskaya, in contradiction to the modern aim that it previously had claimed. This situation changed in 1990 when Nacho Duato took charge of the company. Duato had returned to Spain after a long stay abroad, where he had been totally immersed in the Nederland Dans Theater style of ballet. With visible influences from Jiří Kylián and William Forsythe, he quickly marked a decisive artistic line and took the Compañía Nacional de Danza (as the company is now called) towards a coherence that, with its more contemporary style, had much to do with the country's modernity, adapting to the new circumstances and challenges of Spain in the 1990s. The company shone out in the great performances of 1992, at the Expo in Seville and the Olympic Games in Barcelona.

Those years of tentative first steps have now passed. Choreographers now work in a much more rigorous way, producing work of higher quality in a variety of personal and distinctive styles. A forum is the Centro Nacional de Nuevas Tendecias in Madrid, set up in 1986 and led by Guillermo Heras with critics Roger Salas and Delfín Colomé.

In Valencia, another important centre for modern choreography, Dansa València was set up in 1988 as a platform that brings together the whole Spanish sector in a festival each February, with excellent results. Ananda Dansa Company and the choreographer Vicente Sáez are two good examples of contemporary dance outside Catalonia, where it has been mainly concentrated. Also worth mentioning are the influence of Concha and José Laínez, with their Anxea group, in the Basque country; and, in the Canary Islands, an isolated but noteworthy region, the Ballet del Atlántico, which performs a varied repertory.

Spain now has a modern choreographic culture, which has been fought for tooth and nail, for while society changed dramatically after Franco's death, the old, staid structures took longer to be transformed. This performing art has been greedily devoured by a growing public, and is opening up to an ever-increasing audience.

Creativity in Catalonia: the independent groups

Within Spain, contemporary dance has developed most in Catalonia, for several reasons. First, its closeness to the centre of Europe, both geographically and artistically, means that it has always looked towards vanguard movements taking place outside Spain. Second, given that cultural and artistic life reflects economic conditions, Catalonia was favoured by its relative prosperity compared with other regions during the strong economic imbalances which marked Spain from the Civil War (1936–9) and through the following two decades.

There are other factors worth mentioning however: the performances by Diaghilev's Ballets Russes and by the Ballets and Ballets Russes de Monte Carlo, among other companies, at the Gran Teatre del Liceu in Barcelona during the inter-war period, as well as the acceptance of Dalcrozism, introduced by Juan Llongueras into Catalan society. Furthermore, the Catalan public was used to watching both ballet and indigenous dance forms, which were performed continuously, season after season, first at the Santa Creu Theatre (later named the Principal), and, from its inauguration in 1847, at the Liceu.

Dalcrozism was taught after the Spanish Civil War in the private studio of Joan Llongueras and in some other schools in Barcelona, which were no longer linked to the state system for political reasons, and instead supported by the Catalan bourgeoisie. In contrast, Joan Magriñà took the chair of the Institut del Teatre in 1944 and monopolized it, along with the Liceu and his private school in Petrixol Street, for nearly forty years.

The modernizing process, in which Catalonia always played a leading role, above all in Barcelona, was cut short by the tragedy of the Spanish Civil War, causing the country's economic and cultural regression. A normal rhythm would not be reestablished until the end of the 1970s, with the arrival of democracy, followed by a period of expansion in the 1980s and consolidation in the 1990s.

Independent contemporary dance groups began to proliferate in the 1970s, looking towards France primarily, but also towards Mudra in Belgium and the London Contemporary Dance School, and later towards New York. Initially, the institutional atmosphere dominated by Joan Magriñá yielded scant rewards, and it was at the private schools of Anna Maleras and Herman Bonnin (named as the head of the Institut del Teatre in 1970), both in Barcelona, that new techniques began to be introduced under the supervision of their guest teachers: Giancarlo Bellini from the José Limón Company, Gerard Collins from the Ballet de Marseilles, Gilberto Ruíz Lang from the London Contemporary Dance School, and the two Spanish teachers, Concha and José Laínez, who had trained in The Netherlands. The end of the 1970s also saw Anna Maleras's summer *stages*, to which were later added those organized by the Timbal school. These brought together dancers from other parts of Spain, as well as actors and mime artists, the latter always being well received in Catalonia, right up to the present day.

In 1977, the first example of initially independently funded dance was formally presented, I Mostra de Dansa Independent, also organized by the duo Anna Maleras and Herman Bonnin. With them came Acord, La Gran Compañía, Empar Roselló, Estudi Anna Maleras, Cesc and Toni Gelabert, Anexa, and the Ballet Contemporani de Barcelona, founded in 1974 by Ramón Soler. Another important date was 1979, when seven women founded Heura: Avelina Argüelles, Remei Berderí, Elisa Huertas, Alícia Pérez-Cabrero, Lola Puentes, Isabel Ribas and Carme Vidal, later joined by Angels Margarit. It was in this year that the first international prizes were won: *Laberint*, by Huertas, Pérez-Cabrero and Ribas, won in Bagnolet; and at the Nyons Festival, Avelina Argüelles won with *Absencia* and Isabel Ribas with *Com et dius nena*.

During the 1980s, with democracy re-established, various factors caused the proliferation of independent contemporary dance groups in Catalonia. In 1980, the Department of Contemporary Dance was set up at the Institut del Teatre, unique in the Spanish state. Then, in 1981, La Fábrica was founded by Toni Gelabert and Norma Axenfeldt, a private school which became a Mecca for dancers and teachers from across the world, offering a very avant-garde programme with new forms of teaching – Cunningham and alternative technique, contact improvisation – and choreographic workshops. This produced a great creative fever, and from La Fábrica came such artists and companies as Cesc Gelabert, Juan Carlos García, Danat Dansa, Margarita Guergé, Ramón Oller, Francesc Bravo, María Muñoz, Vicente Saez and others.

Alongside this, in 1983, the Dance Sub-Department in the Department of Culture of the Generalitat de Catalunya was created to award grants, help out with travel costs and programme dance in theatres, all with the aim of financing individual initiatives by independent groups. Also in 1983 the City Council opened the Mercat de les Flors Theatre, and in 1987 the Espacio B at the same theatre, which, under the direction of Andreu Morte, began to co-produce with the biggest companies from Spain and abroad.

All this activity resulted in the formation of a large number of independent contemporary dance groups, above all in Barcelona, whose work was considered original and energetic, and who began to attract international interest and to tour abroad. In the 1980s and 1990s, contemporary dance has been the most exported form of the performing arts, competing with the most avant-garde theatre groups such as Els Comediants and La Fura dels Baus.

One must also add the biennial video-dance shows initiated from 1985 under the leadership of Elisa Huertas, along with the setting up of a professional association of dance, Associació de professionals de la dansa de Catalunya in 1987, which would later reach out across the whole country, all of which contributed towards the organization and diffusion of a little-known art form. The programme for El Grec Summer Festival has also gradually increased its dance content, offering work from both home and abroad, all the while maintaining a high level of quality.

This ideal situation seemed to have reached its zenith by the 1992 Olympic Games, where contemporary dance also had its role to play in the ceremonies. During the 1990s, local choreographers have turned towards the rest of Europe, moving to other countries in search of assistance, where they are treated better, while at home economic cutbacks have restricted the growth that took place in the 1980s. The short-term programming policy does not seem to favour the situation either.

1998, however, seems to mark a change in this process: under the direction of Xavier Albertí, nineteen dance performances and five co-productions (with Mudances, Lanonima Imperial, Mal Pelo, Gelabert-Azzopardi and Sol Picó) were performed at El Grec Summer Festival. Furthermore, the immediate future does bring some good news: IT Dansa has been set up, the young company of the Institut del Teatre led by Catherine Allard, and there are plans to perform dance in the new Liceu Theatre, burnt down in 1994 and reopened in the 1999–2000 season with its own company, to be directed by one of the leading Spanish ballet teachers. There are also plans for a small-scale company at the Teatre Lliure, led by Cesc Gelabert, later to be based in the Ciutat del Teatre, a new centre to be opened in 2000 led by Lluís Pasqual, entrusted to the post by the city council and its former mayor, Pascual Maragall. Here, dance will be given pride of place, with the involvement of the new Institut del Teatre, the new Teatre Lliure and the new Mercat de les Flors. Also worth mentioning is the Education Department's 1997 initiative in incorporating dance studies as part of the general studies at the Aula Oriol Martorell, a music and dance school for primary-age children.

Spanish Dance and Flamenco: Each with Something Special to Say

The term 'Spanish dance' is at best confusing, and certainly inexact. What is Spanish dance? Flamenco, folk dance, the *escuela bolera* or theatrical dance? The answer is simple: all of them. But Spanish dance is commonly seen, not just outside Spain but also within it, as Spanish theatrical dance; that is, the bringing together into one dance work by a choreographer of elements from folk dance, the *escuela bolera* and flamenco. Below we outline, section by section, these constituents that make up Spanish dance.

Folk dance

Folk dance in Spain can be divided into two historical periods, separated by the Civil War. Before 1936, folk dance was conserved in villages as a popular tradition. After the Civil War, the Sección Femenina of the one political party that existed under Franco's dictatorship (The Spanish Falange) decided to commission the women of the Coros y Danzas (a department of the Music Division) to compile information about folk dance. None of the women who worked in dance, music and regional costume had any training in these areas; they were not specialists, but ordinary citizens. The hidden intention behind this recuperation of folk culture was to promote an idea of unity in a politically and socially divided country, through such nationalist acts as the recuperation of traditions involving music and dance.

The Feminine Division's Choruses and Dances worked on this project for forty years (1937–77). This long period meant that the Choruses and Dances put their stamp on the development of dance in Spain. Since its presence was spread out across the whole of the national area (in 1960 it comprised 24,000 members in 1,600 groups), most dance professionals in Spain at present have had some form of direct or indirect contact with the Choruses and Dances. Some dance professionals had come from these groups themselves, whereas others adapted folk dance performance, and sometimes individual members of the Choruses and Dances were employed by the state for propaganda purposes.

The Choruses and Dances have done an important job within folk culture in Spain in terms of presenting and participating in Spanish cultural life, as well as taking it abroad. What is still not known exactly is how adequate it was in conserving folk culture, as practical problems prevailed over the intentions of the political leaders. These difficulties can be reduced to two major ones: a lack of capable personnel in the milieu loyal to the regime belonging to the Choruses and Dances to do the necessary research to compile reliable information, and the shortfall between the designated funds and the ambitious aims set out by the political leadership. In short, the problem of living up to requirements on very tight resources.

One should also mention that in some regions such as Catalonia, Galicia and the Basque country, folk dance groups were formed in opposition groups to the Franco regime, for example the Rey de Viana in Galicia, and the Verdaguer and Rubí *esbarts* groups in Catalonia.

The escuela bolera

The *escuela bolera* represents Spanish classical dance teaching. First encountered in the eighteenth century, and spreading around the world in the nineteenth, it is a mixture of folk dance and classical ballet, characterized by distinctive Spanish movements of the arms and torso, with steps and leaps linked to academic dance. In the second half of this century the *escuela bolera* has been run, taught, and performed by the Pericet family, keepers of traditional knowledge on the subject throughout the century. In 1942, Angel Pericet Carmona (1877–1944) and his son Angel Pericet Jiménez (1899–1973) wrote and compiled the first manual on the different courses that should be included in *escuela bolera* teaching. Today, the school is led by another member of the family, Angel Pericet Blanco.

The Choruses and Dances have influenced and been influenced by the *escuela bolera*, and have used its repertory, with steps and dances from the *escuela bolera* described as 'typical' steps and folk dances from Madrid and Andalusia in existing documents about them. These went on to be danced at folk festivals as 'traditional' Spanish dances.

In the 1960s, dancers started to be concerned about technique, a concern that reached its high point in the 1980s, and directly influenced the *escuela bolera*. The school gradually changed to represent ballet technique, which became not just a fundamental skill or a muscular training but a style to which the *escuela bolera* had to adapt, resulting in important changes to the school's own style. All this, together with the pro-Andalusia movement that has survived from the beginning of the century to this very day, has meant that the *escuela bolera* has been considerably enriched and transformed.

Spanish dance

The creation of a Ballet Nacional de España in 1978, financed by the state, was a turning point for Spanish dance. Most of the good Spanish dance performers entered the new Ballet Nacional, which offered them a measure of security they had not had with their own companies; but it also had direct repercussions on the small Spanish dance companies at that time. Furthermore, the best choreographers of the time were called upon to create or restage their works for the Ballet Nacional. The first director of the company was Antonio Gades whose aims are summarized in his much-repeated sentence, 'The Ballet Nacional should be an institution, not a show'. He did not get what he wanted, and in 1980 was substituted by Antonio, who remained in charge for three years and left an impressive repertoire of works – some his own, like *El Sombrero de Tres Picos or El Amor Brujo*, as well as others, such as *Retratos de Mujer* by Rafael Aguilar. Then, in 1983, María de Avila took over the Ballet Nacional along with the Ballet Lírico Nacional. It was under her direction that José Granero's *Medea* was staged in 1984, one of the most important choreographic works in Spanish dance of the last part of the century. In 1987, José Antonio (not to be confused with the famous Antonio) was appointed director, and in 1993 the Ministry of Culture named as collegiate directors Aurora Pons, Nana Lorca and Victoria Eugenia, who continue as such at present.

It is difficult to talk about Spanish theatrical dance companies since the creation of the Ballet Nacional: few stand out for their quality and creativity, apart from the

Spanish Ballet in Madrid, under the direction of José Granero. This company brought together former members of the independent group founded by Antonio Gades when he stopped directing the Ballet Nacional. José Granero, as director and choreographer, stated that his aim was to 'offer an authentic Spanish dance show, without losing its essence, but with new forms of movement'. Perhaps because his choreographic ideas were so advanced, they did not manage to connect with the public, and unfortunately for Spanish contemporary dance, they disappeared too soon. His language was a mixture of contemporary and Spanish dance, and he introduced modern musicians and composers as well as a more personalized and creative form of choreography. At present, there are several Spanish dance companies, such as those of Antonio Márquez or José Antonio, which are fighting to survive artistically and economically.

Flamenco

Flamenco first took to the stage as a performing art at the beginning of this century, and its name alone evokes Andalusia. For years it has been presented as genuinely Spanish, riding horseback between the exotic and the popular, between the touristic and the intellectual, undefined in the heart of a Spain that was recovering from a civil war which had split national feelings into two contrasting factions. Flamenco has always been a public experience, whether in the theatre, *peña* (club) or private party. Flamenco faithfully reflects the idiosyncrasies of Andalusian culture, where the human being is always the protagonist.

After three years of civil war which left the country destroyed, flamenco succumbed to the nationalistic folkloric dicates of Franco, and became, alongside folklore, a propaganda element of the first magnitude before the rest of the world, and during this time it is impossible to decide, in the words of Gerhard Steingress, whether flamenco was a 'product of a Hispanicized Andalusian culture or of a Spanish culture replaced by Andalusian'.[1]

After the Civil War, with the traditional flamenco refuges exhausted – the *cafés cantantes* (traditional taverns) – and with the wretched era of the 'flamenco opera' that emerged between the two world wars now dead, a popular echo of flamenco song and dance found a place in the Spanish song and variety shows which proliferated in the 1940s and 1950s, being exhibited all over the country in all kinds of settings. This was due to the fact that during the Second World War many international artists came to Spain, then a neutral country, thus 'internationalizing' many aspects of cultural life. These included former artists from Diaghilev's Ballets Russes, who toured Spain, taking advantage of the fact that Spain was not involved in the battle that was raging across the rest of Europe.

During the same period, however, certain stars arose in the flamenco dance world, slowly lighting up the flamenco scene and increasing the historic importance of this unique art form. The art spread its influence from traditional taverns and streets to official theatres, where it gained a real and responsive audience.

Flamenco has developed enormously since the 1920s, largely through a complete break with traditional ways of dancing, as popular inspiration gave way to an intellectual focus on creativity; additionally, it has been subject to major influences from the outside world.

One figure is essential in understanding this phenomenon: Antonia Mercé, 'La Argentina', who flourished during the era of choreographic creativity during the 1920s and 1930s. Mercé was the major star of this new style of flamenco, although her career developed mostly abroad. In her company, Mercé took with her professional flamenco dancers such as Faíco, María la Bella, María la Flamenca, bringing together traditional flamenco dancing with new choreographic tendencies. Antonia Mercé 'La Argentina' died in Bayonne (France) in 1936.

After 'La Argentina', flamenco dancing grew through figures such as Vicente Escudero, who broke all traditional norms in conceiving flamenco from the scenic point of view of sculpture or painting, introducing new influences from avant-garde art movements. Creator of the *seguiriya gitana* (a particular way of flamenco singing), performed for the first time in Madrid in 1940, nobody had previously dared to dance this *palo* of *cante negro*.[2] Inspired by such legendary figures as Lamparilla, El Raspao, or Miracielo, his art, due to its popularity, was pioneering in flamenco history this century. His teaching work enhanced his long career until his death in 1980.

At the same time, another very important figure arrived on the scene, Encarnación López 'La Argentinita'. Creator of such works as *Las Calles de Cádiz* and *Navidad en Jerez*, in which flamenco street artists were incorporated into dramatized shows, she ultimately passed at the peak of her creative form in New York in 1945. She left her legacy and teachings to her sister Pilar, who became one of the most important figures in Spanish dance this century. A woman of unique elegance in her dancing, she brought into her creations the choreographic teachings of her sister Encarnación. Surrounded by intellectuals and influenced by already deceased friends such as Federico García Lorca and Manual de Falla, and with staging and theatrical advice from the writer Edgar Neville, Pilar López produced a generation of flamenco dancers from her company, including Alejandro Vega, Roberto Ximénez, Manolo Vargas, José Greco, and later Güito, Antonio Gades and Mario Maya. All of these became flamenco stars in their own right, and followed what has come to be known as *escuela de Pilar López*.

Two other historic figures must be pointed out: Carmen Amaya (1913–63) and Antonio (born 1922). Amaya was a woman of enormous popular influence who left her mark on a whole era, her strength and performance much imitated by some female flamenco dancers. She revived dancing in *traje de corto* (in trousers), and was unsurpassed at *zapateado* (heel-tapping).

Antonio Ruiz Soler, 'Antonio', was also a landmark in Spanish dance history. Born in Seville, this unique artist was both a classical and flamenco dancer who trained in the best Seville academies in the 1930s with Otero, Enrique el Cojo and Pericet. He started performing alongside the flamenco dancer Rosario, and later created his own company. His career can be divided into two essential parts, the first influenced by more traditional flamenco, the second as a more classical dancer.

His numerous choreographic works dealt with Spanish themes, and include *Sacromonte, Malagueñas y Sevilla, Café de Chinitas, Zapateado, El Amor Brujo* and *El Sombrero de Tres Picos,* among many others. He choreographed dance with *martinete* (Andalusian gypsy song performed without guitar accompaniment) for the first time, and performed it in the film *Duende y Misterio de Flamenco* directed by Edgar Neville in 1952.

In the 1960s, the tourist boom in Spain exacerbated the 'stereotypical'. Even though *tablaos* (*aficionados* bars) had appeared when the *cafés cantantes* disappeared, the real explosion in flamenco occurred when it was discovered to be excellent for tourist business. From the 1960s to the 1980s, shows at the *tablaos* proliferated and many artists were welcomed there, as they were in hotel and holiday centres on the coast.

Yet the influence of these places has not always been negative despite the histrionic image many of them have given to flamenco. Worth mentioning are *tablaos* such as El Guajiro in Seville, which has produced the exceptional Manuela Vargas, as well as one of the best trios to have emerged in flamenco, with Matilde Coral, Rafael 'El Negro' and Farruco. In Madrid, artists like Rosa Durán, 'La Chunga', 'La Tati' and Curro Vélez, among many others, were also *tablao* figures.

In the 1980s, the *tablaos* started to decline, and now only some retain their essence, in Madrid, Seville and Barcelona. Meanwhile, other prominent figures developed their choreographic work, including Antonio Gades, José Granero, Mario Maya, Manolete, Manolo Marín, Cristina Hoyos and Rafael Aguilar. Also worthy of mention is their involvement in Carlos Saura's film trilogy, working with Antonio Gades in *Bodas de Sangre, Carmen* and *El Amor Brujo,* and later, with other artists in *Sevillanas,* giving an image of high-quality flamenco, in contrast to the flamenco performed for tourists at coastal resorts and on cruises.

In the 1990s, flamenco has regained its sense of spectacle in harmony with other dramatic and plastic arts through young artists inspired by their predecessors. Flamenco singing has already become rooted in youth culture, mainly through flamenco-fusion and figures such as Camarón de la Isla who has popularized flamenco and taken it out of the traditional festivals; and flamenco dance too is becoming a major public attraction, filling big theatres once again. Several artists and originators stand out in the present decade, such as Antonio Canales and Joaquín Cortés, both stars of a boom that has once again developed romantic idols, as at the beginning of the century, but bringing with them the glamour of this new era.

Also developing their work, away from the masses but with a quality worthy of the best schools, are such dancers and choreographers as Javier Barón, Javier Latorre, María Pagés, Ana María Bueno, Belén Maya and Carmen Cortés, stars of a new generation who are erupting powerfully onto the flamenco scene, reviving on the one hand the stylistic essence of *cante negro,* and on the other the dramatic and scenic staging of flamenco as theatrical dance. Although the fusion of pure flamenco with other avant-garde and modern aesthetics does not always come off successfully, according to the purists, it is nevertheless unquestionable that flamenco has made great progress in both stage direction and composition in recent years. We are experiencing today, as in 1924 when Antonia Mercé created the first Spanish ballet, the unstoppable development of flamenco, with new and better techniques, and with training which is even more intense than in previous eras, if that is possible.

Conclusion

In conclusion, we can say that in Spain there are two distinct groups of dance: one indigenous, including flamenco, the *escuela bolera* and the less-defined 'Spanish dance', the second, more international, comprising ballet – both classical and modern – and contemporary dance. We can also add folk dance and traditional dance as being somewhere between the two other groups, able to enrich both the authentic dance forms and contemporary dance.

Regional imbalances have also influenced the development of dance in Spain, although at the end of the twentieth century many things have changed since the end of the Spanish Civil War, influenced by the democratization of the country, its laws and institutions. Despite this, Barcelona continues to be the centre for contemporary dance, followed by Valencia; Madrid is the ballet centre, followed by Zaragoza; the *escuela bolera* remains confined to the Pericet family and to some official schools where it has become part of the syllabus; and flamenco is still associated with Andalusia, although to some extent it has spread through the peninsula through cultural centres set up in the big cities, a direct result of the mass immigration from the south to industrial cities during the 1950s and 1960s. We hope that the future will bring a healthy mix of all these strands, without losing their identities, while at the same time remain open to creative developments.

Notes

1 Steingress, Gerhard (1994) *Sociología del Cante Flamenco*, Jerez de la Frontera (Cádiz): Centro Andaluz de Flamenco.
2 *Diccionario Enciclopédico Ilustrado del Flamenco* (1988) Blas Vegas, J. *et al.*, Seville: Cinterco.

Key Texts

Alier, R. and Mata, F. X. (1991) *El Gran Teatro del Liceu: Historia Artística*, Barcelona: Edicions Frances X. Mata.
Anuari 1947–1997 del Gran Teatre del Liceu, Barcelona: Amics del Liceu-Ambit Serveis Editorials.
Avila, R. *et al.* (1988) *Dansa: Noves Tendències de la Coreografia Catalana*, Barcelona: Ambit Serveis Editorials.
Blas Vega, J. *et al.* (1988) *Enciclopedia del Flamenco*, Seville: Cinterco.

Carrasco, M., Casero, E., Colomé, D. and Monés, N. (1995) 'Russian Soul and Spanish Blood: Nationalism as a Construct in the Historiography of Dance in Spain', *Proceedings of the Society of Dance History Scholars*. pp. 249–86.

El de Triana, F. (1986) *Arte y Artistas Flamencos*, Seville: Editoriales Andaluzas Unidas y Bienal de Arte Flamenco.

Gasch, S. (1946) *De la danza*, Barcelona: Barna.

Llorens, P., *et al.* [n.d.] *História de la Dansa a Catalunya*. Barcelona: Caixa de Barcelona.

Muñoz, J. (1997) 'Nacho Duato, Cesc Gelabert, Víctor Ullate and Ramon Oller', in (eds) N. Monés and M. Carrasco *Dansart*, 0, Barcelona: Los Libros de Danza.

Otero, J. (1912) *Tratado de Bailes*, Seville: Tip. de la Guía Oficial.

Puig, A. (1944) *Ballet y Baile Español*, Barcelona: Montaner y Simon.

Table 8 Important dance and political events in Spain (1900 to present)

Year	Dance: artists, works, events	Dance: institutions	Arts scene	Sociocultural and political events
1900		Pauleta Pamies teacher at Liceu School		Monarchy
1903	Joan Magriña born		*Soledades* (Machado)	
1904			Echegarray Nobel Prize for Literature	
1905	La Argentina performs in Madrid			
1906			*Glosari* (d'Ors)	
1907	Vicente Escudero débuts in Madrid taverns		Institut d'Estudis Catalans	
1908	Tórtola Valencia with La Argentina in Barcelona		*Romance de Lobos* (Valle-Inclán)	Electoral victory of Lerroux
1909			Albéniz dies	'Setmana trágica' in Barcelona
				Ferran-Guardia executed
1910			Residencia de Estudiantes	Canalejas president of government
1911	Llongueras studies in Hellerau, Germany		Magiña dies	
1912	Pastora Imperio in Madrid	*Tratado de Bailes* (Otero)		Canalejas assassinated
1913		Institut Catalá de rítmica i plástica		
1914	Carmen Amaya born		*La Vida Breve* (de Falla)	Mancommunita de Catalunya
				Neutrality in First World War
1915			*El Amor Brujo* (de Falla)	
			Goyescas (Granados)	
1917			Picasso and Olga Kokhlova move to Barcelona	

Table 8 continued

Year	Dance: artists, works, events	Dance: institutions	Arts scene	Sociocultural and political events
1918		Course in rhythm therapy (Llongueras)	Institut Escuela	Government of Maura/Cambó
1919		*Le Tricorne* performed in Madrid, produced by Diaghilev *Ballets Russes		
1920			*Divinas Palabras, Luces de Bohemia* (Valle-Inclán)	War with Morocco PSOE Congress Communist Party of Spain founded
1921	'Antonio' born *El Corregidor y la Molinera* premières in Madrid, produced by Diaghilev's Ballets Russes at the Teatro Real Madrid			
1922			Concurso de Cante Jondo Benavente Nobel Prize for Literature	
1923			Fundació Bernat Metge	Dictatorship of Primo de Rivera *Coup d'état* by Primo de Rivera Trade Union leader Salvador Seguí assassinated Clandestine Assembly of CNT in Catalonia
1925			Rafael Alberti Nobel Prize for Literature	
1927	Last performance of Tórtola Valencia in Madrid and Barcelona		*Mariana Pineda* (Lorca) University reform *Manifest Groc* (Dalí)	

Table 8 continued

	Dance	Arts / Literature	Politics / History
1928	First ballet flamenco company, led by La Argentina		
1930	*Avant-garde Dances* (Escudero) Pavlova performs in Barcelona	GATEPAC artists association Law to promote education system	CNT legalized San Sebastian Pact
1931			Second Republic. Constitution, inspired by Weimar Republic
1932	La Argentinita débuts in Madrid	Teatro Univeristario: *La Barraca* led by Lorca *Laia* (Espriu) ADLAN (friends of new arts)	Statutes of Catalonia passed
1933	*El Amor Brujo* with La Argentinita (also 1934)	*Bodas de Sangre* (Lorca) *Tierra Sin Pan* (Buñuel)	'The two dark years'. Anarchist movements Women vote for the first time CEDA and Phalangist movement formed Government of Lerroux and CEDA
1934		*Yerma* (Lorca)	Republican Left formed General strike, peasant strike, general repression
1935	Matilde Coral, dancer and teacher, born Coros y Danzas de la sección femenina	Valle-Inclán and Machado join World Writers Committee Baroja joins Academia Española First surrealist art exhibition	Franco Head of Central State Organization Beginnings of organized underground movement
1936	Antonio Gades born La Argentina dies Amaya and Imperio in film, *Maria de la O*	Lorca executed	Civil War Franco's insurrection

Table 8 continued

Year	Dance: artists, works, events	Dance: institutions	Arts scene	Sociocultural and political events
1938			Machado dies in exile Francoist control of entire mass media	
1939				End of Civil War Franco's dictatorship Neutrality in Second World War
1940		Escudero triumphs in Madrid		State Unions created
1941		First contest of Coros y Danzas		INI (State Industry Board) created
1942		Pericet's Bolero School Handbook published	Miguel Hernández dies in prison	
1944			*Bulletin of the Union of Spanish Intellectuals* published in Paris	
1945	La Argentinita dies in New York			
1946		Pilar López presents ballets	De Falla dies in exile	France closes border with Spain
1947	*Tristan Fou*, Monte Carlo Ballet (Barcelona)			
1948			*Dove of Peace* (Picasso)	Border with France reopened
1949		'Seville kids' Antonio and Rosario in Madrid		
1950		Joan Magriña founded Ballets de Barcelona		
1951				Strikes in Barcelona and Basque Country
1952	*Duende y Mistério de Flamenco* (film, dir. Edgar Neville)	Antonio creates his own company		Spain joins UNESCO

Table 8 continued

1953	Juan Llongueras dies, Barcelona	Rosario founds Ballet de Arte Español	*Bienvenido Mr Marshall* (Berlanga and Bardén)	American aid affects Spanish economy
1954	*El Madarí Meravellós* (Juan Tena)			
1955			Ortega y Gasset dies	Spain joins UN
1956			Juan Ramón Jiménez wins Nobel Prize Baroja dies	Student unrest and strikes
1957	Royal Ballet in Barcelona			Technocrats in power
1958				Spain joins IMF and World Bank
1959	New York City Ballet in Barcelona			Spain enters OECE Stability plan End of autocracy
1960	*Alegre de Concerto* (Juan Tena)		*La Pell de Brau* (Espriu) *Un Millón de Muertos* (Gironella)	Emigration, tourism and foreign investment boost economy
1962	*Escenas Románticas* (Juan Tena)			Strikes and demonstrations
1963	*Los Tarantos*, with Carmen Amaya and Antonio Gades (film, dir. Rovira Beleta) Amaya dies in Begur (Girona)		*El Verdugo* (Berlanga)	1st Development Plan Julián Grimau executed
1965				Government expels Galván, Araguren and Calvo from university Escarré, Abat of Montserrat, exiled
1966	Margot Fonteyn performs in Barcelona			New Press and Information Law Barcelona University closed Organic State Law

Table 8 continued

Year	Dance: artists, works, events	Dance: institutions	Arts scene	Sociocultural and political events
1967		Anna Maleras founds Estudi		
1968			Sitges Teatre Internacional	Strikes and demonstrations Martial Law imposed across Spain
1969	Ballet Nacional de Cuba in Barcelona (directed by Alicia Alonso)		*Tristana* (Buñuel) Menéndez Pidal dies	MATESA scandal New technocrat government
1970				The Cortes declares Juan Carlos successor to Head of State as King General Law of Education PSOE Congress, Felipe González leads
1971			*Luces de Bohemia* (Valle-Inclán, staged Tamayo)	
1972	Kirov Ballet in Barcelona Nureyev performs in Barcelona	Maleras's Grup Estudi opens		
1973	Béjart in Barcelona Angel Pericet Jiménez dies *Acció O* (Gelabert)	The Laínez ANEXA give classes at Institut del Teatre	Picasso and Pau Casals die	New Government: Blanco and Navarro Blanco killed in bomb attack
1974		Ballet Contemporani de Barcelona	*La Prima Angélica* (Saura)	Anarchist Puig Antich executed by Franco Regime gets tougher
1975	*Bodas de Sangre* (Gades, with Hoyos)			Franco dies Juan Carlos King of Spain

Table 8 continued

1976		First summer *stage* organized by Maleras in Majorca	Greek Theatre Festival in Barcelona	
1977		First 'Independent Dance Show' in Barcelona; Coros y Danzas closed down	Teatre Lliure (Puigserver)	General elections; TOP (repressive state machine) dissolved; National Law Courts established; Five labour lawyers assassinated; President Tarradelles returns from exile
1978	Imperio dies	Ballet Nacional de España		Constitution democracy
1979	Cullberg Ballet in Barcelona	Ballet Nacional de Ballet Clásico; Creation of Heura Prize; Avelina Argüelles triumphs in Nyons; *Dansa 79*	*La Fura dels Baus* (Morte)	Statute of Autonomy in Catalonia
1980	Escudero dies	Contemporary Dance Dept at the Institut del Teatre; Biennial Flamenco Festival formed		Elections for the Generalitat de Catalunya
1981	*Bodas de Sangre* (dir. Saura, first of flamenco trilogy, with Gades)	La Fábrica; Dance Festival of Madrid	Tàrrega Theatre Fair	Attempted state *coup*
1982			Mercat de les Flors	PSOE socialist government (González)
1983	De Avila directs both national companies; Culture Dept of the Generalitat creates Dance Sub-department		Theatre Festival of Sitges; Tàrrega Fair; International Itálica Festival; Madrid *movida* boosts contemporary dance groups	

Table 8 continued

Year	Dance: artists, works, events	Dance: institutions	Arts scene	Sociocultural and political events
1984	*Medea* (Granero)	Vianants El Ballet Español de Madrid Danat Dansa Mudances		
1985		Metros Trànsit		Spain enters EEC
1986		Gelabert-Azzopardi Lanómina Imperial		Spain enters NATO
1987		Generalitat awards grants to independent groups The national companies separate again Nats Nuts	Espai B at Mercat de les Flors Ciutat de Barcelona prize of Stage Art	
1988		1st Valencia Dance Festival		General Strike
1989	*Sueños Flamencos* (Hoyos)	10 + 10 Mal Pelo	Auditorium of Madrid IVAM museum, Valencia	Spain has Presidency of EEC The Social Charter
1990		National classical company becomes contemporary Compañia Nacional de Danza under Nacho Duato	Reina Sofía Musuem, (Madrid)	LOGSE (Education Act)
1991		Búbulus	Teatro de la Maestanza, Seville	Maastricht Conference
1992		L'Espai de Dansa opened, Barcelona	Olympic Games, Barcelona EXPO, Seville Madrid Cultural Capital of Europe	
1993		Pons, Lorca and Eugenia direct Ballet Nacional de España		Early General Election

Table 8 continued

Year			
1994			Teatre del Liceu burns down CCCB (contemporary museum, Barcelona)
1995	Joan Magriña dies Antonio dies	Cairón	
1996		La Caldera founded in Barcelona Ballet de la Communidad de Madrid (Ullate) La Porta	Partido Popular government (Aznar)
1997		Dansart	
1998	Ramón Soler dies	Aída Gómez directs Ballet Nacional Taula Activa de Companyies de Dansa de Catalunya IT – Dansa Centro Coreográphico de la Comunidad Valenciana	
1999		Liceu reopened Compañía Nacional de Danza Junîor	

*First visit

9

SWEDEN

Equal rights to dance?

Lena Hammergren

It is a winter evening in downtown Stockholm in 1992, and people are waiting to be let into the Modern Dance Theatre, a venue dedicated to contemporary dance and experimental performance. The performance they have come to see is part of the theatre's annual celebration of the winter solstice. When the audience members are let in from the cold, they are allowed to go on stage, where they are met by something resembling an enormous, rectangular cardboard box, its sides covered with peepholes. In order to see the performance, the spectators are forced to kneel or sit on the stage floor to see through the small openings. Through wide-angle lenses, they see seven women in long white gowns, huddled together on lengths of white fabric. The dancers rise slowly and begin to move in sequences taken from the classical ballet *The Sleeping Beauty*, but executed in reverse order.

The audience's experience of the dance is unusual. The wide-angle lenses lend a sense of distance and space while the construction of the cardboard box as the theatre stage invites laughter. The spectators are made aware of their neighbours, with whom they must jostle for the best viewing spots, and of their own bodies, which they must ceaselessly hold in uncomfortable positions so that they do not miss what is happening behind the walls of the box. Because everything is played out on-stage, the spectators also become actors; many of them take the opportunity to study eagerly the behaviour of other members of the audience from the vantage point of comfortable chairs in the auditorium.

This performance was given only once and was seen by about 200 people, many of whom were themselves professionally involved in the Swedish dance and art communities. In the light of the exclusivity of the performance, it could well be considered odd to use it to illuminate the situation of the art of dance in Sweden. Actually, it provides a felicitous point of departure for a description of twentieth-century dance from both aesthetic and cultural–political perspectives.

The title of the work was *A Winter's Dream*. It came about through the collaboration of two independent performance artists, Bogdan Szyber and Carina Reich, and dancers from the Royal Swedish Ballet. The performance was part of a working project, the purpose of which was to allow artists from different dance environments to meet and thus to bridge the gap between state-subsidized dance institutions and freelance dance artists. The latter group receives less subsidy, less regularly. However, the aesthetic and ideological message of the work was not about the harmonious melding of these disparate dance worlds. Rather, the message was formulated as an ironic comment on the conventions that have constituted the basis for dance and the dance experience throughout the history of western dance since the Renaissance.

The dancers were perceived as being confined by aesthetic conventions, thereby destroying the illusion of magnificence and space imparted by the conventional theatre stage; the allusion to 'the Beauty' is lost in torpor. The performance also emphasized the spectators as voyeurs in the literal sense. The classical ballerinas, virtuosi of their art, were transformed into mechanical music-box figurines, their avenues of expression wholly controlled by the need of the audience to see better or simply to stretch their legs, an ideal of consumption worthy of modern Swedish political and economical development.

A number of important factors meaningful to the history of twentieth-century Swedish dance can be differentiated in *A Winter's Dream*. One is the renaissance of classical ballet; another is the flowering of modern dance and independent, non-institutional dance; and a third is the confluence between these ideals of dance. Furthermore, the production was influenced by a theatricality that is a distinguishing feature of Swedish contemporary dance. Finally, it exemplifies the cultural politics of its day and reveals the strengths of the cultural ideology as well as its weaknesses.

The Renaissance of Ballet

In Sweden, the 1950s is frequently referred to as the 'renaissance of classical ballet'. This analysis of Swedish dance history is founded upon the successful improvement of technique by the Royal Swedish Ballet at the end of the 1940s, achieved with the help of foreign teachers and choreographers. Furthermore, the company changed the repertoire policy that had been advocated throughout the opening decades of the twentieth century to become directed towards performing the classical ballets in their entirety, rather than just selected scenes. The first was *The Sleeping Beauty* in 1942 (compare Szyber's and Reich's choice of ballet), but it was not until 1950 that full-evening ballets became more frequent. Antony Tudor, who was engaged as artistic director, staged *Giselle* in 1950. This was followed by *Swan Lake* (1953), under the direction of Mary Skeaping, who succeeded Tudor as artistic director. The ballet was a great success with the public, thereby cementing the position of dance as of equal status to the opera repertoire.

The rebirth and rise of dance was furthered by tours during which the Royal Swedish Ballet presented short selections from the classical repertoire on stages large and small across Sweden, and by the production, in the 1950s, of a series of pedagogical demonstrations designed especially to be shown at schools. Both were part of a drive to take the ballet to 'the people', an educational programme that may be compared with the English Ballet for All group, a project organised by the Royal Ballet in London in which Mary Skeaping was also involved.

The characterisation of the earlier years of the twentieth century as a period of decline for the development of the Royal Swedish Ballet is germane to this historical description. Around the turn of the century, a succession of German ballet-masters were appointed, all of whom are regarded as relatively unimportant to the development of the ballet. However, under their leadership important changes occurred within the company. Several boys were accepted to the ballet school and, by 1902, the first of them had achieved the rank of 'principal student' and could thus complement the ballet-masters, who had been essentially the only male dancers in the ensemble during the late nineteenth century. Thereby was laid a part of the foundation which eventually allowed the staging of items from the classical ballet repertoire in their entirety.

Yet another aspect which serves to distinguish the 1950s as the renaissance of the ballet was the concentration on revue dances during the 1930s and 1940s, which was later considered to have corrupted the classical ideal. Naturally, this perception is founded upon the strict division between so-called high culture and popular culture. However, such distinctions were not imposed at the time, and crossing the borders between genres was common. Many of the classical ballets performed at the opera during these decades bore traces of the visually lavish set decoration and costuming of the revue culture, and several of the Royal Swedish Ballet's dancers and choreographers also worked in revues. This expanded the previously narrow labour market for the artists and thus created what was, for Sweden, an unusually flexible situation for the art of dance.

The specific mix of revue and classical ballet disappeared increasingly after the Second World War. When Tudor was appointed in 1949, the opera house was instead prepared to stage, beyond the classical ballets, dramatic works that incorporated modern and classical technique. Such works included Tudor's own *Lilac Garden* (1936, Swedish première 1949) and Birgit Cullberg's *Miss Julie* (1950), based upon the Strindberg drama. The glorious days of the theatrical revue ballet were over, to be replaced by revue dance presented on film, made by Swedish as well as American film directors. Cinema was to be the next great popular Swedish form of entertainment.

Regional ballet companies

The history of the Royal Swedish Ballet dates from the eighteenth century; complementary regional ballet ensembles were not formed until the first half of the twentieth century. The Gothenburg Opera was founded in 1920, presenting ballet primarily as part of operettas and operas. It was not until the end of the 1960s that dance was afforded a more clearly limned profile within the theatre's repertoire. The truly significant public success came when Ulf Gadd began as artistic director in 1976. He was educated at the Gothenburg Opera Ballet School and was therefore well acquainted with the history of the theatre. He sharply criticized the tradition of consigning classically trained dancers to roles as extras in operettas. Gadd created a series of ballets of emphatically theatrical character and also made reinterpretations of classical ballets. An important aspect of Gadd's intentions was to teach the history of dance to the public. In *Diaghilev's Russian Ballet* (1980), he blended social criticism with the biographies of artists, stylistic references and a psychological drama centred around the figures of Nijinsky, Diaghilev and Isadora Duncan. The ballet company is still active, with a mixed repertoire, and has taken an interest in working with the region's freelance choreographers.

The other regional ballet company that still exists, if in changed form, was founded in Malmö in 1944. It was incorporated into the Malmö City Theatre, which presented musicals, operettas and theatre. (Since 1995, the ballet company has existed as an autonomous organization called the Skåne Dance Theatre.) In contrast to the opera houses in Stockholm and Gothenburg, Malmö wanted to direct its efforts towards a modern and flexible theatre architecture where the stage proscenium was eliminated. It was to be a 'people's theatre' of 1,700 seats for which tickets would cost no more than entry to the cinema. As in Gothenburg, there was a delay before dance was given a more prominent role, but generally speaking, the theatre has never managed to attain success with its ballet repertoire equal to that of the Gothenburg Opera. The new, modern ideals that had influenced the design of the theatre building never achieved a significant breakthrough with regard to the ballet repertoire. Audiences were drawn to the theatre primarily by such classical productions as Bournonville's *Napoli* during Elsa-Marianne von Rosen's time as director, from 1979 to 1987.

New Ideals: Modern Dance

In tandem with the rejuvenation of the classical ballet ideal in the 1950s, the decade brought about the establishment of modern dance in Sweden on a serious level. As in many other countries, modern dance was first glimpsed in Sweden in the early twentieth century through guest performances given by Isadora Duncan and other avant-garde dancers in the same spirit. Modern dance was also spread by Swedish dancers who travelled to dance schools abroad and later established companies in Sweden. Anna Behle was one of the first to study with both Duncan and Émile Jaques-Dalcroze. In 1907, she opened her own school of eurhythmics in Stockholm, teaching both children and adults. Later, she would also teach at the Academy of Music; and the University College of Music to this day offers training in Dalcroze-inspired techniques. Furthermore, one can draw a direct line from Behle via students and teachers to the training of children's dance teachers at the University College of Dance in Stockholm.

During this time, dancers and teachers were directed towards private schools and performances at private theatres. The status of dance artists was low and they began to think about how society's interest in this marginalized art form could be heightened. To achieve this aim and simultaneously to narrow the already established gap between dancers associated with institutions and freelancers, the

Swedish Dance Teachers' Association was founded in 1939. The collaboration between the genres of modern dance and ballet was clearly highlighted by the involvement by the board of directors of the modern dancer Ronny Johansson, whose career had been mainly conducted in Germany, and Sven Tropp, principal dancer at the Royal Swedish Ballet. Because the primary purpose was to improve working conditions for the members of the association, they took forceful action to forestall the entry into the country of foreign dancers who were turning towards Sweden as a result of the oncoming war. After the war, this position changed and increasing numbers of foreign teachers were able to obtain work permits. This expression of national protectionism is a sensitive issue in the history of Swedish dance; it has long been ignored but has now become the object of critical discussion.

However, there were other members of the dance community who assumed the opposite standpoint on this matter. The year prior to the establishment of the Teachers' Association, another organization called the Society for Promotion of Dance was formed. With the support of some members of the organization, Gertrude Engelhardt, a student of Mary Wigman, was permitted to work in Sweden. Yet another of the accomplishments was the presentation of dance performances with mixed programmes alongside lecture series on various dance-related subjects. The society's programme activities thus became an excellent forum for a meeting of dance genres involving independent dancers, dancers from the Royal Swedish Ballet, and, eventually, jazz dancers.

Absolute dance versus dramatic dance

Without excessively oversimplifying this historical description, the establishment phase of modern dance can be coupled primarily with two female choreographers, both born in 1908: Birgit Cullberg and Birgit Åkesson. In addition to their positions as central figures within Swedish modern dance, they also represent the conflicting ideals of the absolute as opposed to the dramatic dance, which created the dynamic in the central European dance community during the 1920s and 1930s.

Birgit Åkesson travelled to Wigman's school in 1929, but soon distanced herself from purely expressionistic dance. She worked out her own more abstract vocabulary of movement and often danced without musical accompaniment. It was an ideal of movement that stressed kinetic purity and poetic expression from the interplay of the various parts of the body. Birgit Cullberg, who studied at Dartington Hall in England, chose another path. Inspired by the Jooss–Leeder technique, she came to work within the dramatic dance tradition with an emphasis on the psychological and social course of events, and employed a fusion of classical and modern dance techniques. The 1950s became an important decade for them both. They staged ballets for the opera house in Stockholm and thus reached a larger audience than they had previously enjoyed. Their careers would briefly converge with the founding in 1963 of the first Swedish educational programme for choreographers at the Choreographic Institute in Stockholm (later the University College of Dance).

Subsequently, Cullberg's and Åkesson's professional lives followed completely different paths. Åkesson began extended research into African dances in countries south of the Sahara before she choreographed a number of solo dances in the 1980s, commissioned by Swedish Television. Despite her limited choreographic output, the aesthetic ideals upon which her dances are based led to her becoming the most important source of inspiration for the young generation of dancers and choreographers of the 1980s. Following her years at the Royal Swedish Ballet, Cullberg founded her own company in 1967. It was a part of the state institution for the touring of theatrical performances, the National Theatre Centre.

Birgit Cullberg was succeeded as artistic director of the Cullberg Ballet by her son, Mats Ek. Under Ek's direction and with his choreography, the group reached a completely new and larger audience during the 1980s. Like Cullberg's ballets, Ek's dances were frequently based on social themes, for example *St George and the Dragon* (1976), which embodied the meeting of the industrialized world with the ancient folk culture of the Third World, and *Soweto* (1977), which, despite the exclusively white ensemble, was inspired by the racial difficulties in South Africa. Ek's reinterpretations of the classical repertoire were equally successful. In *Swan Lake* (1987), the Prince is depicted from a Freudian perspective, with a strong sexual bond with his mother. Furthermore, the Swans are played by both men and women and the finale is more ambivalent than in the traditional version; the Prince is united with the Black Swan. In 1993, Mats Ek left the company for a successful career as a freelance choreographer. Following a short guest appearance by Carolyn Carlson as director, the Cullberg Ballet has since been led by two former dancers with different backgrounds: Lena Wennergren from the Cullberg Ballet and Margareta Lidström from the Royal Swedish Ballet. The company still tours throughout Sweden, and is also considered to be one of the greatest international ambassadors for Swedish ballet by virtue of its countless tours abroad.

Equal Rights to Culture

During the period immediately after the Second World War, a range of reform programmes were instituted in Swedish society: the right to paid holidays from work and old-age pensions, educational reforms of various kinds, and the establishment of publicly financed health insurance. No particular cultural policies were established, but the state did provide financial support for the arts with funds generated by state lotteries. It was during the 1960s that the nation's cultural life began to be regarded as a state concern that demanded the formulation of a unified cultural policy. In 1963, the responsibility for culture was moved from the Ministry of Commerce to the Ministry of Education, and the formulation of a system of central government subsidies was begun.

In 1969, a commission gathered to create the foundations for a new social-democratic cultural policy. This was finally established in 1974 and the Swedish National Council for Cultural Affairs began to administrate its implementation. The new cultural policy emphasized collaboration between state, county and municipality, and was dedicated to dispersing culture throughout the country, counteracting the effects of commercialism and making culture available to previously marginalized groups, particularly children, youth, the disabled and the working class. 'Equal Rights to Culture' became the pivotal concept of the new cultural perspective.

Alternative movements

The foundation of a state cultural policy can be seen as a tardy reaction to the changed Swedish social climate. During the 1960s, Swedish citizens turned their attention towards the surrounding world. Different groups protested against the Vietnam War, the space programmes in the USA and the Soviet Union, environmental destruction and the exploitation of the Third World. This wave of protest also extended to questioning the condition of the foundations of democracy inside Sweden. People realized that the nation was composed of various national and ethnic minorities, especially people from Greece, Italy and countries in Latin America. This situation was initially a consequence of the mass labour immigration of the 1950s, but later also a result of Sweden's programmes for refugees. Within the performing arts, the new mentality was most noticeable within theatre, in terms of staging plays about socio-political issues, for example the Greek colonels' *coup*, undemocratic traditions in Swedish schools, the revolution in Cuba, and the Swedish miners' situation. Cultural life became more clearly polarized. The widest gap existed between the institutions and the young artists who formed independent groups and eventually organized themselves into national centres in order to influence cultural policies more effectively.

The Dance Centre was formed in 1971 in Stockholm in order to coordinate the administration of performances by independent dancers and choreographers and to deepen the public's interest in dance in various ways. Characteristic of the early dance groups was their search for a more intimate format and their desire to interact more closely with the audience. The groups worked with outreach programmes in schools, day nurseries and libraries, and a wide variety of workplaces. These outwardly directed, itinerant activities also affected the choice of repertoire for the groups. They created dances with political messages, addressed feminist issues and ecology, and explored the psychological relationships between people. Movement workshops, in which audiences, adults and children alike, were invited to participate, were frequent events. However, these socio-political ideals would change during the 1980s as modernistic tendencies – that is, a focus on dance as 'pure' form – became increasingly clear.

The members of the Dance Centre worked most often with modern dance techniques, but there were also a number of groups that, in keeping with the more open attitude towards the world outside Sweden, specialized in performing folk dances from countries and cultures such as Spain and Latin America. This diversity would eventually lessen. During the last few years of the 1970s, discussion of the status of dancers became more prominent. The folk dance groups were found to be too tradition-oriented and too amateur. Certainly, they often had higher incomes than the other members, but that was shown to be a result of their frequent work as lecturers, instructors, and so on. The prevailing opinion was that this situation prevented dancers and choreographers from asserting their status as professional artists, and that it could thereby affect state allocation of subsidies. Discussion about this influenced the National Council for Cultural Affairs, which reduced grants to the folk groups. The authorities clearly indicated that it was newly created dances and more experimental approaches to choreography that would be given financial support. For a time, this limited policy resulted in an almost symbiotic relationship between the dance groups and the subsidizers, and caused many groups to work in the same production forms and with similar modes of expression. The dance community found itself divided into separate sections with little communication between those who were considered 'true' artists and those conceived merely as craftspeople. Even though the folk groups remained members of the Dance Centre, the situation marked them with a kind of artistic inferiority, which to this day has hindered a sharing of different dance experiences. The situation is particularly interesting to look at in comparison with tendencies in the Swedish theatre. Some of the most creative theatre performances of the 1980s and 1990s have grown out of a will to combine elements from Swedish and foreign folk dance and theatre traditions, thus creating new acting styles. Critics and audiences alike have acclaimed Peter Oskarsson's work because of the weaving together of, for example, the Swedish folk dance 'polska' (a spinning couple-dance introduced to Sweden during the sixteenth century) and movements from Chinese and Indian dance and theatre.

One result of the more transparent cultural climate that prevailed during the 1960s and 1970s was the investment in new educational programmes. The Ballet Academy was founded in 1957 in Stockholm, and it later became a centre for dance as a whole – classical ballet, historical dance, dance of other cultures, children's dance and modern dance. Its initiator was Lia Schubert, a dancer and teacher from Austria, who collaborated with Folkuniversitetet, an organisation connected with Stockholm University devoted to providing higher education to the public more informally than is possible through the university itself. During the first few years, the Ballet Academy also became a meeting place for amateur and professional dancers as well as actors, musicians and visual artists.

It was also through the efforts of the school that the genre of jazz dance was introduced to Sweden, with the assistance of guest teachers such as Walter Nicks, Talley Beatty, and Vanoye Aikens. Jazz dance soon attracted the greatest interest. From 1961, regular performances in the style were given, in which students from the school and professional dancers from the Royal Swedish Ballet participated. The Ballet Academy also introduced the Graham technique, and for some years in the early 1970s cooperated with the London School of Contemporary Dance .

With regard to both the independent groups and the various educational programmes, one can state that the freer, more permissive cultural climate of the 1960s and 1970s has since become more constricted, and not solely as a result of the new economic crisis of the late 1980s. Even though the social-democratic cultural policy paid homage to the rights of all to culture, it was to be moulded and controlled in detail as the state saw best. Politicians were torn between wanting to support quality and artistic competence while furthering their concomitant conclusion that artists must tour the country, must give many performances, must attain larger audiences and must address children and youth especially if they are to obtain government support.

Bogdan Szyber's and Carina Reich's *A Winter's Dream*, in common with their other productions, says a great deal about the state's inability to create a flexible structure to encompass the diversity of dance. Szyber and Reich have worked with mime and performance art since the 1980s. Above all else, their site-specific performances have inspired the public and critics to sing their praises, but one cannot say that the National Council of Cultural Affairs has been equally accommodating. The Council has had difficulty determining the genre of their art in order to place them in the correct category for subsidy. Is it theatre, visual art, sculpture or dance? Suspending twenty-seven actors from the pillars of a water tower in *Beautiful Sadness* (1989), or installing twenty-four plastic-wrapped actors wound in narrow water hoses on a statue in downtown Stockholm in Birger *Jarl's Fountain* (1993), does not yield ticket revenues, a regular repertoire or accurate audience figures, nor does it shed light on audience categories. Consequently, the artists receive very little government support. From the standpoint of the politics of culture, artistic quality is subjugated to the societal need for culture as a provable, collective benefit. As an ironic comment upon the state's inability to proffer equal rights to culture, Szyber and Reich toured the countryside, presenting their performance piece *Poetry for Creature* (1990) only to cows and geese.

The Contemporary Structure

Gradual structural changes have occurred within the dance sector since the end of the 1980s. Today, the independent groups no longer set the tone. Now, a few choreographers whose artistic potential is deemed to be higher than that of others – and who have managed to give many performances – work in project form.

The changed cultural climate of the most recent decades has stimulated a new cultural policy, established in 1996. Dance, which was previously coupled with music or theatre, is addressed independently for the first time. The cultural policy now being followed stresses the building of an infrastructure. The cultural proposition of 1974 had succeeded in creating a sound infrastructure for theatre, through such methods as the establishment of a number of regional theatres with permanent companies. The difficulties experienced by the dance community in creating a similar structure have in part stemmed from a lack of appropriate performance venues, a limited labour market, deficient assumption of responsibility at the regional level, an undeveloped network of producers and the high costs of touring. Furthermore, it may be stated that dance, despite its great dependence upon government subsidies, has a significantly lower total subsidy level than theatre.

176

So, the cultural policy of 1996 laid emphasis upon the establishment of regional dance centres. This was, however, nothing new for the dance sector, though it had not previously been formulated in cultural–political terms.

The East Goth Ballet started in the 1970s. The company was incorporated into the county theatre of Norrköping and Linköping in eastern Sweden. Despite an increasingly successful repertoire including works by young Swedish choreographers, the company has had difficulty in asserting its position *vis-à-vis* its stronger theatre partner. In accordance with the new cultural policy, the state supported its activities but local authorities were more doubtful about its value. In the regional debate about the future of the company, one of the arguments put forth was that money designated for culture should instead be spent on health care and education. In 1997, the company closed down.

Not all regions subscribe to this line of reasoning, even in the face of the general problems of the 1990s with respect to financing the social structure. Since 1988, in Örebro, a community in central Sweden, the choreographer Lena Josefsson has been active with her Company Raande-Vo. Josefsson, whose choreography reflects a unique blend of contemporary dance techniques and music and dance styles from Tanzania, where she was brought up, is one of the few choreographers who has been given continual support for her dance group. In 1997, however, she accepted the position as artistic director of the Skåne Dance Theatre, and brought some of her dancers with her. They have provided an interesting mix with the more classically trained dancers who have remained in the company after its dissociation from the Malmö Music Theater (formerly the Malmö City Theatre). In the northern regions of the country, a completely new dance company was started in 1995. Northern Dance is a company of six dancers and is led by American Jeanne Yasko, who was trained in the Humphrey–Limón tradition, a style which to some extent still colours her own choreography. Still further north, a collaborative project of a more unusual sort was begun in 1996. The Barents Dance Company is both a network and a dance group, its members from the northernmost parts of Sweden, Norway, Finland and Russia. So far, the performances have been influenced by the dancers' different backgrounds in modern dance styles, ballet and Russian character dancing.

Three independent dance venues in the large urban areas of Sweden also constitute an important part of the infrastructure. The Modern Dance Theatre in Stockholm was the first of these, founded in 1986 upon the initiative of choreographer Margaretha Åsberg. In 1987, the Young Atalante venue was created by three choreographers from the Rubicon group, based in Gothenburg. And finally, in 1996, the Dance Station in Malmö opened as a guest performance venue for contemporary dance. It was founded in 1991 under another name as a collaboration between several independent theatre and dance groups. Along with the extensive guest performance programmes, the venues also function as home stages for the artists who founded them. The venues are financed by both state and local funds, yet must still wage a constant battle for survival and are forced to make do with limited human resources.

177

The problem of finding a platform in Sweden for productions in larger formats and for international guests has been a knotty one. Unlike Denmark, which regularly hosts large international dance companies, Sweden has lacked venues with sufficient capacity. It was, therefore, seen as a triumph when the House of Dance was founded in Stockholm in 1991. The premises had formerly housed the Stockholm City Theatre and had a wide stage suitable for larger dance performances and a smaller, more flexible stage known as the Blue Box for experimental works. When the Dance Museum moved in with its archives and collections, the profile of the House of Dance as a centre open to a wide variety of dance activities was reinforced. The museum holds collections relating to Scandinavian folk dances and western theatrical dancing, as well as items from African, Chinese and Indian dance cultures. In 1999, however, the museum moved to a new building, close to the Royal Swedish Opera. Over the years, the House of Dance has succeeded in drawing a young and diverse public and has staged performances offering a blend of dance genres to eager audiences: classical ballet, modern dance, jazz dance, performance art, non-western dance and musicals.

Discussion about quality and innovation in opposition to democratic ideals (of the 'everyone can dance' ilk) has been a recurring feature in the Swedish dance community over the latter half of the twentieth century. The debate held through the late 1970s and early 1980s about professionalism within the Dance Centre was an expression of this, but it has also come to influence the 1990s. However, unlike in the earlier debate, the opinions of the dance community now prove to be not nearly as unanimous. Some of the more successful freelance choreographers no longer wish to be represented by the Dance Centre, because they feel that in order to remain active they need other types of economic support and other organizational forms beyond the needs of the majority of the Centre's members. It is felt that one central organization can no longer represent all parties as it once had done. There is a greater multiplicity of layers within the dance community than had existed in the 1970s. Furthermore, efforts should be directed at improved quality rather than towards continued focus on diversity, which is considered the current motto of the Dance Centre.

The eventual result has been that a small number of choreographers gathered in a joint production office located in the House of Dance. In 1999, however, the production office closed down. Because the original plans had called for the building to house a working dance group, a choreographers-in-residence programme was also begun in 1996. The theatre chose its choreographers from the new production group. Per Jonsson was to be the first, a choice probably motivated by Jonsson's position as the most successful independent young choreographer. He had also worked with large classical ballet companies since his breakthrough in 1984 with *Shaft*, a dance performed by three men moving along three paths of soil, each ending in a sheet of iron suspended from the ceiling. The movement vocabulary is typical of Jonsson's works: a blending of basic human gestures and often fast-paced, more abstract movements. In 1999, Jonsson died and his career tragically ended.

The choreographer-in-residence for 1997 was Christina Caprioli. She initiated an educational-cum-performance project including workshops, lectures and reconstructions in collaboration with invited American choreographers from the postmodern era of the 1970s: Yvonne Rainer, Steve Paxton and Douglas Dunn. Caprioli, born in Italy, had danced with Dunn in New York, and wanted to bring the traditions that had formed her own career to her young dancers and to a young audience to whom the 1970s represented an unknown historical past. Caprioli also works with young amateurs in the suburbs of Stockholm and has created an educational youth programme in modern dance, which was held in the rehearsal halls of the theatre. This may well be the beginning of a new structure based upon the will to seek new paths for the development of the art of dance beyond those legitimized and institutionalized by the state.

Furthermore, choreographer Efva Lilja has worked since the 1980s with a different distribution and production structure. Together with her dance company, she offers rural communities a project called 'Dance for a Week'. The project brings a number of different performances, workshops and lectures to various sites in the community schools, day nurseries, libraries, local stages, shopping centres, the streets and the town square – so that as many people as possible can encounter dance in their familiar environments, but also in the most unexpected places. Thus Lilja is adhering to the ideal of the early 1970s.

Aesthetic Ideals and Ideology

In 1976, Margaretha Åsberg staged *Lifeboat* outdoors on a barge moored at one of the many docks in Stockholm. The dance has been characterized as the introduction of a new aesthetic vein within Swedish dance, more like performance art than modern dance. The performance opened with a woman rising from a wooden coffin. She wandered between large troughs filled with grass, sand and earth in which various actions were played out: scrutiny of the face in a mirror, wrapping of the body with twine, a game with stones. The piece concluded with a ritual purification in which the woman smeared her naked body with flour before covering herself with earth. The dance was at once concrete, through the dancer's unemotional execution of the different actions, and theatrical, through its utilization of powerful symbols.

Even if *Lifeboat* was unique at the time, one can discern a direct link between it and the productions of Szyber and Reich, as well as the dances staged in various open-air environments by other contemporary choreographers, such as Efva Lilja and the Tiger Group. The latter is a production group based around two choreographers (initially three). They work with a kind of theatricalization of everyday movements, often stressing a feminine world in which buckets, brooms, bags and other ordinary objects appear. Another link between the 1970s and the 1990s is this interest in the relationship between body and object. Conversely, a point of differentiation is that artists in the 1990s have most often abandoned Åsberg's use of 'universal' rituals and her belief in cross-culturally understood symbolic codes, and instead reinforced the feature of the dances as ironic or provocative theatrical comment upon contemporary-life situations.

Åsberg's later dances were to encompass shifting aesthetic ideals. She started the Pyramids group in 1979 (later a production title as opposed to a company title) with both professional dancers and amateurs. The same year, she created the first Swedish minimalist dance, again entitled *Pyramids*. She also choreographed dances with text such as *The Atlantic* (1989), based on a short story by Marguerite Duras, and *The Transmuted Paradise* (1991), based on a text by Heiner Müller. In these pieces Åsberg experimented with limiting traditional acting, using speech on a more artificial level rather than using it for demonstrating the contents of the text.

Åsberg's choreographies were particularly influential during the 1980s for several reasons. Her background as a dancer with the Royal Swedish Ballet lent her sufficient status to win over the more conventional critics. She had also come into contact with Birgit Åkesson, had danced in some of her dances at the opera and had been her student at the Choreographic Institute. Because many of the dancers and choreographers of the younger generation came to work in Åsberg's own productions, she became an important connecting link back to Sweden's early modernist dance.

The new choreographers of the 1980s were fascinated by Åkesson's dance technique, which emphasized the forms of the movable body with no pronounced symbolism or theatrical character. Many were also inspired by the compositional forms of Merce Cunningham and by the idea of creating 'pure' dance. Thus they came to embrace many of the aesthetic features of classical modernism in art, defined by the art theoretician Clement Greenberg and similar to what we define as minimalism in dance: the absence of outside references, concentration on the essential qualities of dance, the form of movements in time and space, and new structures that replaced climax with repetition and fragmentation. These tendencies thus stood in sharp contrast to the more socio-political dance expressionism of the 1970s as reflected in the dances of both members of the Dance Centre and the Cullberg Ballet, also in contrast to Åsberg's interest in the relationship between body and art object.

In trying to characterize and summarize the predominant aesthetic ideals during the last three decades of Swedish modern dance, the 1970s can best be described as revealing an interest in socio-political dance, in theatricality, supported by the introduction of performance art; the 1980s as marked by aesthetics closer to the ideals of Cunningham or Yvonne Rainer with attention to the nature of movement as such, disregarding narrative, character, and expressionism; and the 1990s by its reintroduction of meaning, theatricality, performance art and virtuosic dancing.

Equal Rights, Equal Dancing?

In 1994, the National Council of Cultural Affairs and the Ministry of Health and Social Affairs partially financed a film designed to stimulate interest in dance. The film is a composition of a number of sequences depicting different types of dance: children practising classical ballet and doing Spanish dances, contemporary Swedish modern dance, social dances in various settings performed by people of different age groups, and dance in theatrical contexts. The dances are accompanied by a single musical piece, Ravel's *Bolero*, except during the final seconds when the credits are rolled and the various musical genres are played along with the dances they represent. The ideology of the film is that all dance is enriching, physical, universal and sensual. Dance liberates us and carries us into a community far more expansive than the limited landscapes bounded by intellect, age, sex or ethnicity.

This ideology is one that has permeated and continues to affect how dance is viewed in Sweden. In this form, the ideology expressed by the film has lent support to the politicians' belief in culture as a collective benefit. It has also contributed to elevating the status of the dance community and the acceptance of dance within the educational sphere. That the dance film can also be experienced as repressive of important cultural differences, as neglectful of gender, as holding a Eurocentric view of dance by virtue of the selected dances and music, and as excessively emphasizing dance as a bodily and sensual experience alone, has not been given equal attention.

The perception of dance as both aesthetic and ideological has become noticeable only over the most recent few years, though some earlier steps in that direction can be discerned. Efva Lilja has, among other things, focused on the age of the dancer and has worked with older professional dancers and amateurs. The young choreographers Jens Östberg and Lars Max Bethke work with a mix of 'high culture' and an MTV-inspired aesthetic, thus trying to break the boundaries between fine art and popular culture. The only existing company that works exclusively with jazz dance, the Modern Jazz Dance Ensemble, also works under the banner of popular culture, for example by using cartoons as subject-matter. Kenneth Kvarnström has created provocative dances with elements of sexuality and violence, thus questioning the assumed 'positive' value of dancing. Several choreographers have also begun to work consciously with constructions of masculinity and femininity. Seen in general, a re-theatricalized aesthetic has coloured the choreographies, with a lucid staging of certain cultural and societal conventions, not least those of the genre conventions of dance itself.

Conversely, perspectives of ethnic identity have been glaringly absent. Within the framework of the present debate about the founding of a forum for world culture, clear lines are still being drawn between Swedish cultural life and the cultural manifestations of other parts of the world. Even though, as an American critic once remarked, Swedes of today have an appetite for 'exotic' dances, expressed in social dancing, workshops, or performances, these trends seldom address nationality or ethnicity from a point of view whereby such identities are questioned. Sweden, the land of equality, is still incapable of seeing that it is possible for an artist to create a dance in the borderland between the native and the foreign, allowing different cultural values to interact, dissolve, and form into hybrid identities that lack authentic or traditional essence. There is still a close link with the manner in which the folk groups of the 1970s tried to conserve a dance tradition, instead of exploring new terrain. The kind of dance that expresses a multiplicity of intersecting local voices has yet to gain a foothold.

Key Texts

Anderson, K. and Münster-Swendsen, J. (eds) (1991) *Dance, Dance, Dance: Nordic Dance*, Copenhagen and Stockholm: Nordic Theatre and Dance and Danstidningen.

Engdahl, H. (1991) *Swedish Ballet and Dance: A Critic's View*, Stockholm: Swedish Institute.

Hall, F. (1953) 'Birgit Åkesson: Post-Expressionist Free Dance', *An Anatomy of Ballet*, London: Andrew Melrose, pp. 220–6.

Häger, B. (1989) *Ballets Suédois*, Paris: Jacques Damase.

Hammergren, L. (1992) 'The Import(ance) of Fragmentation', in *American Dance Abroad: Influence of the United States Experience*, Proceedings of the Society of Dance History Scholars, pp. 175–85.

Näslund, E. (1978) *Birgit Cullberg*, Stockholm: Norstedts.

Peter, F.-M. (ed.) (1998) *Birgit Åkesson: Postmodern Dance from Sweden*, Köln: Wienand.

Skeaping, M. and Ståhle, A. G. (1979) *Balett på Stockholmsoperan*, Stockholm: Nordstedts.

Vail, J. (1998) *Kulterella koreografier*, Stockholm: Carlssons.

Table 9 Important dance and political events in Sweden (1900 to present)

Year	Dance: artists, works, events	Dance: institutions	Arts scene	Sociocultural and political events
1900			To Damaskus I (Strindberg)	
1903	*Cléo de Merode			
1905	*Isadora Duncan		Cinemas grow in number	
1906		Anna Behle's school established		
1907	*Anna Pavlova			
1908				
1910			Skådebanan (organization for 'peoples' theatre')	
1911	*Jaques-Dalcroze		Max Reinhardt visits Sweden	
1912				
1913	Michel Fokine to Royal Ballet, Ballets Russes dances		Society for Theatre History	
1916			Ballet Primadonna, film by Mauritz Stiller with dancers from Royal Ballet	
1917				Liberal/Social Democrat
1919				Entertainments tax
1920		Les Ballets Suédois (dir. Rolf de Maré till 1925)		Social Democrat
1921			Gothenburg Opera	
1925			First city theatre recieves state subsidies	
1927			Radio theatre	
1929				Liberal
1930	Birgit Åkesson to Wigman's school		Stockholm exposition introduces functionalism	

Table 9 continued

Year	Dance: artists, works, events	Dance: institutions	Arts scene	Sociocultural and political events
1931	Julian Algo (Laban pupil) director, Royal Ballet			
1932				Social Democrat
1933			National Theatre Centre	State investigation of theatre situation
1934	Åkesson's début in Paris and Stockholm *Ballets Jooss			
1935	Birgit Cullberg to Dartington School			
1936				Social Democrat/Liberal
1938				
1939				
1940		Society for the Promotion of Dance Swedish Dance Teachers Association	'That Unknown Trojan Horse' anti-Nazi song by Karl Gerhard banned by the censor	
1942	Culture-propaganda (Cullberg), anti-Nazi ballet			
1944		Cullberg tours with National Theatre Centre	Malmö City Theatre	
1945				Social Democrat
1946		Swedish Dance Theatre (dir. Cullberg and Ivo Cramér, till 1947)		
1947			First theatre company performing for schoolchildren	
1949	Antony Tudor, director Royal Ballet			
1950	Miss Julie (Cullberg)	Dance Museum (director, Bengt Häger)		

Table 9 continued

1951				Social Democrat/Liberal
1953	Mary Skeaping, director Royal Ballet			
1954	*Martha Graham			
1956	Skeaping starts choreographing historical dances for the Drottningholm Theatre *New York City Ballet		Long Day's Journey Into Night (O'Neill), world première	
1957	Sisyphus (Åkesson), first choreography for Royal Ballet	Ballet Academy		Social Democrat
1958	*Merce Cunningham		Museum of Modern Art	
1959				National Supplementary Pension Act
1960			Stockholm City Theatre	
1961	Ballet Academy's *Jazzballet 61* (first full-scale jazz dance performance)		'Movement in Art' (Duchamps, Calder, Rauschenberg), at Museum of Modern Art	Pension-like grants to artists
1963	Echoing of Trumpets (Tudor)	Choreographic Institute		Cultural section formed at Ministry of Education
1964			Three state theatre schools open	End of public lotteries used for subsidies
1965			Pistol Theatre starts producing political theatre	
1967	Erik Bruhn, director Royal Ballet	Cullberg Ballet		
1968		Cramér Ballet	A Play About School (Pocket Theatre) attacks undemocratic traditions	New state investigation of Swedish culture
1969			Theatre Centre (independent groups)	National Council for Cultural Affairs
1970	Miraculous Mandarin (Ulf Gadd's breakthrough)	Choreographic Institute renamed National School of Dance		

Table 9 continued

Year	Dance: artists, works, events	Dance: institutions	Arts scene	Sociocultural and political events
1971		East Goth Ballet Dance Centre (independent groups) L'Étoile du Nord (first company performing 'happening'-like events)		
1973		Dance Theatre (company performing political dances) Dance (magazine published by Dance Museum)		
1974			Gee, Girls Freedom Is Near! (Garpe, Osten) first major Swedish women's lib. play House of Culture (exhibitions, venues)	New cultural policy
1975	Cramér, director Royal Ballet Lifeboat (Åsberg)	Viva Mexico (folk dance company)		
1976	The Batman (Mats Ek's first choreography)			Liberal
1977		Wind Witches (dir. Eva Lundqvist)		
1978		National School of Dance renamed National College of Dance (later University College of Dance)	Royal Dramatic Theatre stages The Storm, debating nuclear power	Performing arts and art schools reorganized, national colleges (later university colleges)
1979	Pyramids (Åsberg) first minimalist dance	Pyramids (dir. Margaretha Åsberg)		
1982	Giselle (Ek) first version of the classics Où (Efva Lilja, first choreography)	The Glass House (first dance venue in Stockholm founded and run by an independent dance group, Wind Witches)		Social Democrat
1983			First international festival with Latin American theatre companies living in exile	

Table 9 *continued*

1984	Shaft (Per Jonsson's breakthrough) *Pina Bausch and Tanztheater Wuppertal	Caprioli Dance Company (dir. Christina Caprioli)		
1985	Mats Ek, director Cullberg Ballet	Swedish Choreographers Association Swedish Dance Committee, member of the ITI Dance Committee		
1986	Lunar Pond (Kenneth Kvarnström, first choreography)	Modern Dance Theatre, Stockholm		
1987		Young Atalante, Gothenburg		
1988		First university programme in dance theory, Stockholm University	The Big Wrath, Peter Oskarsson's first production of theatre performances using a mixture of Swedish and Asian folk culture	
1989	Two solo dances for television by Åkesson			
1991		House of Dance Dance Magazine		Liberal
1992		Åsberg first professor in choreography at University College of Dance		
1994	*Ballett Frankfurt	Education of modern dancers starts at University College of Dance Jens Östberg wins Bagnolet competition, France		Social Democrat
1995	Jonsson choreographs for Rambert Dance Company			
1996	Visions of Earthly Paradise (Szyber/Reich), performed in London	Dance Station, Malmö	Robert Wilson lectures at Stockholm City Theatre	New cultural policy
1997	Performances of American postmodern choreography from the 1970s		Nobel Prize in literature to Dario Fo	

*First visit

10

UNITED KINGDOM

An expanding map

Bonnie Rowell

Towards an Un-unified Theory

Dance in the UK has both a complex and diverse recent history. It offers up for analysis neither a straightforward dialectical position between those elements that uphold the status quo versus those that resist, nor neatly compartmentalized and homogeneous subgenres. What it does do is offer a reflection of Britain's search for a position in the world in light of fundamental economic, social and cultural changes since the Second World War. Our position on the world map has changed in terms of our relationship with America and Europe as well as our relationship with the former empire. Our position at home has changed in terms of a rapid shift in the racial make-up of our population. At the same time, postmodern theory reflects an international shift in, among other things, the status of art, in the relationship between 'high art' and popular culture, as well as foregrounding the representation of 'other' voices: reflecting feminist perspectives, disability issues, racial minority issues. Of course, some people in our society have resisted change, while others have wholeheartedly embraced these new representations, new interests and influences. But dance perhaps highlights these tensions more than any other art because of the unique way in which it has developed during this century.

While dance illustrates these tensions, it can also be viewed as a special case among the arts. Most notably there is its youth as an acknowledged art form, and its materials are human beings – that is, 'thinking' and interacting bodies – the body as site for political and social tension has been a feature of the era. These two aspects serve to make the situation ever more complex as groups within the dance world vie with each other to consolidate and reinforce dance's standing, some by creating – and preserving – a tradition, some by embracing this newness and proclaiming dance to be at the forefront of radicalism. The cultural theorist Jim Collins has pointed out that the many apparent contradictions deriving from these diverse and conflicting voices lead us to a situation which defies former theories of cultural analysis. He writes: 'Cultural production is no longer a carefully coordinated "system", but provides a range of simultaneous options that have destabilized traditional distinctions between High Art and mere "mass culture"' (Collins 1989: 2).

Social historian Arthur Marwick would seem to endorse this point of view when he cautions against talking about *general* changes in political direction, or putting too much credence in changes of government as a reflection of people's *actual* political beliefs: 'There is a danger in speaking at all of "*the* British experience", perfectly respectable and acceptable though that phrase is as a piece of shorthand as long as it is never allowed to obscure the fact that different individuals, different groups, in reality meet with different experiences' (Marwick 1982: 8).

Or again, the novelist Salman Rushdie has proclaimed in relation to the integration of different cultures within our society: 'If history creates complexities, let us not try to simplify them' (cited in Jeyasingh 1995: 191).

Academics then, both at the cutting edge and at the more traditional end of theoretical debate, would seem to agree that trends, categories, chronological historical overviews are no easy things to read and determine, even less so our very recent history. What then do we make of dance, a relatively underdeveloped art form, at least until this century, and one with far less weight of scholarship to support its study?

Since the war, we have seen the Royal Ballet consolidate its status as a national flagship on the one hand, promoting a classical heritage to which it can lay only questionable claim, as we shall see, while displaying home-grown works as diverse as those by the classicist Frederick Ashton and the realist–expressionist Kenneth MacMillan. In the 1990s, it has made a foray into the works of such iconoclasts as the Americans William Forsythe and Twyla Tharp. These choreographers, together with its own Ashley Page, are concerned in one way or another with undermining and questioning the status and conventions of classical ballet as it has been traditionally viewed, as well as consciously drawing upon an aesthetic of popular culture. All these choreographers have reflected, in their own way, some part of the cultural debate.

On the other hand the modern dance contingent has absorbed both Graham- and Cunningham-style 'modernisms' within a very short space of time.[1] Ballet Rambert changed its repertoire in 1966 to a modern one and began to explore highly expressionistic and political statements with the choreographies of Norman Morrice and John Chesworth plus the works of Americans Glen Tetley and Anna Sokolow. Then Robin Howard established the London School of Contemporary Dance (LSCD) in 1966 and the London Contemporary Dance Theatre (LCDT) in 1967, with teaching and repertory based firmly within the Graham aesthetic. From the beginning, however, there was also a marked interest in the technique and choreographic processes of Merce Cunningham, in part stemming from the enthusiasm of Richard Alston and Siobhan Davies for this style, both early students at LSCD. The modern dance community has also learned from European modern dance artists, notably those influenced by Pina Bausch, which are of a more extreme expressionist/physical-theatre bent. Thus modern dance[2] in this country can by no means be seen as homogeneous, embracing as it does aesthetic polar opposites under a single banner.

In addition, towards the middle of the period under discussion, there has been a 'British' New Dance movement that sought to subvert what it saw as the stranglehold of British classicism as well as the increasing institutionalization of modern dance, doing so by means of polemical subject-matter, though often borrowing from American movement styles and theories of the body such as contact improvisation and release. Last but not least, we have seen the expansion of non-western dance from its inclusion on the agenda of the Arts Council some twenty-one years ago under the separate heading of 'ethnic arts', to the acknowledgement of a cultural diversity within Britain that has touched all art forms. What we now see is evidence of a greatly increased awareness of the population in its totality, and so alongside the expansion of African, Afro-Caribbean and South Asian dance[3] we have disability groups claiming equal prominence. Issues of feminism, of gender representation, sexual orientation and age discrimination are equally concerns at the forefront of social awareness and dance reflects these concerns, sometimes covertly, sometimes more directly.

Some examples serve to illustrate this complex situation. There are signs that a mature generation of choreographers within the modern dance genre, such as Alston and Davies, nod in the direction of a more traditional aesthetic; that is they are more concerned with continuing the 'modernist' project of exploring the medium of dance itself, and in so doing align themselves with the status quo of which they once stood outside. But, while neither choreographer includes overt polemical material, both still represent a politics of the dancer and of the dancing body, reflecting current thinking albeit in subtle form. Or again, there are the dances of Shobana Jeyasingh, which, though drawing freely upon the techniques and imagery of Indian dance, in particular Bharata Natyam, could also be seen as explorations of the medium in its own right, in other words, displaying concerns which parallel those of Alston and Davies. Jeyasingh's choreography would seem to exemplify an analysis by the American anthropologist Joan Erdman (1996). She argues that Indian dance has always looked to adapt to the present situation for its continuance and asks why we should expect South Asian dance to be any more – or less – preoccupied with the preservation of its cultural heritage than is western dance?

Or she may be compared with the approach of Adzido and its representation of African traditions, with its emphasis on roots, homeland and difference. How dance reflects our sense of identity as well as its search for artistic identity therefore represent major concerns of this chapter.

This variety and pluralism of vision perhaps constitutes, finally, a rejection of any notion or ideal of 'progress', a notion at the very heart of the modernist movement, which implied a painstaking building of cultural understanding within rigid limits, often imposed from a western and minority perspective. These have been rejected in favour of the individual voice that draws upon all experiences and all traditions of art – and of life – as source material and as inspiration.

This chapter will therefore address all these tensions in terms of those forms that offer resistance to the status quo as well as those that uphold and support it, in terms of its institutions, its subject-matters as well as its audiences. It will also seek to explore the erosion of this dialectic. Second, it will explore the current status and nature of the medium itself in terms of representations of the body as well as the medium's relationship with the other arts. Third, it will explore the search for identity: national identity in terms of our political relationship with America and Europe, or in terms of our multicultural population and the representation of its 'other voices'.

Education, Status and Funding

One feature of the 1970s which must not be underestimated in relation to the development of a different public consciousness of dance was the steady growth of a dance presence within the British public education system, to a level perhaps unprecedented in Europe. There had been some infiltration of ideas from both American and European modern dance traditions prior to this. Most notably, Kurt Jooss had based his company at Dartington in Devon in 1933 and Rudolf von Laban founded his Art of Movement Studio first in Manchester in 1946, then in Addlestone, Surrey, from 1953. With the exception of Jooss's company, however, dance within education had little contact with the profession. Then from the mid-1970s, Robert Cohan set up schools and college residences, with dancers and students from the recently established London Contemporary Dance Theatre and London School of Contemporary Dance. A group of colleges and polytechnics, following the success of the American university model, began to offer dance at degree level and beyond.

These links between the profession and the mainstream educational system have had a twofold effect. First, the status of dance has been enhanced as a subject worthy of serious consideration on a par with the other arts. Second, there is a new generation of articulate dance practitioners better able to represent the profession within the community and within its institutions at all levels. It is perhaps timely then to look at whether levels of public funding have followed these trends.

Public subsidy for dance began with the Arts Council of Great Britain (ACGB), which was set up in 1946 as a result of the activities of the Council for the Encouragement of Music and the Arts (CEMA) during the war years. Dance was for a long time comparatively poorly funded under the auspices of the Music Panel, with a Dance Theatre Sub-Committee. In 1978, a Dance Advisory Committee was established, finally, in 1980, a Dance Panel, with direct link to the Arts Council.[4] As we shall see, the 1970s and 1980s saw an unprecedented growth in dance activity, with modern dance firmly established and with a proliferation of new dance groups arising from the newly established schools and college-based courses, encouraged by Dance Umbrella[5] – an organization committed to promoting British dance artists. Dance, which had been historically underfunded, was now struggling to develop an essential infrastructure concomitant with its growth in activity. By

191

1985, the director of the Dance Umbrella Festivals, Val Bourne, was warning that, given contemporary trends with the emphasis on private sponsorship, future festivals might be forced into giving priority to larger, more prestigious overseas companies (ones with higher levels of public subsidy than in the UK), rather than to independent and new British artists whom it had previously been used to promoting (editorial for 1985 Dance Umbrella programme).

After 1993, the pattern of increase in overall Arts Council funds stopped and for the financial years 1994/5 and 1996/7, overall funding actually dropped (Art Council of England 1998: 20–1). However, dance has received £23 million in both 1997/8 and 1998/9 financial years and there is now a slight increase promised for 1999/2000. The first National Lottery grants were made in 1995, beginning with capital projects, for example transforming two major venues for dance – Sadler's Wells and the Royal Opera House, but also encompassing regional – as well as London-based projects.

While the arts in general have struggled to maintain their levels of funding, dance has had to contend first, with a historical situation in which it was the 'poor relation' and thus chronically underfunded in relation to the other arts. Second, it has had to deal with an increase in activity at all levels, an increase possibly unparalleled within the other arts.

The Expanding Map: Resistance and Consolidation

The tensions between the need to establish a respected dance community in the twentieth century and the equally pressing needs to be a part of the modern and postmodern movements' radical cultural changes are nowhere more apparent than within ballet. The post-war years added to these tensions in terms of Britain's need to regenerate its political, economic and social self-esteem. These tensions are emergent within ballet in terms of seeming contradictions: on the one hand between ballet's apparent agenda and that of the other arts; and on the other hand between different sorts of artistic statement within the repertory.

A comparison between our ballet companies' repertories and other arts events will serve to point up the many contradictions inherent within the relationship between dance and its audience in the immediate aftermath of the Second World War. The year 1956 saw Richard Hamilton's 'This is Tomorrow' exhibition in which Britain was exposed to major innovations within the visual arts. The same year witnessed the first production of John Osborne's *Look Back in Anger*, which, alongside novels such as Kingsley Amis's *Lucky Jim* (1954) and John Braine's *Room at the Top* (1956), sought to undermine the cosy class structure of Britain. The previous year had seen the opening of Mary Quant's first Bazaar in the King's Road (in Chelsea, London), which paved the way for the 'swinging sixties' fashion market and helped put Britain at the hub of popular culture in the West. In light of these events, cultural activity in general can be seen to be extremely buoyant and forward-looking, with the public emerging from many years of economic and social hardship, and appearing to be avid for change.

Dance audiences on the other hand seemed avid only for revivals.[6] There had been an upsurge in public interest during the war years, due to the tours undertaken by the Vic-Wells company and the Ballet Rambert. Ballet's new-found popular appeal was capitalized upon by, for example, Festival Ballet,[7] which toured mixed programmes of popular works throughout the 1950s. Some attempts were made to encourage young talent: for example choreographic platforms such as Ballet Workshop at the Mercury Theatre, the Sadler's Wells Choreographic Group and the Sunday Ballet Group, which staged works by new choreographers as well as new composers and designers. However, the incorporation of new works into the repertories of our major companies, though provoking hot debate within the dance press, was often ill-received by audiences, and nineteenth- and twentieth-century classical revivals tended to dominate. Beth Genné offers a possible explanation.[8] Within the repertory of the Royal Ballet in the 1930s and 1940s she argues, were 'classics' that had spurious claim to the term: *The Sleeping Beauty* was only some fifty years old and preceded Isadora Duncan by just one decade! She notes too that Balanchine's rediscovery of *Swan Lake* resulted in *Apollo* in 1928, whereas de Valois decided to attempt to reconstruct the ballet as exactly as possible. Reasons for this retroactivism are clear and understandable, according to Genné, for de Valois had a keen historical sense and recognized the need to divorce British ballet from what was perceived as its less than respectable music-hall past as well as to create a 'canon': a classical background as exemplar of style and technique and in so doing, align ballet with the other arts.

Genné goes on to point out that de Valois was all too aware of the evolutionary status of ballet, and of a consequent need for tradition to go alongside innovation in order to nurture this evolution. A number of British contemporary composers had been used in ballet and with the success of John Cranko's *The Prince of the Pagodas* (1957) with its commissioned score by Benjamin Britten it was hoped that these collaborations would persist or even proliferate. But it was to be many years before these pieces gained major audience popularity. It must also be remembered that de Valois's own dances had featured within the repertory of the 1930s and 1940s, and these were highly expressionistic statements that owed much to her experience at the Abbey Theatre in Dublin and to the modernist influences of the poet Yeats, to the European influences of Kurt Jooss, and to her collaborations with contemporary artists and musicians.

The directorships and choreography of Ashton and MacMillan perhaps highlight these polarities within the Royal Ballet to keenest advantage. Ashton was the arch-classicist: a parallel to Balanchine in some ways but with a sentimental eye on British history and British countryside. Yet Macaulay (1996b) has pointed out that Ashton in his own way displayed a modern sensibility: as seen in *Monotones* (1965), which owes much to the Cunningham company's visit in 1964, or, more covertly, in the sexuality displayed by Lise in the final *pas de deux* of *La Fille mal gardée* (1960). Or again, there are two extraordinary dances from the 1930s and 1940s: *A Wedding Bouquet* (1937) to music by Lord Berners with words by Gertrude Stein and *Scènes de ballet* (1948) to a Stravinsky score. It was Ashton too who commissioned

Nijinska to revive *Les Biches* in 1964 and *Les Noces* in 1966 for the company, both radical statements of 'high' modernism.

Ashton's successor Kenneth MacMillan, on the other hand, sought more openly to subvert the classical technique, importing an attitude to weight and use of the torso from modern dance. He also looked to explore radically new subject-matters for ballet: sombre, often harrowing explorations of psychological themes based upon historical events or literary sources. During the 1990s we have seen a move to preserve the Ashton legacy and the Ashton style. On the other hand, MacMillan's widow Deborah, who has artistic control of his legacy, has encouraged the casting of a male dancer in the role of chosen maiden in the reconstruction of his *The Rite of Spring* (1962), tutored by Monica Mason, the dancer on whom the role was created. The reasons given for this departure are first, that MacMillan had considered the possibility of a man in the role, but more radically within the context of this debate – that ballet can only be preserved as a living art by looking to the future.

More recently the debate has been intensified as we have seen mixed receptions for pioneering works by Forsythe. His dances actively seek to subvert dance classicism by deconstructing (a term he himself uses) classical ballet technique and by recontextualizing it within a non-linear structural form set against fragmented classical music scores or electronic scores by his collaborator Thom Willems. The effect is to present ballet within a new and exciting context, or perhaps more importantly to show fresh and challenging possibilities for classically trained dancers, not just in terms of their technical accomplishment, but also their expressive potential.

Turning the Tables: High Art and Popular Culture

An alternative dimension to this debate concerns the postmodern erosion of boundaries between high art and popular culture with the cross-fertilization of ideas between genres. The latter part of the twentieth century has seen the frequent absorption of popular cultural influences, not just into avant-garde dance works, but also into the mainstream. Conversely, values associated with 'high art' have been incorporated into more populist statements. In the 1990s, choreographers such as Matthew Bourne and Lea Anderson have reappraised ballet's past narratives. Neither Bourne's nor Anderson's work can be said to be overtly political; in fact they do not pose a critique of ballet so much as simply ignore the boundaries between ballet and other genres. Bourne unashamedly courts the box office, offering spectacular and widely accessible performances in non-traditional dance venues for non-dance audiences. His company, Adventures in Motion Pictures, once predominantly composed of Laban Centre graduate dancers like Bourne himself, has increased in size to incorporate both ballet and modern-technique-trained dancers. *Highland Fling* (1994), for the small-scale company retold the story of *La Sylphide* in a punk-populated Glaswegian setting, while *Swan Lake* (1995) had a cast exclusively of male swans and featured in the Odette/Odile role,

Adam Cooper, then a member of the Royal Ballet. The latter dance brought to the attention of non-traditional and traditional ballet audiences alike the possibilities of the genre to incorporate new representations of the male dancer. The central male relationship was undoubtedly an important reason for the considerable media attention, though the message was less to do with homoeroticism, more to do with the combination of male strength and sensitivity displayed in some strong choreography and performances. In both dances too, there was the sense of an honest reappraisal of the notion of the ideal which is at the heart of ballet classicism, updated to a contemporary context.

Anderson's dances continue to be more intimate, but incorporate popular music plus an advertising artist's eye for catchy visual compilations. Her *Le Spectre de la rose* (1994) saw a televisual reinterpretation of the Fokine theme danced by her male company, the Featherstonehaughs, in rose-petal suits, as an ensemble with no soloists. The final leap, this time in slow motion and from the top of a derelict building, paid homage to the original, yet sought to comment both on its hyperbolized technical accomplishment as well as on the new era of dance and televisual effect.

Anderson's subject-matter has tended towards a fascination for 'high art' forms with a liking for 'diva-esque' costumes, and yet, with some notable exceptions, for example *Parfum de la nuit* (1988) to Bellini's music, which directly confronted the image of the 'diva', she has tended to use commissioned scores by contemporary musicians, drawn from a small band of close associates. Within the mainstream of modern dance, Christopher Bruce has employed popular music by the Rolling Stones, Bob Dylan and John Lennon to explore and question cultural stereotypes. What can be seen, then, is a sense of the erosion of traditional boundaries together with a much more confident approach towards dance conventions. We see choreographers from all dance forms posing a critique while at the same time maintaining a sense of respect for dance's history.

Dance Politics

The New Dance movement of the 1970s was begun by a group of dancers calling themselves X6 after the name of the dance space in London's Docklands where they used to meet. The emphasis for them was liberation, newness and radicalism, but they also rejected what they saw as foreign models for dance and became increasingly self-conscious about developing a British form of dance, dealing with endemic concerns. There was a social and political emphasis from the beginning, so far as subject-matter was concerned, but also in terms of audience involvement and the use of small intimate performance spaces. Of primary importance was the journal they began in 1977, also called *New Dance*, which encouraged the airing of concerns and debate about the nature of the art form. The community dance thrust sprang from their work in the 1980s in which important links were forged between the concerns and needs of different groups within the community and the profession.

In 1981, former Royal Ballet dancer and X6 member Jacky Lansley made *I, Giselle*, which re-evaluated the representation both of women in general and the classical ballerina in particular within our society. This was a hard-hitting and uncompromising piece that had an overtly feminist agenda, but also drew upon Lansley's knowledge of and deep respect for the original. Earlier still, Emilyn Claid, Mary Prestidge and Lansley had made *Bleeding Fairies* (1977) also for the X6 Collective, a dance that 'made the point that ballerinas are real, flesh and blood (and menstruating) women, not ethereal and romantic beings' (Mackrell 1992: 30).

In the last decade, we can see polemical subject-matter and the representation of minority voices most clearly in the works of companies like DV8 Physical Theatre and CandoCo. Lloyd Newson's company DV8 have consistently addressed issues of gender stereotyping and sexual orientation in a direct and sometimes harrowing way, but they have also questioned all forms of accepted cultural behaviour, from religious belief to dance training. *Dead Dreams of Monochrome Men* (1988) broke new ground in its exploration of the psychological state of the serial killer Denis Nilsen, based upon Brian Master's book *Killing for Company* (1985). Its interval-less performance at the ICA lasted nearly one and a half hours and allowed no late entrants, having the effect of capturing its audience as voyeuristic witnesses to torture and death – perhaps forcing the audience members to consider their roles as outsiders. More recently, *Enter Achilles* (1995) portrayed male stereotypes in a more humorous way, as beer-swilling machos tormenting more sensitive 'new men'. Newson draws upon popular music and cultural icons such as Superman to make his point, but he also looks to folk culture and his ensemble 'lager lout' dance in *Enter Achilles* to eastern European folk music made a poignant pastiche of classical ballet.

It is apparent, then, that the shibboleths of dance are being questioned. Of late, the dancer has been subjected to similar scrutiny. The traditional notion of the dancer as the malleable material of the choreographer with its concomitant value system of the body as object – as finely tuned expressive tool – has given way to a notion of the dancer as person and as thinking, feeling collaborator within the process of choreography.

The Medium of Dance: Representations of the Body and of the Dancer

Different attitudes to the body were rife in the 1960s, with the work of the New Dance contingent and with the influences of Steve Paxton, Mary Fulkerson and respectively contact improvisation and release work. These dance forms sought a new attitude, releasing the dancer from the hierarchy of the choreographer–dancer relationship and made the dancer agent for the movement in improvisational or improvisation-based dances. But there also emerged a new attitude to the body itself and how to treat it in a more sensitive and respectful way. Some choreographer–performers such as Rosemary Butcher and Gaby Agis continue this project, releasing the dancer to be participant in the making of the dances and providing non-stressful dance forms in which the body is less subject to the rigours of physical virtuosity required of ballet and, increasingly it seems, of modern dance. Butcher's dances, for example, can be seen to use dancers in a gentle way, creating expression in terms of subtle accumulations of gesture and relationship and gradually changing outlines of structure. Her dances are informed by her interest in collaborations with musicians, visual artists and architects, and her abstracted dance statements, rooted as they are within human emotion, link her to artists like Richard Long. Comparisons have also been made between some of her dances and the systems music of the 1970s and 1980s, with composers such as Philip Glass and Steve Reich. *Flying Lines* (1985) exemplifies this style and contains passages of both dance and musical improvisation. The visual artist Peter Noble provided an installation of kite-like flying shapes, accompaniment was composed and performed by Michael Nyman and the starting point for all three was the looping movement of kites flying. The result is a lyrical exploration of shape and space rooted in the humanity of the dancers, which suggests human aspiration to flight. Butcher has stayed true to this aesthetic and in the 1990s her minimalism counters current trends.

In some ways Alston and Davies can be seen to work within a similar aesthetic, but with a greater degree of technicality required of the dancer, though this never transgresses a respect for the dancer as person. Alston's movement style is eclectic, beginning with a Cunningham attitude to rhythm, direction changes and torso mobility, but with a release-based attitude to weight. His work has over the years acquired a more balletic appearance, continuing the classical values of form and line, yet he has never lost an attitude to the dancer that first acknowledges, the dancer's input to the choreography and second, the dancer's expressive potential as personal to that performer, over and above the demands of the technique. His reworking of *Soda Lake* for Rambert in the late 1980s did not seek to recreate the solo he made for Michael Clark in 1981 so much as acknowledge the differing inputs of new male and female dancers, their physiques, their personalities and their particularized style.

In a similar way, Davies absorbed the lessons of contact improvisation and release-based technique from her study leave in the United States in the 1980s and incorporated these lessons into her own very personal style. In later years, this style acknowledged the inputs of all her dancers from Scott Clark to Gill Clarke and her 1997 reworking of *White Man Sleeps* (1988) saw a version that was changed from its original statement in its exploration of play and work to incorporate the strengths of her current company. It is interesting that our first generation of contemporary choreographers is interested in reviving work, adding an important dimension to the heritage debate, usually the preserve of classical ballet. But implicit within the work of them all is a new politics of the body, as well as a new attitude to choreography and the collaborative nature of the medium, which is being increasingly and more openly acknowledged.

There are contradictory statements from elsewhere. Some American visitors during the Dance Umbrella festivals of the 1980s, such as Molissa Fenley, upheld a notion of fine-tuned athleticism that played into the hands of the populist body-image of gymnasium workouts. Recent work from Europe and Canada displays highly dramatic and expressionistic forms and often treats the body as site for social and physical violence. Dance companies like DV8, V-Tol and Random have all incorporated high-energy, risk-taking, extreme forms of physical activity into their repertories in the 1990s. The result at its best makes a spectacular and expressive impact. Critic Jann Parry has made the point: 'While there is a variety of motives for going to extremes, the most obvious one is the visceral impact it has on the audience: you sense the shock, the risk, the pain in your own body. It's good for expressing anger, frenzy, despair – or for finding out what happens when the body is pushed to its limits' (Parry 1997: 7).

What happens when the body is pushed to its limits seems quite often to include injury and these forms often embrace the same sorts of extreme pressures endemic to more traditional dance forms. This could be seen in some ways as tantamount to the denial of the dancer as person – the very reverse of the desired artistic effect.

DV8's latest performance *Bound to Please* (1997) exposes the dancers' insecurities and the dance world's obsession with 'physical perfection and beauty'. *Bound to Please* includes the 60-year-old dancer Diana Payne-Myers in its exploration of the image of the dancer and the constraints placed upon her (and him) by a public little interested in their humanity. In his programme notes Lloyd Newson writes: 'At times dance feels very juvenile to me: until we re-define our notions of what dance is, what a dancer looks like and how a dancer moves; until older, fat and disabled dancers can be encouraged to keep performing and to talk about their lives, the form will remain young and immature. We must encourage dancers to use more than just their bodies'.

Matthew Hawkins, one-time Royal Ballet dancer, has also collaborated with Payne-Myers in *Matthew and Diana on Manoeuvres* (1994); Mark Baldwin, former Rambert dancer, has choreographed for a company of mature dancers. Perhaps these choreographers have taken their cue from Jiři Kylián's 'mature' company, Nederlands Dans Theater 3, for whom Bruce has created work, or perhaps it is the influence of choreographers such as the American Mark Morris for whom age, shape and size present no limitations to expressive potential. Whatever the instigation, it seems that Newson's appeal for dancers to use more than just their bodies is being heeded.

CandoCo is perhaps the best-known fully professional company integrating disabled and able-bodied dancers. Their dance video *Outside In* (1995), to Victoria Marks' choreography, combines strong gymnastic performances with sensitive release-based explorations of each other's bodies. CandoCo dancers can cover the dance space on two hands just as vigorously and become embroiled in poignant relationships every bit as eloquent as their able-bodied counterparts, if not more so. The company has, strangely, been accused of conservatism, of lacking the political hard edge, perhaps because of their lack of polemical subject-matter, but the company has surely radically changed the way that we think about physical ability in dance, just in the way in which people with disabilities are represented within the performances.

The debate has not been localized within the modern or postmodern dance camps. Within the Royal Ballet a new generation of powerful women and men have stamped their mark on the choreography. Dancers such as Sylvie Guillem, Darcey Bussell and Deborah Bull have had works made on them to suit their own particular physicalities and expressive qualities. Guillem has covertly questioned the choreographer's ultimate authority by changing the steps when it suits her and has provoked strong controversy as a result. Deborah Bull was invited to speak at the Oxford Union and showed herself to be in possession of an acute intellect, far removed from the traditional ballet stereotype. Both dancers have worked with modern dance choreographers: Guillem with Jonathan Burrows and Bull with Davies. Indeed Burrows provides another example: Royal Ballet School-trained, appearances in Butcher's choreography, all the time maintaining that his work is getting closer and closer to classical ballet, even while he rejects its vocabulary in favour of 'the distinctly demotic flat-footed steps crocheting floor patterns in *The Stop Quartet*, the slicing arms, the upper-body jacknifes [sic] into a four-legged crouch' (Meisner 1996: 3). Or again there is Page, who came up through the Royal Ballet School and Company, but spent time exploring new styles and new forms under the auspices of Dance Umbrella during the 1980s.

The Royal Ballet dancer, then, can become agent of her or his own expression rather than tool of someone else's. Moreover choreographers have risen to the bait, and we have seen in the works of Forsythe, Tharp and Page a new questioning of the roles of male and female in dance as well as within the portrayal of relationships. Here is choreography 'freed from the language of boys and girls', in Stephanie Jordan's words,[9] with reference to the outdated language of the ballet school that has stereotyped gender from the classroom onwards and never allowed dancers the image of full maturity.

The Medium's Relationship with the Other Arts

Almost as soon as it had become established, LCDT spawned an interest in a post-Graham aesthetic on the part of some of its alumni. This was partly due to the art-school training of some of the new students of dance, and their awareness of contemporary issues, most notably within American contemporary art. Students such as Alston and Davies were acquainted with the work of Robert Rauschenberg, Jasper Johns and Andy Warhol and through them became acquainted with the work of John Cage in music and Merce Cunningham in dance. But it was also due to LCDT's founder, Robin Howard and his encouragement and support of experimentation from the outset, his exposure of the students to British performance art and to visiting American theatre artists alongside avant-garde artists of a post-Cunningham, post-Judson Theatre aesthetic such as Meredith Monk, Yvonne Rainer and Twyla Tharp. It has been noted that at this time LSCD could easily have become a centre for radical theatre (Jordan 1992: 32). It could also be this interest in conceptualism and pop art that helped to pave the way for links with popular music.

Endemic within the punk movement of the 1980s was an anarchic anger and an implicit, though unformalized, critique of the status quo. Some choreographers harnessed this aggression, exploiting its energy and displaying, in Baudrillard's terms, its obscenity.[10] Michael Clark is one such, and his 1982 *Because We Must* used the music of Lou Reed and the Velvet Underground among others to lay bare the souls of the choreographer and dancers and to proclaim loudly that ballet was dead. The stage show contained nudity, pornographic text, portrayed graphic sex acts and discussed cocaine taking. All this was set against the portly figure of the late Australian fashion designer Leigh Bowery, who performed as well as providing some outrageous costumes. At one point, three white-clad female dancers danced a lyrical Cunningham-inspired trio to be interrupted by a fourth female, naked except for red boots and wielding an audibly working chainsaw. The message was clear – *ballet blanc* meets Archaos. The dance was exhilarating in its energy and iconoclasm and represented Clark's choreography at its best – poignantly expressive and absurd in equal measure – pure Dada. That punk's statements held an implicit political consciousness cannot be denied, but it was a self-destructive consciousness, an element that was highly apparent within Clark's work at the time, too.

Dance has harnessed the aesthetic and to some extent the content of the other arts. More recently, there has been seen an interest in the dancing body and in the ontology of dance by artists in other fields as well as academics from other disciplines – from sociology, cultural studies, anthropology and philosophy. A sociology of dance is now thriving, because dance deals with the social body. But it also deals with the biological body, as is clear from the influence of the 'aerobics' boom; as well as with the artistic body, that is the body as shape and form through time and in space. Perhaps it is time to connect these three within our consciousness.

Questions of Identity, Geographic and Artistic

It is apparent that the major agenda for dance in the UK in recent decades has been the search for identity – in terms of its relationship with the dance representations of the US on the one hand and Europe on the other. To some extent, dance reflects the shifting political situation here – but only to some extent. It has also had to deal with radical changes in the UK's demographic population and has had to represent other cultures now part of that population – to absorb these cultures, but also to preserve their heritage. It has had to represent interests and views of people who have in the past had lesser voices – feminist issues, gay rights, disabled people who have been excluded from the activity, certainly on the theatrical stage. And all this against a backdrop of dance finding its artistic identity – that is as an art form in its own right independent of the other arts for its expression, even when it draws upon their skills as it does in physical theatre. Dance has had to argue its identity as an art form that has its own very special nature and requirements.

In relation to America and Europe, companies now seem to be increasingly multinational. DV8 began in Britain, has a choreographer who is Australian by birth, and the company contains dancers from all over the world, but this is true of many other companies. What then of the Ashton style, the English style, the understated lyricism of Second Stride during their first American tour that was said to be so English in the early 1980s?[11] Perhaps these things are all of the past and, while that past is well worth preserving in some forms, it is the present that keeps the form alive. But Alastair Macaulay maintains, perhaps this Englishness is apparent now in the works of Anderson whose dances display 'an utterly English conception of character: light, defined principally by social behaviour, close to caricature', reflecting the English class system: theatrical and mimetic in 'from the waist up' delineation of character (Macaulay 1996a: 23). But Anderson does it in a knowing way, in a way that proclaims knowledge of its loss and looks forward to new identities.

In a similar vein, the dances of Shobana Jeyasingh do not seek to preserve a pure form of Indian dance: even though she draws upon images from its various forms, she also makes reference to the conventions of western modern and postmodern dance. Jeyasingh describes her background: 'For me, my heritage is a mix of David Bowie, Purcell, Shelley and Anna Pavlova, and it has been mixed as subtly as a samosa has mixed itself into the very English cuisine in the last ten years or so: impossible to separate' (Jeyasingh 1995: 193). Her dances are challenging to an audience uneducated in the Indian forms from which she quotes and the conventions that she explores, and relatively few are versed in both western and South Asian dance styles. But as an Indian living in England, Jeyasingh would argue, how else is she to choreograph? She has asserted that 'authentic tradition' is an impossibility, indeed that its pursuit is a 'retrogressive opposition to the project of modernity' (Jordan 1996: 39). Instead, Jeyasingh's dances are explorations into the possibilities of dance movement to communicate 'without cultural baggage', to find a dance language that is 'objective'. The idea that there can be meanings that are not cultural meanings would seem to fly in the face of current wisdom concerning the process of understanding artworks, but within her dances this problem is confronted. Certainly, within her movement style, set within the context of multicultural conventions, the dancer and the dancer's individuality are once again foregrounded and we catch glimpses of the dancer as person, living within and making sense of complex surroundings.

Multiculturalism has been a feature within the arts in general in this country since the late 1970s. We had seen a huge influx of immigrants predominantly from the West Indies and the Indian subcontinent during the 1950s, encouraged by the British government as a measure to augment the labour force. During the 1970s there was a proliferation of dance companies featuring non-western forms, due to a new generation of British-born people of African, Afro-Caribbean and Asian descent who needed to proclaim their sense of cultural identity. Towards the middle of the decade, African dance received funding through the Manpower Services Commission and various community programmes as a means to conceal and reduce the tension caused by unemployment figures within this group. Thus, the African Peoples' Dance Movement emerged initially from a community base, funded through government employment schemes.

There has since arisen a lively debate concerning representation of all forms of dance experience from the African, Afro-Caribbean and Asian communities in all their complexity, and interests range from the preservation of cultural heritage through to the fusion of this heritage with contemporary western experience. The American academic and writer Henry Louis Gates, Jnr. has noted that, twenty-five years ago, cultural forms for black people were borrowed piecemeal, essentially unmodified. Yet today a culture that 'is distinctively black and British can be said to be in full flower, both on the streets and in the galleries' (Gates 1997: 2), and he notes too that it is now hip for white youths to speak with a Jamaican accent. Cultural theorist and Professor of Sociology at the Open University, Stuart Hall, has identified this phenomenon in similar terms: 'For the first time, being black is a way of being British' (ibid.). Gates goes further, adding: 'In no small measure, black culture simply is youth culture in London today' (ibid.). What is significant in all these observations is the diversity and complexity of cultural reference: 'It's reached a point where a lot of artists who began by identifying themselves with ethnic minority groups have moved outwards into engaging in a more culturally diverse mainstream'; 'The hope it offers [is] of a consciousness that is cultural rather than racial – that has the capacity to acknowledge difference without fetishising it, the freedom to represent without having to be representative' (ibid.).

These ideas echo those of Homi Bhabha in his manifesto for 'Re-inventing Britain' – a 1997 conference organized by the British Council, which looked at how 'very different British identities are being formed and re-formed across and between cultures' (Wadham-Smith and Ingrams 1997: 2). Today, we see a questioning of the very notion of 'ethnic minority dance', as Homi Bhabha's concept of the 'new cosmopolitanism' testifies, a concept that transcends and replaces the 1980s notion of multiculturalism, and that transcends concepts of identity – be it ethnic, class, gender or national identity (Bhabha 1997: 9).

Aside from the issue of dance forms stemming from and contributing to the identity of minority groups, dance plays other roles in relation to geographical identity within the UK. For a start, there have been moves to decentralize dance activity and to build centres of dance culture outside of the capital. Thus, the project of National Dance Agencies began in the 1990s,[12] and there are now eight such centres across different regions of England.

But place achieves a new importance today as we regroup and find new identities beyond the old national and regional boundaries, as the local, regional community becomes increasingly significant in a global world. Scotland, which has now (since 1997) won its claim for separate nation status, has its own well-established Scottish Ballet, also a contemporary repertory company, Scottish Dance Theatre and a number of independent groups. Dance work often makes reference to specifically Scottish themes or to indigenous dance forms. Recently, dance has featured increasingly strongly at Edinburgh's International Festival and at Glasgow's New

202

Moves Across Europe, neither of which organizations look to England for models. But perhaps most significant for Scottish dance are the projects that foster dance training and choreographic development within the new nation, and large lottery funding will support two such projects. Up till now, dance students and choreographers have often had no option but to journey south in order to pursue their careers. Dance Base is to create a new, professional-standard dance centre in Edinburgh. A new Scottish School of Contemporary Dance is to be established in Dundee, and at the first National Dance Forum, a cross-section of the Scottish dance community was invited to debate just what curriculum such a professional training school should offer, seizing the opportunity to learn from but not necessarily emulate tried models from other countries.

Dance Comes of Age

So what do we have today? We have dances as diverse as those of DV8 and the Royal Ballet, of Bourne and Jeyasingh and all of these have their own agendas and choreographic concerns, their own subjects and particularized dance styles. Pervading it all, we see emerging a new way of looking at the dancer and a new status for her or him – one whose agency within the dance statement is finally acknowledged. Moreover, the dancer's body has become a site for political statement in itself and all dance must now at the very least recognize that the body cannot be neutral and neither can the dancer – both are charged with political implications. Implicit within this is a new ontological status for dance itself – as collaborative art. Collaboration between choreographer and dancer has long been recognized by DV8 for example, where responsibility for the choreography is cited as belonging to the company with Newson as director. We have also seen Newson call for a new maturity among dance-makers and performers, and for representations of the community as it *really* is. Perhaps the final say should lie with CandoCo's artistic director, Adam Benjamin: 'The entry of disabled students into the most exclusive world of dance raises issues of aesthetics, politics, personality, sexuality . . . the lessons we learn, therefore will be more than academic; they will have an impact not only on dance as an art form, but on the way we perceive, treat and respect each other as human beings' (Benjamin 1995: 47).

Notes

1 It was not until the 1960s that the modern dance movement really made a significant appearance in the UK – several decades after the US and the rest of Europe. This was prompted by visits by the Martha Graham Company, first in 1954, then again in 1963, closely followed by the companies of Paul Taylor, Alvin Ailey, Murray Louis and Merce Cunningham.

2 LSCD started to use the term 'contemporary' to refer to the techniques it was currently offering as well as to the dance style of the LCDT repertory. This term for a while became common currency and synonymous with 'modern' in relation to the dance styles being introduced at that time. For consistency, I use the term modern to

describe these dance styles, the term also providing a helpful distinction with later postmodern developments, though both these terms are problematic, not least, as Sally Banes notes, in the relationship between their usage within dance and within the other arts. See Sally Banes, *Terpsichore in Sneakers*, Middletown Connecticut, Wesleyan University Press, 1987.

3 These terms are not ideal, covering as they do many differing dance styles and diverse cultural roots. However, I am prompted in their use as a shorthand by the debate reproduced within Parthasarathi (1993).

4 In 1994, funding responsibilities were devolved to three bodies (the Arts Council of Northern Ireland already being separate): the Arts Council of England (ACE), the Scottish Arts Council (SAC), and the Arts Council of Wales (ACW).

5 The Dance Umbrella Festivals were begun in 1978 by a Royal Ballet trained dancer, Val Bourne, and persist to this day in robust form. The original idea was to present a showcase festival along the lines of the New York Dance Umbrellas, which celebrated British contemporary work, as well as exposing the fast-growing dance audience to important innovative foreign companies. In the first few years, these were almost exclusively American, but from the mid-1980s European companies became frequent visitors. Dance Umbrella expanded from a largely London-based event to simultaneous showings at regional centres, contributing in no small part to the decentralization of dance that was to become a feature of the late 1980s.

6 See Peter Williams's series 'The 21 Years That Changed British Ballet', *Dance and Dancers*, beginning December 1970 and running through to March 1972.

7 Later known as London Festival Ballet, then English National Ballet.

8 'Creating a Canon: Ninette de Valois and the Vic-Wells Repertory', a talk given by Beth Genné for the Society for Dance Research Study Day 'The Birth of the Royal Ballet' at the Royal Festival Hall, London, 31 July 1997.

9 In 'The Power of Centre: Dancing and Debating towards the Millennium', a paper given by Jordan at the World Dance Alliance Conference, Melbourne, July 1996.

10 Baudrillard argues that in a postmodern age, communication is all invasive and undifferentiated, therefore obscene. Baudrillard, J. (1983), 'The Ecstasy of Communication', in H. Foster (ed.) *Postmodern Culture*, London: Pluto, pp. 126–34.

11 See Jowitt, D. (1983) 'On a Sound Footing', *Dance and Dancers*, January: 16–17.

12 These had their roots in the recommendations of the 1989 Devlin Report: *Stepping Forward*.

References

Arts Council of England (1998) *Annual Report*.

Benjamin, A. (1995) 'Unfound Movement', *Dance Theatre Journal*, 12(1): 44–7.

Bhabha, H. (1997) 'Re-Inventing Britain – A Manifesto', *British Studies Now*, 9: 9–10.

Collins, Jim (1989) *Uncommon Cultures: Popular Culture and Post-modernism*, London: Routledge.

Erdman, J. (1996) 'Dance Discourses: Rethinking the History of "Oriental Dance"', in (ed.) G. Morris, *Moving Words – Re-writing Dance*, London: Routledge, pp. 288–305.

Gates, H. L. (1997) 'Black Flash', the *Guardian*, 'The Week' section, 19 July: 2.

Jeyasingh, S. (1995) 'Imaginary Homelands: Creating a New Dance Language', in (ed.) J. Adshead, *Border Tensions: Dance and Discourse. Proceedings of the Fifth Study of Dance Conference*, Guildford, Surrey: University of Surrey.

Jordan, S. (1992) *Striding Out: Aspects of Contemporary and New Dance in Britain*, London: Dance Books.

Jordan, S. (1996) 'Networking Dances: "Home and Away" in the Choreography of Shobana Jeyasingh', in (eds) C. Hillis and U. Dawkins, *New Dance from Old Cultures*, Braddon, ACT: Ausdance, pp. 39–43.

Macaulay, A. (1996a) 'Aspects of Englishness', *Dance Theatre Journal*, 12(4): 22–8.

Macaulay, A. (1996b), 'Gender, Sexuality, Community', in (eds) S. Jordan and A. Grau, *Following Sir Fred's Steps. Ashton's Legacy*, London: Dance Books, pp. 115–26.

Mackrell, J. (1992) *Out of Line: The Story of British New Dance*, London: Dance Books.

Marwick, A. (1982, 2nd edn, 1996) *British Society Since 1945*, London: Penguin.

Meisner, N. (1996) 'Closing in on ballet', *Dance Theatre Journal*, 13(2).

Parry, J. (1997) 'Defining the Cutting Edge', in (ed.) L. Sanders, *At the Cutting Edge*, Proceedings of the 1996 NDTA/daCi conference.

Wadham-Smith, N. and Ingrams, L. (1997) 'Identity, Transnationalism and the Arts', *British Studies Now*, 9: 2.

Key texts

Adshead, J. (ed.) (1995) *Border Tensions: Dance and Discourse. Proceedings of the Fifth Study of Dance Conference*, Guildford, Surrey: University of Surrey.

Devlin, G. (1989) *Stepping Forward: Some Suggestions for the Development of Dance in England during the 1990s*, London: Arts Council Dance Department.

Jordan, S. (1992) *Striding Out: Aspects of Contemporary and New Dance in Britain*, London: Dance Books.

Jordan, S. (1992) 'American Dance Abroad: Influences of the United States Experience', *Proceedings of the Society of Dance History Scholars*, Fifteenth Annual Conference, Riverside, CA: University of California Press.

Mackrell, J. (1992) *Out of Line: The Story of British New Dance*, London: Dance Books.

Marwick, A. (1982, 2nd edn, 1996) *British Society Since 1945*, London: Penguin.

Parthasarathi, S. (ed.) (1993) *What is Black Dance in Britain?*, London: Arts Council.

White, J. (ed.) (1985) *Twentieth-Century Dance in Britain: A History of Five Dance Companies*, London: Dance Books.

Table 10 Important dance and political events in the UK (1900 to present)

Year	Dance: artists, works, events	Dance: institutions	Arts scene	Sociocultural and political events
1900				Conservative Government Labour Party formed Edward VII
1901				
1904		Imperial Society of Teachers of Dancing		
1906				Liberal Government
1908	*Isadora Duncan *Maud Allen *Anna Pavlova		*The Mask* (Craig ed.)	
1909		*Dancing Times*		
1910		Margaret Morris opens her school	*Salomé* (Wilde) Coronation Exhibition	George V
1911	*Diaghilev's Ballets Russes			
1914			*Pygmalion* (Shaw) Vorticist Exhibition	First World War
1915			Entertainments Tax	
1916				Easter Rising, Ireland
1918				End of First World War Women given the vote at age 30
1920		Marie Rambert school British Ballet Organization Association of Operatic Dancing		
1921			*Four Plays for Dancers* (Yeats)	Eire independent from UK
1922			*Ulysses* (Joyce) banned *The Waste Land* (Eliot) BBC formed	
1924		Cecchetti Society merges with ISTD	Wembley Empire Exhibition	Labour Government

Table 10 continued

1926	A Tragedy of Fashion (Ashton)	Marie Rambert Dancers Academy of Choreographic Art		General Strike
1928			Lady Chatterley's Lover (Lawrence) banned	Women given the vote at age 21
1929				Wall Street Crash
1930				
1931	Façade (Ashton)	Camargo Society The Ballet Club Vic-Wells Ballet Sadler's Wells Ballet School	Belshazzar's Feast (Walton)	Commonwealth
1933	Les Rendezvous (Ashton)	Ballets Jooss		
1935	The Rake's Progress (de Valois) Façade (Ashton)	Ballet Rambert Markova-Dolin Ballet Association of Operatic Dancing becomes Royal Academy of Dancing	Fourth Symphony (Vaughan Williams)	Conservative Government
1936	Lilac Garden (Antony Tudor)		First television broadcast	Edward VIII George VI
1937	Dark Elegies (Tudor) Checkmate (de Valois) Les Patineurs (Ashton)			
1938	Rudolf Laban arrives in UK		Dear Octopus (Dodie Smith)	Munich Crisis
1939			Council for the Encouragement of Music and the Arts Entertainments Nationals Service Association (ENSA)	Second World War
1940		International Ballet		
1941		Sadler's Wells Ballet	A Child of Our Time (Tippett)	

Table 10 *continued*

Year	Dance: artists, works, events	Dance: institutions	Arts scene	Scoiocultural and political events
1945		Art of Movement Studio (Laban)	Council of Industrial Design *Peter Grimes* (Britten)	Second World War ends Labour Government
1946	*Symphonic Variations* (Ashton) *American Ballet Theatre	Sadler's Wells Ballet moves to Royal Opera House, Covent Garden	Young Vic Arts Council of Great Britain First Edinburgh festival	United Nations Assembly National Health Service
1947		Metropolitan Ballet		India independence
1948	*Cinderella, Scènes de ballet* (Ashton)		*The Red Shoes* (Powell and Pressburger)	British Nationality Act
1950	*New York City Ballet	Festival Ballet *Dance and Dancers*	*ARK* (journal of the Royal College of Arts) Aldeburgh Festival	Korean war
1951	*Pineapple Poll* (John Cranko)		Festival of Britain Royal Festival Hall opens	Conservative Government
1952			*Waiting for Godot* (Beckett) *Oh Calcutta* (dir. K. Tynan)	Elisabeth II
1954	*Martha Graham			Anglo-Egyptian Suez Canal Agreement
1956	*Bolshoi Ballet	Sadler's Wells Ballet becomes Royal Ballet Western Theatre Ballet	*Look Back in Anger* (Osborne)	Suez crisis
1957				National Service ends
1958	*The Burrow* (MacMillan)			Notting Hill race riots
1959			Obscenity trial: *Lady Chatterley's Lover* published	

Table 10 continued

1960	La Fille mal gardée (Ashton) The Invitation (MacMillan)			Nigeria, Cyprus independence
1961	*Kirov Ballet	Royal Ballet visits Russia	Royal Shakespeare Company War Requiem (Britten)	Tanzania independence
1962	Nureyev guest artist with Royal Ballet	Benesh Institute opens		Jamaica, Trinidad independence Immigration Act
1963			National Theatre opens	Profumo affair
1964	Martha Graham in Edinburgh *Merce Cunningham *Paul Taylor *Alvin Ailey The Dream (Ashton)		Council for National Academic Awards (CNAA) First World Theatre season Shakespeare quartercentenary	Malawi, Zambia independence Labour Government
1965	Romeo and Juliet (MacMillan) Monotones (Ashton)		The Homecoming (Pinter) The Place Saved (Bond)	Rhodesia unilateral declaration of independence
1966		London School of Contemporary Dance Ballet Rambert becomes contemporary	Equivalent 8 (Carl André exhibits at the Tate Gallery)	
1967		Language of Dance Centre International Dance Teachers Association London Contemporary Dance Theatre	Rosencrantz and Guildenstern Are Dead (Stoppard) Sergeant Pepper (The Beatles)	Demonstrations against Vietnam war Sexual Offences Act decriminalizes homosexuality, legalizes abortion

Table 10 continued

Year	Dance: artists, works, events	Dance: institutions	Arts scene	Sociocultural and political events
1968	*Embrace Tiger and Return to Mountain* (Glen Tetley)		Lord Chamberlain Stage Censure abolished Welfare State International (WSI) *Hair*	Student riots Armagh riots: resurgence of Irish 'troubles'
1969	*Cell* (Robert Cohan)	The Place Scottish Ballet Northern Ballet Theatre	New Activities Committee (Arts Council) for 'fringe' ventures	
1970			*The Female Eunuch* (Greer)	Conservative Government
1972		Strider		Amin expels British Asians from Uganda UK joins EEC
1973		Mary Fulkerson at Dartington Hall Laban Centre	*Flowers* (Kemp) Women's festival at Almost Free	
1974	*Troy Game* (Robert North)			Labour Government Miners' strike
1975	*Stabat Mater* (Cohan)	Rosemary Butcher Dance Company Extemporary Dance Theatre	Gay theatre season at Almost Free *Black Slaves, White Chains* (Mathura) *Parliament in Flames* (WSI)	
1976	*A Month in the Country* (Ashton)	X6 Dance Collective ADMA BA Hons Laban Centre	Minority Arts Advisory Service (MAAS) *The Arts that Britain Ignores* (ACBG)	

Table 10 continued

1977	Rainbow Bandit (Richard Alston) Cruel Garden (Christopher Bruce, Lindsay Kemp)	New Dance MAAS Movers (first 'black' dance co.)		Racial Discrimination Act
1978	Mayerling (MacMillan)	Dartington Festival Dance Umbrella Council for Dance Education and Training		
1979	*Trisha Brown *Lucinda Childs	Academy of Indian Dance	Regional Arts Associations Black Theatre Co-operative	Conservative Government (Thatcher) 'Winter of Discontent'
1980		Chisenhale Dance Space MA Dance Studies, Laban Centre Dance education and training in Britain (Gulbenkian Report) Labannews	Britain's New Arts (Commission for Racial Equality) The Romans in Britain (Brenton)	Zimbabwe independence Unemployment tops 2 million
1981	Soda Lake (Alston) Plain Song (Siobhan Davies) I, Giselle (Jacky Lansley)	BA Hons Surrey University Phoenix Dance Company		Maze Prison hunger strike Inner-city race riots (Brixton, Southall, Toxteth) Greenham Common
1982		BA Hons LCDS Second Stride	Channel 4	Falklands War
1983		Dance Research Labannews becomes Dance Theatre Journal	Barbican Theatre opens Eyre's Guys and Dolls	
1984	*Pina Bausch (Edinburgh) Further and Futher into Night (Ian Spink)	Green Candle Dance Company The Cholmondeleys	Arts Council diverts £6 million from London to the regions	Miners' strike
1985		Northern School of Contemporary Dance		

Table 10 continued

Year	Dance: artists, works, events	Dance: institutions	Arts scene	Sociocultural and political events
1986	*The Snow Queen* (David Bintley) *No Fire Escape in Hell* (Michael Clark)	*The Place of Indian Dance in British Culture* (Arts Council) DV8 Physical Theatre	English Shakespeare Company	Greater London Council abolished
1987	*Because We Must* (Clark)	Adventures in Motion Pictures (AMP)	Renaissance Theatre Company	
1988		Siobhan Davies Dance Company *Choreography and Dance*	*Satanic Verses* (Rushdie)	
1989	*The Prince of the Pagodas* (MacMillan)	Shobana Jeyasingh Dance Company National Resource Centre for Dance ADiTi (National Organisation for South Asian Dance) London Festival Ballet becomes English National Ballet	*Towards Cultural Diversity* (Arts Council)	
1990		Sadler's Wells Royal Ballet becomes Birmingham Royal Ballet		
1991		The Data Place Candoco *Dance Now*	10 Regional Arts Boards	Abolition of 'Poll Tax'
1992	*Winnsboro Cotton Mill Blues* (Davies)			Gulf War
1993				Maastricht Treaty National Lottery
1994		Richard Alston Dance Company	Damian Hirst (Turner Prize)	
1995	*Swan Lake* (Matthew Bourne)			
1997		Benesh Institute merges with RAD	*Cultural Diversity* (Arts Council)	Hong Kong back to China Labour Government

* First visit
Compiled by Andrée Grau and Sanjoy Roy

INDEX

213

215